Galatians

Galatians

PETER OAKES

Baker Academic
a division of Baker Publishing Group
Grand Rapids, Michigan

Published by Baker Academic
a division of Baker Publishing Group
P.O. Box 6287, Grand Rapids, MI 49516-6287
www.bakeracademic.com

Printed in the United States of America

Library of Congress Cataloging-in-Publication Data

Oakes, Peter (Peter S.)
    Galatians / Peter Oakes.
        pages cm. — (Paideia : commentaries on the New Testament)
    Includes bibliographical references and index.
    ISBN 978-0-8010-3275-2 (pbk.)
    1. Bible. Galatians—Commentaries. I. Title.
  BS2685.53.O25 2015
  227'.4077—dc23   2014043638

Unless otherwise indicated, all Scripture quotations are the author's own translation.

Contents

Contents

Figures

Foreword

Paideia: Commentaries on the New Testament is a series that sets out to comment on the final form of the New Testament text in a way that pays due attention both to the cultural, literary, and theological settings in which the text took form and to the interests of the contemporary readers to whom the commentaries are addressed. This series is aimed squarely at students—including MA students in religious and theological studies programs, seminarians, and upper-division undergraduates—who have theological interests in the biblical text. Thus, the didactic aim of the series is to enable students to understand each book of the New Testament as a literary whole rooted in a particular ancient setting and related to its context within the New Testament.

The name "Paideia" (Greek for "education") reflects (1) the instructional aim of the series—giving contemporary students a basic grounding in academic New Testament studies by guiding their engagement with New Testament texts; (2) the fact that the New Testament texts as literary unities are shaped by the educational categories and ideas (rhetorical, narratological, etc.) of their ancient writers and readers; and (3) the pedagogical aims of the texts themselves—their central aim being not simply to impart information but to form the theological convictions and moral habits of their readers.

Each commentary deals with the text in terms of larger rhetorical units; these are not verse-by-verse commentaries. This series thus stands within the stream of recent commentaries that attend to the final form of the text. Such reader-centered literary approaches are inherently more accessible to liberal arts students without extensive linguistic and historical-critical preparation than older exegetical approaches, but within the reader-centered world the sanest practitioners have paid careful attention to the extratext of the original readers, including not only these readers' knowledge of the geography, history, and other contextual elements reflected in the text but also their ability to respond correctly to the literary and rhetorical conventions used in the text. Paideia commentaries pay deliberate attention to this extratextual repertoire in order to highlight the ways in which the text is designed to persuade and move its readers. Each rhetorical unit is explored from three angles: (1) introductory matters; (2) tracing the train of thought or narrative or rhetorical flow of the argument; and (3) theological issues raised by the text that are of interest to the contemporary Christian. Thus, the primary focus remains on the text and not its historical context or its interpretation in the secondary literature.

Our authors represent a variety of confessional points of view: Protestant, Catholic, and Orthodox. What they share, beyond being New Testament scholars of national and international repute, is a commitment to reading the biblical text as theological documents within their ancient contexts. Working within the broad parameters described here, each author brings his or her own considerable exegetical talents and deep theological commitments to the task of laying bare the interpretation of Scripture for the faith and practice of God's people everywhere.

Mikeal C. Parsons
Charles H. Talbert
Bruce W. Longenecker

Preface

Unity in diversity in Christ. People of all kinds eating together through common relation to Christ. A trip to Jerusalem that finds unity. Unity broken at Antioch. An argument building to oneness in Christ. An ethic centered on love, the key virtue for unity.

At stake is the Galatians' *pistis*: their trust in Christ and, consequently, their fidelity to Christ. If these gentiles run off down the road toward dependence on Jewish law, they forget what Christ has done on their behalf on the cross.

Particular thanks are due to the following:

Andrew Boakye, David Harvey, Nijay Gupta, and James Dunn for reading and offering valuable comments on part or all of the draft commentary;

John Barclay and Tom Wright, and to John Elliott, Philip Esler, and other Context Group colleagues for helpful discussion of key points;

the Nordic Theology Network, University of Helsinki, and Stockholm School of Theology, especially Rikard Roitto;

George Brooke, Todd Klutz, Sarah Whittle, and other colleagues in the Ehrhardt Seminar at Manchester;

PhD students during the writing of the commentary: Elif Aynaci (and, for the photographs, her brother Burak Karaman), Soon Yi Byun, Stephen McBay, Richard Britton, Isaac Mbabazi, Jonathan Tallon, Sungjong Kim, and Pyung-Soo Seo;

Robert and Dawn Parkinson and everybody at Didsbury Baptist Church;

Conrad Gempf and Robert Morgan for classes on Galatians, and to many fellow students, especially Sean Winter, Brad Braxton, and Moyer Hubbard.

Thanks are also due to the many great scholars whose published work has helped in understanding Galatians—above all to my former Manchester colleague, Martin de Boer,[1] whose commentary is now the benchmark for thorough work on the letter. The present commentary was essentially completed in 2013. I look forward to future opportunities to interact with many more recent works, especially that of N. T. Wright,[2] significant commentaries by Douglas Moo[3] and by Andrew Das,[4] and the important collection edited by Mark Elliott, Scott Hafemann, N. T. Wright, and John Frederick.[5]

Finally, my thanks go to all who have helped bring the commentary through to completion: to the series editors, especially Bruce Longenecker, and to the editorial committee, especially Loveday Alexander; to James Ernest, for repeated help over the several years it took to write; to Wells Turner, Rachel Klompmaker, Mason Slater, and the rest of the production and marketing teams at Baker Academic; above all, for endless work and support, to Janet.

---

1. *Galatians: A Commentary* (Louisville: Westminster John Knox, 2011).

2. *Paul and the Faithfulness of God*, 2 vols., Christian Origins and the Question of God 4 (London: SPCK; Minneapolis: Fortress, 2013).

3. *Galatians*, Baker Exegetical Commentary on the New Testament (Grand Rapids: Baker Academic, 2013).

4. *Galatians*, Concordia Commentary (St. Louis: Concordia, 2014).

5. *Galatians and Christian Theology: Justification, the Gospel, and Ethics in Paul's Letters* (Grand Rapids: Baker Academic, 2014).

Abbreviations

General

//	parallel to	m²	square meters
§	section	NT	New Testament
AT	author's translation	OT	Old Testament
esp.	especially	trans.	translated by, translation (in)
frg.	fragment	x	when preceded by a numeral, designates how often an item occurs
lit.	literally		

Bible Texts, Editions, and Versions

LXX	Septuagint, the Greek Bible	NIV 1984	New International Version (1984 edition)
MT	Masoretic Text: the Hebrew Bible	NRSV	New Revised Standard Version
NIV	New International Version (2011 edition)		

Ancient Manuscripts and Papyri

ℵ	Codex Sinaiticus	𝔓⁴⁶	Papyrus 46
B	Codex Vaticanus	P.Brem.	*Die Bremer Papyri*. Edited by U. Wilcken. Berlin, 1936.
𝔐	Majority Text		

Ancient Corpora

OLD TESTAMENT

Gen.	Genesis
Exod.	Exodus
Lev.	Leviticus
Num.	Numbers
Deut.	Deuteronomy
Josh.	Joshua
Judg.	Judges
Ruth	Ruth
1–2 Sam.	1–2 Samuel
1–2 Kings	1–2 Kings
1–2 Chron.	1–2 Chronicles
Ezra	Ezra
Neh.	Nehemiah
Esther	Esther
Job	Job
Ps(s).	Psalm(s)
Prov.	Proverbs
Eccles.	Ecclesiastes
Song	Song of Songs
Isa.	Isaiah
Jer.	Jeremiah
Lam.	Lamentations
Ezek.	Ezekiel
Dan.	Daniel
Hosea	Hosea
Joel	Joel
Amos	Amos
Obad.	Obadiah
Jon.	Jonah
Mic.	Micah
Nah.	Nahum
Hab.	Habakkuk
Zeph.	Zephaniah
Hag.	Haggai
Zech.	Zechariah
Mal.	Malachi

DEUTEROCANONICAL BOOKS

Add. Esth.	Additions to Esther
1–2 Esd.	1–2 Esdras
Jdt.	Judith
1–4 Macc.	1–4 Maccabees
Sir.	Sirach/Ecclesiasticus
Wis.	Wisdom of Solomon

NEW TESTAMENT

Matt.	Matthew
Mark	Mark
Luke	Luke
John	John
Acts	Acts
Rom.	Romans
1–2 Cor.	1–2 Corinthians
Gal.	Galatians
Eph.	Ephesians
Phil.	Philippians
Col.	Colossians
1–2 Thess.	1–2 Thessalonians
1–2 Tim.	1–2 Timothy
Titus	Titus
Philem.	Philemon
Heb.	Hebrews
James	James
1–2 Pet.	1–2 Peter
1–3 John	1–3 John
Jude	Jude
Rev.	Revelation

OLD TESTAMENT PSEUDEPIGRAPHA

Apocr. Ezek.	Apocryphon of Ezekiel
As. Mos.	Assumption of Moses (see T. Mos.)
2 Bar.	2 Baruch (Syriac Apocalypse)
4 Bar.	4 Baruch
4 Ezra	4 Ezra
Jos. Asen.	Joseph and Aseneth
Jub.	Jubilees
Pss. Sol.	Psalms of Solomon
T. Job	Testament of Job
T. Mos.	Testament of Moses

DEAD SEA SCROLLS

4QMMT   *Some Observances of the Law*
          (4Q394–399)

RABBINIC WORKS

Letters preceding the names of Mishnaic
tractates indicate sources: Mishnah (*m.*),
Tosefta (*t.*), Babylonian Talmud (*b.*), and Je-
rusalem/Palestinian Talmud (*y.*).

'Abot R. Nat.   'Abot de Rabbi Nathan
Ber.   Berakot

APOSTOLIC FATHERS

Ign. *Eph.*   Ignatius, *To the Ephesians*

Ancient Authors

ARISTOTLE

Eth. Nic.   *Nicomachean Ethics*

ATHENAEUS

Deipn.   *Deipnosophistae*

CICERO

Amic.   *De amicitia*
Inv.   *De inventione rhetorica*
Nat. d.   *De natura deorum*

EPICTETUS

Disc.   *Discourses*

JOSEPHUS

Ant.   *Antiquities of the Jews*
J.W.   *Jewish War*

JUSTIN

1 Apol.   *First Apology*
2 Apol.   *Second Apology*

PHILO

Contempl.   *On the Contemplative Life*
Post.   *On the Posterity of Cain*

PLATO

Euthyd.   *Euthydemus*
Gorg.   *Gorgias*
Rep.   *Republic*

PLUTARCH

Per.   *Pericles*

SENECA (THE YOUNGER)

Clem.   *De clementia*
Ep.   *Moral Epistles*

STOBAEUS

Flor.   *Florilegium*

TACITUS

Agr.   *Agricola*

Reference Works

BDF   *A Greek Grammar of the New
        Testament and Other Early
        Christian Literature.* Edited
        by F. Blass and A. Debrunner.
        Translated and revised by Rob-
        ert W. Funk. Chicago: Univer-
        sity of Chicago Press, 1961.

LSJ   *A Greek-English Lexicon.* By
        H. G. Liddell, R. Scott, H. S.
        Jones, and R. McKenzie. 9th
        ed. with rev. supplement. Ox-
        ford: Oxford University Press,
        1996.

Galatians

Introduction

How should we prepare to study a text? What steps can we take to alert us to the range of issues that may be relevant? To help prepare us for analyzing Galatians, we will do four things. First, we will take an initial look at Galatians, together with relevant external evidence such as early use of Galatians, to give us a provisional idea of the nature of the text. This will provide the basis for a second step, consideration of what contexts (in the widest sense) are relevant for understanding the text. Our third step will be analysis of the structure of Galatians. Finally, we will give a brief overview of some ways in which people have interpreted and used Galatians.

The Nature of the Text

Our initial look at Galatians will be in three parts. We will begin by gathering basic data about its language, size, date, sender, and recipients. Then we will look at form and content, including, for instance, seeing what words are most frequent. Last, we will gather basic evidence about the situation for which the letter was written.

Basic Data about Text, Date, Sender, and Recipients

The work known as Paul's Letter to the Galatians is a text of about 2,230 words, written in a form of Greek differing somewhat from that of classical Athens but similar to that of other NT texts and some other writings of the late Hellenistic to Roman Imperial period. The earliest text of Galatians is found in the papyrus $\mathfrak{P}^{46}$, dated about AD 200 (Gal. 1:1–6:10 is at the University of Michigan; 6:10–18 is in the Chester-Beatty Library, Dublin). The text of Galatians is extremely stable in the manuscript tradition. Of the limited number of textual variants that raise significant questions, none extends to more than a few words.

The earliest really clear use of Galatians is by mid-second-century writers such as Marcion (see "Issues in the Reception of Galatians," below). He and other writers of that period viewed Galatians as an authoritative text, coming from the hand of the apostle Paul. Galatians makes reference to events that extend, at the very least, to about sixteen years after the death of Christ (see esp. Gal. 2:1). Taking the earliest conventional date for the crucifixion, AD 30, this puts Galatians as dating from 46 or later. Taken together with the evidence of the earliest clear use of Galatians, this places the maximum possible year range as about 46–140.

We are probably safe in narrowing the range much further. There is general agreement that the text actually was written by Paul. Since Paul probably died in about 67, Galatians is now limited to about twenty years in the middle of the first century. We can take another five or so years off this because there is broad agreement that Paul wrote Galatians earlier than his imprisonment in Rome in the early 60s. This gives us a range of about 46–61, quite a specific historical context. To narrow the date range any further leads us into controversial areas, which we will examine in discussing "Contexts for Understanding Galatians."

The text presents itself in the form of a Greek letter. The sender describes himself as "Paul, an emissary" (*apostolos*, traditionally "apostle"), adding that "all the brothers and sisters with me" (*hoi syn emoi pantes adelphoi*) are cosenders (1:1–2), although the letter has no obvious signs of communal authorship. Paul is a name on thirteen of the letters in the NT. He is also the main character in the second half of Acts of the Apostles.

The letter is addressed to *"the assemblies [ekklēsiais] of Galatia"* (1:2), and at one point Paul addresses the recipients, *"Oh, foolish Galatians!"* (3:1). Galatia was a Roman province in the center of Asia Minor (modern Turkey). The Galatians, or Gauls, after whom the province was named, were Celtic tribes who had rather bizarrely ended up establishing sizable kingdoms in the upland heart of Asia Minor after arriving (en masse, with their families) as mercenaries involved in wars of the third century BC. The kingdoms were incorporated into a Roman province in 25 BC (Mitchell 1993a, 1, 14–16, 61). In Paul's day, the boundaries of the province covered a much broader area than the original upland Gallic kingdoms. This leads to a debate about the letter's destination, which is connected to questions of dating, discussed below. However, we can certainly say that, broadly, the geographic and political context of the recipients is central Asia Minor under Roman provincial governance.

Another key point about the recipients is that they are presented as having been brought to Christian faith by Paul (4:12–20). They are also presented as being gentile: Paul describes them as previously "not knowing God," "enslaved to beings that by nature are not gods" (4:8), and as considering

Figure 1. View of the mountains along the highland route from Iconium (modern-day Konya) to Pisidian Antioch (Yalvaç).

undergoing circumcision (5:3). (On all this, see discussion on "Expected Hearers and the Implied Reader," below.) The geographical context of the sender, Paul, is not specified.

Form and Content of the Text

In terms of form, Galatians is broadly in the style of many other Greek letters. However, the text includes autobiographical narration (1:11–2:14; 4:12–15), and much of the letter consists of argument. In several sections this takes the form of citation and application of Scripture. In 4:21–31, there is something like an allegory based on Scripture. There is also much exhortatory material. In Gal. 5:19–21 is a list of vices, followed by a positive list in 5:22–23, which largely consists of virtues. Hans Dieter Betz and other scholars argue that the form of Galatians follows the norms of Greco-Roman formal rhetoric, although others have questioned this (see below).

Unlike the case of letters such as 2 Corinthians and Philippians, few scholars have questioned whether Galatians is a single text rather than a composite formed from more than one earlier text. Exceptions include Joop Smit (2002), whose analysis in terms of formal rhetoric leads him to see 5:13–6:10 as a later addition that does not fit the main rhetorical structure, and Thomas Witulski (2000), who argues that 4:8–20 addresses a different situation (related to the imperial cult) from that of the rest of the letter (related to Jewish law). Witulski has some adherents (Pilhofer [2010, 292–95] supports the force of the idea).

However, there is a strong overall consensus that Galatians was written as a single letter.

An initial read-through of Galatians shows that the content includes two particularly prominent elements. The letter opening and narrative in Gal. 1 lay particular emphasis on the divine origin of Paul's authority and message, an emphasis linked to a rebuke of the recipients for turning away from this message at the instigation of third parties. The second element is an argument relating to Jewish law. This argument could be seen as the major topic of the letter from 2:15 to the end, coming to a practical focus in a warning against the recipients undergoing circumcision (5:3; cf. 6:12). Alternatively, one might see a third prominent topic emerging in 5:13–6:10, in the form of discussion of ethical issues.

To delve a bit deeper, we can analyze the content of the text in lexical (word choice) terms. The sidebar shows the number of occurrences of various Greek words or word groups (groups of words derived from the same stem, like the English words "slave," "enslave," and "slavish"). Five groups are particularly frequent. The very high frequency of *Christos* (Christ) contributes to marking the letter as strongly Christian (some "Christian" texts have few distinctively Christian features). The frequency of *nomos* (law) shows how central the topic is. The *-angel-* word group is about announcement. In Galatians, this is mainly either *euangelion* (gospel) or *epangelia* (promise), indicated by brackets. The final very common word group is *pistis/pisteuō* (words relating to trust, or fidelity). The unusual frequency of both "law" and "faith" makes the relationship between them potentially a key point for study of the letter.

Among the moderately frequent word groups, a few combinations of related terms stand out clearly. There is a great deal of terminology about Jews and gentiles: *peritomē* (circumcision), *ethnē* (gentiles), *Ioudaios* (Jew),

Frequency of Some Lexical Groups in Galatians

Christos	Christ	38
-nomos	law	33
theos	God	31
-angel-	messenger, gospel, promise	29
pist-	faith, trust	27
pneuma	Spirit/spirit	19
sarx	flesh	18
Iēsous	Jesus	17
[-euangel-	gospel	15]
anthrōpos	human being	14
huio-	son, adoption	14
dikaio-	righteous, consider righteous	13
perit-	circumcision, circumcise	13
-adelphos	brother/sister	12
-graph-	write, Scripture	12
-doul-	slave, enslave	12
-erg-	work	12
ethn-	gentile	11
eleuther-	free, freedom	11
zōē/zaō	life/live	11
[epangel-	promise	11]
Ioudai-	Jew, Jewish	9
chari-	grace, give	9
Abraam	Abraham	9

Abraam (Abraham). Another interesting combination is *douleia* (slavery) and *eleutheria* (freedom). Another possible pair relates to the makeup of humans: *sarx* (flesh) and *anthrōpos* (human being). Readers with knowledge of Greek ideas about the person may also expect that *pneuma* (spirit) belongs here too. Most Christian readers will, on the other hand, expect to link it with *theos* (God) and maybe with *Christos*. We shall have to see what fits the text.

A logical further step would be to look at semantic groups, that is, sets of terms that are related in meaning even though they may be lexically different. For instance, the *douleia* (slavery) lexical group in Galatians forms part of a wider semantic group of terms relating to slavery and freedom. Along with the *-doul-* terms, this semantic group includes *paidiskē* (slave girl), *eleutheria* and related forms (freedom/free/set free), and probably *exagorazō* (redeem).

Consideration of semantic groups in Galatians, generally, further reinforces the areas of interest inferred from the lexical groups. One addition is the semantic field of life and death, which is expressed in various terms, including crucifixion. Another analytical approach would be to look for points that are highlighted by the structure of the letter. For instance, "There is no Jew or Greek" (Gal. 3:28) comes at a climax in Paul's argument. However, these initial surveys alert us only to some, but not all, important aspects of the letter. In the exegesis of the text, we will argue that a key theme of the letter is concern for unity. This happens not to be expressed by frequent repetition of unity-related words, so it is not picked up by lexical surveys.

What the Letter Implies about Its Situation

Paul does not explicitly set out his purpose for writing. However, we can find quite a lot of evidence about the situation, as perceived by Paul, from what he writes about the three (human) parties who are primarily involved: his Galatian addressees, Paul himself, and those described with terms such as "some people who are harassing you" (1:7). This third group we will call "Paul's opponents" (see below).

Paul addresses his audience as being in the process of going wrong in some way that involves departing from what he has taught them:

> "turning away from the one who called you in the grace of Christ, to a different gospel" (1:6)
>
> "O foolish Galatians, who cast the evil eye on you?" (3:1)
>
> "turning back again to the weak and poor elements, to which you are wanting to enslave yourselves again" (4:9)
>
> "I fear about you, in case somehow it is in vain that I have labored for you" (4:11)
>
> "I am in despair about you" (4:19–20)
>
> "Who cut in on you to stop you from obeying the truth?" (5:7)

In 1:6 they are turning "to a different gospel." This implies another message that they see as Christian. In 3:2, Paul demands to know whether they received the Spirit "by works of law . . . or by a message of trust." The implication is that they are starting to adopt "works of law." In 4:9–10, Paul wonders at their turning back "again to the weak and poor elements. . . . You are observing days and months and seasons and years." Some sort of calendrical observances are involved in their changing behavior. In 5:2 he warns, "If you get circumcised, Christ will be of no use to you." Paul sees at least some Galatians as inclining toward circumcision.

Some further, reasonably likely points about the situation can be derived by mirror reading from the imperatives in the letter. Mirror reading has to be done with due caution (Barclay 1987). However, Paul is very sparing in his use of instructional imperatives in Galatians, which makes his use of them quite marked. He instructs the Galatians to do the following: to be like him (4:12); to stand firm (in freedom) and not take on again a yoke of slavery (5:1); not to use freedom as an opportunity for the flesh but to serve one another in love (5:13); to watch out that they are not destroyed by one another, if they bite and devour one another (5:15); to walk by the Spirit (5:16); to restore (humbly) a person caught in a sin (6:1); to bear one another's burdens (6:2); each to test their own work (6:4); to share good things with their instructor (6:6); not to give Paul trouble (6:17). Although the instructions in this list look rather varied, the one theme that does seem to emerge is a call for love and mutual support. This finds further reinforcement elsewhere in Gal. 5, where Paul several times gives love a central place in discourse and where his counsels point to a likely concern about their disunity (5:15, 20, 26).

Paul writes a considerable amount about himself in the letter. To some extent this is done (in classic rhetorical fashion) as narrative that sets up the argument. A clear instance is Paul taking Titus to Jerusalem, with Titus then not being compelled to be circumcised (2:1–5). To some extent Paul also presents himself as a model, as is clearest in the first direct instruction: "Be like me" (4:12). However, there is also a marked defensive tone in what Paul writes about himself:

"Am I now seeking to win favor from people or from God? Or am I seeking to please people?" (1:10)

"I did not see any of the other emissaries except James, the brother of the Lord. See, before God! I am not lying in the things I write to you!" (1:19–20)

"Have I become your enemy by telling you the truth?" (4:16)

"Let no one cause me trouble, for I bear the marks of Jesus on my body." (6:17)

Paul perceives his reputation as having come under attack. In particular, he seems to feel the need to defend the idea that he did not learn his gospel message from the apostles at Jerusalem. Since an accusation in that area is not an obvious corollary of the issues, such as circumcision, that we have seen as directly affecting the Galatian Christians, it seems probable that accusations against Paul's reputation, and particularly about the origins of his message, are part of the situation of the letter.

The third group prominent in the situation is Paul's opponents. He writes less about them than we might expect. Paul describes them as "some people who are harassing you and wanting to pervert the gospel of Christ" (1:7; cf. 5:10, 12). They have possibly "cast the evil eye" on the Galatians (3:1). They are "zealous for" the Galatians, but "not in a good way. Instead, they want to exclude you, so that you will be zealous for them" (4:17).

> ## Naming the People Whom Paul Opposes
>
> Scholars struggle to find a good term to describe the group whom Paul is opposing. Use of the term "Judaizers" (e.g., Bruce 1982, 25), is fraught with lexical and historical difficulty (see comments on 2:14). Reuse of Pauline terms such as "agitators" (e.g., Jewett 2002) is methodologically sensible but gives a pejorative impression. "Teachers" (e.g., Martyn 1997a, 13) is reasonable, although it is maybe too specific about their general role. We will use what appears the most neutral term, "Paul's opponents" (e.g., Dunn 1993, 9), that is, people whom Paul opposes. As Robert Jewett (2002, 343) argues, it is possible that they did not present themselves as opposing Paul. However, Paul certainly opposes them.

They have "cut in on" the Galatians, so as to "stop you from obeying the truth" (5:7). They "want to make a good showing in flesh, . . . compelling you to be circumcised . . . so that they would not be persecuted. . . . They are wanting you to be circumcised so that they might boast in your flesh" (6:12–13). It is hard to be sure what circumstances Paul sees his opponents as being in that relate to "boasting" and to avoiding persecution (see comments on 6:13). However, it seems clear that a key part of the situation of Galatians, as Paul sees it, is that a number of Christian Jews (contra Nanos 2002) have spoken to gentile Galatian Christians, encouraging them to adopt circumcision.

Drawing these points together, the evidence from statements in Galatians that directly relate to the audience, to Paul, or to his opponents suggests that, as Paul sees it, the situation leading to the writing of the letter includes the following: some Christian Jews have encouraged gentile Galatian Christians to adopt circumcision; someone has also made accusations against Paul, especially about his gospel having come from other people; at least some of the Galatian Christians have given Paul the impression that they are inclined to be circumcised and to take on other practices based on Jewish law, including calendrical ones; there is probably some disunity among the Galatian Christians.

Contexts for Understanding Galatians

What contexts are relevant for understanding various aspects of the nature of Galatians, as analyzed above? We will offer a survey of some prominent ones, then discuss the controversial matter of the letter's specific geographical and chronological contexts.

Our first characteristic of the text is that it is in Greek: more specifically, "Hellenistic" or Koine (*koinē*, "common") Greek. In our commentary on the text, we shall therefore need to consider word usage and syntax in ancient Greek texts, especially those in Koine Greek or, thinking chronologically, those from around the first century AD. Other NT texts are clearly crucial to this. Especially other texts written by Paul will help us understand his particular vocabulary and syntax. Of course, these may vary over time and may be affected by his general use of scribes (trained writers, not "the scribes" mentioned in the Gospels) to write down the letters (Rom. 16:22; cf. Gal. 6:11). However, linguistic use in other Pauline Letters is not (usually) the same as assuming that the ideas in each letter are the same. For instance, we can argue, lexically, that *nomos* ("law") in Galatians and Romans usually refers to the Jewish law, but that does not mean that Paul necessarily takes the same attitude to the Jewish law in both letters. There is considerable disagreement among scholars about how many NT letters were written by Paul. For purposes of linguistic comparison, this commentary will assume a minimalist position, that Romans, 1 and 2 Corinthians, Galatians, Philippians, 1 Thessalonians, and Philemon (the seven "undisputed" letters) are by Paul. Needless to say, discussion of whether some or all of the other six NT letters attributed to Paul were written by him is beyond the scope of this commentary.

Our second characteristic is that the text is drawn on by second-century Christian writers as being authoritative and that it is then carefully preserved in the extensive NT manuscript tradition. A significant context for understanding Galatians is the set of ways in which early Christian writers understood and used it. However, the amount of very early usage that gives us much help with interpretative decisions is extremely limited. The earliest major use is by Marcion, about a century later (available only through writings of his opponents, esp. Tertullian), involving a reading of Galatians radically at odds with that of most other Christians (see below). Beyond Marcion, the third- and fourth-century worlds of Origen, John Chrysostom, and Augustine involve situations for Christians so different from those of Paul that their interpretations shed much more light on their own ideas than on Paul's. Yet their writings, especially those in Greek, do remain a significant, if problematic, context for understanding Galatians. A further point about early Christian reading of Galatians is that the letter was read as part of an emerging canonical collection of texts. The canon (beyond Paul's Letters) comes into this commentary in three methodologically distinct ways: other NT texts offer linguistic evidence of Koine Greek usage among first-century Christians; other NT texts offer evidence of the situation and ideas in the Jesus movement at the time of Galatians; readers of this commentary are assumed to be interested in the relationship between ideas in Galatians and those in other parts of the canon.

The third characteristic of the text is that it falls within the period AD 46–61. This places it in a certain period of the social, cultural, and political history of the region: preindustrial, Greco-Roman, Roman Imperial, in the reign of Claudius (to 54) or Nero (in his early period, which is usually seen in relatively positive terms), in the decades leading up to the Judean revolt against Rome (66–73). Each of these wider or narrower characterizations of the period points to a range of social, cultural, and political contexts. Among the social contexts are, for instance, the economic structures of first-century society and factors such as patronage. Among the cultural contexts are, for example, popular philosophical movements and the effects of classical Greek literature and philosophy. Among the political contexts are the structures of empire and their relation to the imperial cult.

The date range also relates to stages in the development of the Jesus movement. It has spread well beyond Judea and Galilee. It has drawn in significant numbers of gentiles, but the leading figures in the movement are still Christian Jews rather than gentiles. There has not yet been any organized state persecution of Christians. Other parts of the NT are clearly a particularly important source for understanding aspects of the context in the development of the Jesus movement.

Our fourth characteristic of Galatians is that it generally follows Greek letter form. This means that we will discuss the text in relation to the norms of writing seen in other literary and nonliterary ancient letters written in Greek.

Our fifth and sixth characteristics of the text are that it is addressed to "the assemblies of Galatia" and that it is sent by Paul. Here we reach the heart of the contextual issues. All the other contexts must themselves be contextualized and prioritized according to their relationships to the experiences of Paul and of the Galatians (as understood by Paul). Imperial context, linguistic context, and all the others need to be understood from the viewpoint of Paul and the Galatians—from within their worlds.

The shared world of Paul and the Galatians is the world of the house church. This exists at a certain type of social location in first-century life. It also exists at a location within the Jesus movement of its day. To help us think concretely about this, we can make use of a model house church (see sidebar "Pompeian Model of Craftworker's House Church"). This model relates to house churches hosted by craftworkers, something we know to have happened in Rome (Rom. 16:5; probably, more precisely, an apartment church: Jewett 2007, 64–65) and that was probably common elsewhere (cf. Acts 18; 1 Thess. 2:9; 4:11).

There are other models of house-church social structure that could also be relevant for thinking about the Galatian assemblies. In Rom. 16 we have what

Pompeian Model of Craftworker's House Church

Forty people, such as these:

1. Householder (house ca. 300 m² ground plan including outside space), wife, children, a few (male) craft-working slaves, (female) domestic slave, dependent relative.
2. Several other householders (houses ca. 20–250 m²), some spouses, children, slaves, other dependents.
3. A few members of families with non-Christian householders.
4. A couple of slaves with non-Christian owners.
5. A couple of free or freed dependents of non-Christians.
6. A couple of homeless people.

Oakes 2009, table 3.6

This model was constructed by using the archaeological remains of a craftworker's house at Pompeii, of a size large enough to accommodate a substantial group meeting. The remains (and other Pompeian evidence) were used to consider the size of group that could meet there, the likely structure of the craft-working household, and the likely social profile of a group in which the craftworker's house was the largest domestic space available. (The numerical indicators in the model—"several," "a few," "a couple"—are rough representations of probabilities of such social types forming part of such a group; see Oakes 2009, 46–89.)

may well be two household churches: "those of the household of Aristobulus" (Rom. 16:10) and "those of the household of Narcissus who are in the Lord" (16:11). Each of these sounds like a Christian group consisting of members of a single large household, probably mainly slaves. A model of such a household church would look somewhat different from our model craftworker-hosted house church. Also probably somewhat different would be a house church hosted by Gaius, mentioned in Rom. 16:23 as host to the whole assembly in Corinth. He might well be wealthier than a craftworker, although not necessarily a member of the town's social elite. A house church in his home might be larger than our model and begin higher up the social scale.

There are various possible model house churches and, in any case, the towns of Galatia are not Pompeii. However, the nature of Greco-Roman society means that the house churches of Galatia are almost certain to have consisted of the kind of innately hierarchical group of people seen in our model. This is, first, because of the hierarchy of the Greco-Roman household, which provides a key building block for a house church. Second, it is because Greco-Roman society centered on "vertical" social ties rather than "horizontal" ones. That is, the most common and economically important links were between richer/more powerful and poorer/less powerful: patronage ties, landlord-tenant interactions, creditor-debtor interactions, owner-slave interactions. Socioeconomic solidarity among people of equal status tended to be weak. For instance, although workers in a particular trade might meet together in associations (e.g., the Roman *collegia*), these were primarily social rather than functioning at all like modern trade unions (Stevenson and Lintott 1996, 352). In fact, interactions between equals were often more characterized by competition, whether economic or in terms of competing for honor (see, e.g., Malina and Pilch 2006, 334–35).

The structural priority that Greco-Roman society gave to "vertical" relationships means that a group such as a house church, constructed by starting with a (whole or part) household, was usually bound to draw in a social range spreading downward, economically, from the level of the host householder—broadly the kind of social group in our Pompeian model craftworker house church. We might want sometimes to nudge the top end up in social status. We might occasionally want to build a model from a single household. However, at the level of detail useful for exegesis of a NT text addressed to Christian groups in Greco-Roman towns, the overall socioeconomic shape of an appropriate model house church is still going to look much like our model. So, for example, when a text implicitly encourages people to "remember the poor" (Gal. 2:10), it seems safe to use our model to suggest that fewer than one in five of the letter's recipients are likely to be in control of a household's finances. To take another example, even if a copy of texts from the Septuagint Greek

© Janet Oakes 2007

Figure 2. Atrium of craftworker's house in Pompeii (region I, block 10, house 7).

Expected Hearers and the Implied Reader

An important step in interpretation is to consider the audience that the author expects to be writing for. "Expected hearers" (or "expected readers," although this text would tend to be read aloud) are, in principle, a construct of the mind of the author. In practice, they will have much in common with actual people whom the author has encountered or heard of and for whom he or she is now writing. Extratextual evidence about those people, such as evidence from archaeology of the area where they lived, can therefore be valuable evidence to help interpretation, although with the caveat that the author might possibly have had limited awareness of the circumstances of the hearers. Another key source of evidence about the expected hearers is the text itself (intratextual evidence). If the text is coherent, it will be constructed in such a way that it implies a certain type, or types, of reader. This "implied reader" (a construct from the text) is useful evidence of the expected hearers (a construct in the mind of the author, yet normally with significant similarities to a particular group of real people).

The practical upshot of this argument is that because, in principle, understanding of the intended meaning of a text involves attention to the expected hearers of the text, interpreters with an interest in the intended meaning should draw on both extratextual evidence and intratextual evidence. A concern for the implied reader alone is not sufficient, or even sustainable, despite the way in which many scholars present their work. Extratextual evidence, whether it is, say, the meaning of Greek words in other texts or the range of social values common in first-century Mediterranean societies, is vital for understanding a text.

Another problem with focusing solely on the implied reader is that it unrealistically and problematically limits Paul's expected audience. The implied reader of Galatians is a free, male gentile inclined to adopt circumcision. This was probably only a limited minority of the people for whom Paul was writing. Probably at least about half were women. Some were probably slaves. Some may have been Christian Jews. Proper interpretation includes consideration of how we can fairly expect the text to have been heard by all the types of people for whom it was probably written.

translation of the Hebrew Bible were available to the recipients of Galatians, our model implies that only a few of the members of a house church would likely have had sufficient education to read it. These kinds of conclusions look reasonable to use for exegesis despite the range of differences that undoubtedly existed between any actual Galatian assembly and our model. Without using such a model, many key elements of the reality of the social situation of the Galatian Christians almost inevitably become neglected. As a result, exegesis will tend to miss significant issues.

That the letter is sent by Paul also brings in a range of more specific contexts. For understanding Paul, we have the help of his other letters, although

English Words for First-Century Realities

Several scholars have drawn attention to the pitfalls of using English words such as "Jew" and "Christian" to represent people and situations in the first century (e.g., Esler 2012; Horsley 2005; Mason 2007). There are two key problems. First, modern readers tend to conceive of these terms in relation to their experience of present-day Jews and Christians, with a possible overlay of a historic sense of how Judaism and Christianity have developed over the centuries. Second, biblical scholars have extensively used these terms in ways that do not correspond to the historical situation. Philip Esler (2012) cogently argues that the people referred to as *Ioudaioi* in Greek texts were essentially an ethnic group rather than a religious group, even though, as an ethnic group, they were strongly characterized by particular religious beliefs and practices. Richard Horsley (2005, 2) argues, also cogently, that the first-century followers of Jesus do not fall easily into the patterns that later came to constitute Christianity as an institutionalized religion. These scholars urge the abandonment of the terms "Jew" and "Christian" for study of the first century and favor words such as "Judean" and "Jesus-follower."

Esler's reading of the first-century situation and of the misuse of terms by scholars looks correct. However, I think that most readers of this commentary will think of the English word "Jews" as denoting an ethnic group (typically, but not always, with strongly religious characteristics). I also see the discontinuities between the religious practices of first-century Jews and Christians from those of today. However, there is also strong ethnic (in Hutchinson and Smith's sense [1996, 6–7]) continuity in Judaism: for instance, in seeing Jerusalem as in some sense home. There is also, for both Judaism and Christianity, a fair amount of continuity in some key religious beliefs and practices. Theologically and politically, there is often virtue in reform movements that hold current authorities to account by use of narratives of origins. This is one factor that makes me inclined to take a "glass-half-full" approach to the issue of terminology and keep the terms "Jew" and "Christian" for first-century study, albeit with the kind of needed provisos as are eloquently argued by Esler and Horsley. With great reluctance, I also use "Judaism" to translate *Ioudaïsmos* in 1:13–14—mainly because my alternative paraphrase runs to thirteen words! For this and discussion of Steve Mason's argument about *Ioudaïsmos*, see comments on 1:13. Some others terms will, however, be avoided. "Christianity" sounds too institutional for the first century. I tend to write "Jesus movement." "Church" too easily evokes a building or hierarchical institution, although the term "house church" is valuable in expressing the key setting for early meetings. I will use "assembly" to translate the Greek *ekklēsia*.

without assuming that he always expresses the same views. The six disputed letters that various scholars see either as by Paul or not by Paul will, respectively, either be further direct evidence of his ideas or indirect evidence from people seeking to write in his name and tradition. Similar points hold for the portrait of Paul in Acts. More broadly, the world of ideas expressed in other first-century Christian texts gives some help in understanding him, as does, more broadly still, the corpus of early Jewish texts that express the views of his culture and of the Pharisaic party to which he belonged (Phil. 3:5).

Sources to help us understand the specifically Galatian audience are fairly scarce. However, Susan Elliott (2003) has done interesting work on the cult of the Magna Mater in the region, Thomas Witulski (2000) and Justin Hardin (2008) have considered the imperial cult in the province, and Clinton Arnold (2005) has discussed the significance of "confession stelae" from the western part of the region. It is noticeable that all this contextual evidence is cultic. That reflects the state of archaeological study in the region. There have been no discoveries of extensive, well-preserved, urban domestic remains from this period to help us understand more about living conditions.

The most prominent lexical and semantic content of the letter, as surveyed above, suggests various topics that could relevantly be explored within the range of contexts above. So we are interested in Jewish or Greco-Roman texts or material remains relating to topics such as law, the nature of a person, interaction with the divine, slavery and freedom, interactions between Jews and gentiles, *pistis* ("trust," "fidelity"), inheritance, and crucifixion. Many more could be added.

What the letter implies about its situation reinforces the contextual significance of the development of Paul's mission and, more broadly, of the Jesus movement, especially in Jerusalem. It also raises further topics to be considered in various contexts: topics such as loyalty to founding figures; desertion; boasting; modes of rebuke; modes of argument, possibly including formal rhetoric (see below).

All this sets an agenda that can be followed in only a limited way in the scope of a single commentary. However, the above, or something like it, is the real contextual agenda for studying a text such as Galatians. There is also a complex agenda of linguistic analysis. Other agendas could be added too. Although this commentary can tackle the agendas in only a limited way, the writing of a commentary does offer a strategic opportunity to set up the overall range of issues in the hope that other interpreters will pursue them even where this commentary does not manage to do so.

Specific Geographical and Chronological Contexts

Galatians offers three useful clues about its geographical destination. The clearest is that it is addressed to "the assemblies of Galatia" (1:2). In 3:1, Paul confronts his audience, O . . . *Galatai*. More subtly, in 2:1 he mentions Barnabas without introduction and in 2:13 implies that the audience would have expected good things of him.

The Greek word *Galatia* is simply a transliteration of the Latin name of the Roman province created in 25 BC by the absorption into the Roman Empire of a group of areas, most of which were previously controlled by Celtic rulers allied to Rome (Mitchell 1993a, 61). In Paul's time this province covered a great area of central Asia Minor, running from Paphlagonia in the north to coastal Pamphylia in the south. As Paul tends to use names of provinces elsewhere (e.g., Gal. 1:21; 2 Cor. 1:1; 8:1), there would normally seem to be no difficulty in seeing Paul as addressing a range of Christian assemblies spread about in some parts of the province. Our knowledge of Paul's missionary practice elsewhere would suggest that the assemblies were probably mainly in towns, but some spread into surrounding villages would also be possible.

The Greek word *Galatai* (3:1) normally refers to Celts, Gauls, Galatians—all the same thing (e.g., Schmidt 1994, 15–16). This sounds as though it ought to help us narrow down the geographical destination of the letter. It sounds as though Paul is just addressing one ethnic group. Is there a part of the province in which the population essentially consisted of this ethnic group alone? Our best resource for helping to answer this is epigraphic evidence. Although inscriptions are not equally representative of all socioeconomic groups, they

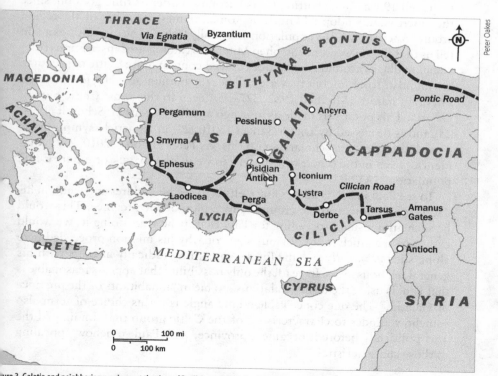

Figure 3. Galatia and neighboring provinces at the time of Paul's letter. Drawn by the author, after Mitchell (1993a, map 3), with Zimmermann 2013; cf. Strobel 2013).

do provide useful data across quite a wide range. Let us consider two areas, one in the south of the province, the other in the north.

Although Cilliers Breytenbach is correct that Celtic political control and hence, to an extent, occupation had extended into substantial parts of the south of what became the province (1996, 152–67), inscriptions suggest that they only formed a small minority there. Bradley H. McLean's catalogue (2002, 87–96) of inscriptions from the museum at Konya—the site of the Roman colony of Iconium, one of the main centers in the region—contains hardly any Celtic names. In contrast, there are, for instance, large numbers of ethnically Phrygian names (cf. Mitchell 1993a, 175). The Phrygians were the predominant ethnic group in central Asia Minor when the Celts arrived in the third century BC (Mitchell 1993a, 175), and then Phrygians persisted in the population.

Moving to the north of the province, the list of "Galatian priests of the Divine Augustus and the Goddess Rome" shows that there were at least some Celtic members of the elite in the provincial capital, Ancyra. For instance, Albiorix was priest in AD 26/27 and his son, Aristocles, held the office in 34/35 (Mitchell 1993a, 108; spotting Celts becomes harder as time goes on, since they increasingly adopted Greek or Roman names). So what of the region around Ancyra? Was the population essentially Celtic? The inscriptions again tell us that the answer is no. Stephen Mitchell's catalogue of inscriptions from ancient villages around Ancyra does indeed contain more Celtic names than are found at Iconium, but they are still heavily outnumbered by, for instance, Phrygian names (Mitchell 1982, 377–95), even in this most Celtic part of Galatia. This point was made as long ago as 1994 by Karl H. Schmidt (1994, 28) and is discussed by Dieter Sänger (2010, 20) in an article symptomatic of a shift in German scholarship on this. As Peter Pilhofer (2010, 277) comments, "Even in the center of Galatia can we in no way talk of a pure Celtic population" (AT).[1]

To see Paul in 3:1 as addressing Celts is to see him addressing what, in his day, was a minority ethnic group in any region of the province. This would be such an unusual proceeding for Paul that, if he were doing it, we would expect to see much more obvious signs of why his mission proceeded here along such *ethnically* specific lines—something radically at odds with his general religious ideas. Instead, the only possibility that appears reasonable is that Paul is using the term "Galatians" to mean "inhabitants of the province of Galatia." The one conceivable ethnic angle is if this choice of term also somehow alludes to characteristics of the Celtic group that dominated the area politically before it became a province, with Paul somehow appealing to those characteristics.

---

1. The German original reads, "Selbst im Zentrum Galatiens kann keineswegs von einer rein keltischen Bevölkerung die Rede sein."

The casual mention of Barnabas in 2:1 suggests that we should look to the account of Paul's mission in Acts 13–14 for the most likely area of Galatia in which the "assemblies" of Gal. 1:2 were located. According to Acts, that was the one mission in which Paul and Barnabas worked together (Acts 13:2; 15:39). There are serious difficulties in coordinating the chronology of Galatians with that of Acts, but it remains a major first-century piece of evidence about Paul's mission and weighs in favor of the assemblies of 1:2 being especially, although not necessarily exclusively, ones on the arc of the Acts 13–14 mission, along the main road system linking the Roman colonies and other towns of the more fertile southern inland region of the province, north of the mountains of Rough Cilicia but south of the more arid steppes of central Galatia. Martinus C. de Boer (2011, 4–5) argues the contrary, that the absence of Barnabas from the account of Paul's mission in 4:13–15 and the negative comment about him in 2:13 make it unlikely that the audience of Galatians was in the southern area, evangelized by Barnabas and Paul together. However, the topic of 4:13–15 relates to Paul's own visual appearance: mention of Barnabas would not be relevant. On 2:13, Paul makes it clear that Barnabas's behavior was unexpected—"even Barnabas"—as it would be if Barnabas was viewed positively by an audience who had been evangelized by him.

How did scholarship ever go down the rather curious road of the North Galatian hypothesis? A key factor is that the boundaries of the province changed, with the southern parts being reassigned to other provinces in a series of stages over the centuries after Paul. This meant that church fathers inevitably assumed that Paul was writing to the northern area around Ancyra (Sänger 2010, 13; Mitchell 1993b, 154–60). A second factor was that epigraphic evidence was quite hard to find, although much has actually been available since the turn of the twentieth century. A third factor, which heavily complicated scholarship in the past century, was that scholars generally entangled the geographical and chronological questions. Those defending the South Galatian hypothesis generally did so in order to defend the chronology of Acts. Conversely, those attacking Luke's chronology tended to make the North Galatian hypothesis a key plank in their platform. The move among some German scholars to support the "Province" hypothesis (rejecting the North Galatian idea), while advocating a very late date for Galatians (Pilhofer 2010, 271, 275–82), should hopefully free scholars from thinking that the geographical and chronological questions are necessarily intertwined.

Our initial consideration, above, of the date of Galatians placed it first between AD 46–140 (between the crucifixion plus sixteen years, and the period of first clear use of the text) and then 46–61 (up to Paul's imprisonment in Rome). The latter date is an argument from silence: Paul does not mention being a prisoner, despite doing this in other letters (e.g., Phil. 1:13; Philem. 9), and there probably would have been a rhetorical advantage in doing so in Galatians. In fact, we can probably move this from 61 back to 58. The chronology of Acts

Light from Acts on Galatians and Vice Versa

Acts sheds light on Galatians. Luke's narrative of the early mission offers historically likely evidence to fill in some gaps in Galatians. Conversely, at these same points of contact, Paul's discourse in Galatians offers evidence from a primary source to support, or sometimes to raise questions about, aspects of the narrative in Acts. Key points of contact are as follows:

Gal. 1:1, 11–12, 15–16. Paul speaks of receiving his gospel via a revelation of Christ. Acts presents this as an encounter in a vision of the resurrected Jesus (9:3–6; 22:6–10; 26:13–18).

Gal. 1:2; 3:1. Paul writes to Galatia. Acts describes a mission in South Galatia and journeys through other parts of the province (13:13–14:25; 16:1–7; 19:1).

Gal. 1:6–7; 2:4; etc. These passages refer to some Christian Jews opposing the Pauline mission as being too lax in relation to Jewish law. Acts attests groups with such attitudes (11:2–3; 15:1, 5; 21:20–22).

Gal. 1:13–14, 23. Paul's zealous persecution of Christians is described in Acts 8:1–3; 9:1–2; 22:3–5; 26:9–12.

Gal. 1:17. This verse curiously mentions Paul returning to Damascus, assuming something like the narrative of Acts in which his encounter with Christ had happened in that vicinity.

Gal. 1:18; 2:1. These verses mention visits to Jerusalem. Paul visits Jerusalem several times in Acts (9:23–29; 11:30 and 12:25; 15:4–30; 18:22–23; 21:17–23:30). Coordinating Gal. 1:18 and Acts 9:23–29 is not difficult chronologically, although there are questions in reconciling to whom Paul spoke. Coordinating Gal. 2:1 with any one visit in Acts is notoriously difficult. Conversion in the mid 30s, + 14 years, sits awkwardly with the death of Herod Agrippa in Acts 12:20–25, probably AD 44 (Josephus, *Ant.* 19.8.2) and possibly with Gallio as proconsul in Acts 18:12, dated epigraphically to around AD 51. Acts scholars have proposed various harmonizations or ways of understanding Luke's approach to chronology (e.g., Alexander 1993).

is probably correct in seeing Paul as imprisoned at Caesarea for two years up to the change of governor from Felix to Festus (Acts 24:27), which likely took place in AD 59/60 (Bruce 1983, 345–46). This takes us back prior to the date preferred by Werner Foerster, who argues for Galatians being written from Myra in Lycia, when the boat taking the imprisoned Paul to Rome stopped at this port near the south end of Galatia in AD 60 or 61. Foerster's argument (1964, 135) that the phrase "and all the brothers with me" (Gal. 1:2) fits the shipboard situation seems outweighed by the force of Paul's silence about his imprisonment. Another argument from silence suggests going back a couple of years earlier than 58, to at least 56 and probably further. The silence in question

Gal. 2:1, 10, 13. Here there is mention of Barnabas, who features in Acts 4:36; 9:27; 11–15, mainly as someone with whom Paul worked in mission, especially in southern Galatia.

Gal. 2:2. This verse refers to a revelation, which could be the prophecy of Acts 11:27–30 (irrespective of difficulties coordinating the chronologies).

Gal. 1:18–19; 2:6–9, 11–12, 14. These verses refer to Peter, John, and James "the brother of the Lord" as leaders of the Jerusalem Christians. The status of these three is narrated in Acts (Peter in chaps. 1–12; 15:7; James in 12:17; 15:13; 21:18; John in chaps. 3–4; 8:14, 17, 25).

Gal. 2:11. This verse refers to Antioch. We should probably rely on the narrative of Acts to take this as a reference to Antioch in Syria rather than Antioch in Pisidia (13:14; 14:19, 21), which was in Galatia. The depiction in Acts is of Syrian Antioch as the key early center of the gentile Jesus movement and Paul's mission (11:19–29; 13:1; 14:26; 15:22–35; 18:22).

Gal. 3:2. This verse describes receiving the Spirit following preaching, as in Acts 2:38; 8:15–17; 9:17; 10:44–47; 11:15–16; 19:2–6.

More generally, Acts provides a narrative of the spread of the Jesus movement both from Jerusalem around the Mediterranean and from being a group of Jesus's Jewish direct disciples to being a network of gentile and Jewish groups nurtured by mobile leaders such as Paul, Apollos, Prisca, and Aquila. The narrative of Acts has almost always been the framework within which Galatians has been interpreted. Taken in general terms, it makes good sense of the letter. In some cases it should make us think again about aspects of Paul's narrative. For instance, although the pro-gentile-mission portrayal of Peter in Acts raises issues about Luke's aims and so forth, it should also caution us against jumping to the conclusion from Galatians that Peter's sympathies were with Paul's opponents (see above). However, commentators who try to interpret passages in Galatians by tightly linking them to texts in Acts (e.g., Gal. 2:1–10 with Acts 15) are probably underestimating the complexities of assessing Luke's specific knowledge and approach.

is about Paul's collection for "the holy ones in Jerusalem" (Rom. 15:25–26). The contrast between Galatians and the letters written during the collection is particularly striking, given that Paul has an opening to write about it when he mentions "remember[ing] the poor" at 2:10. I am persuaded by Bruce Longenecker's argument (2010, 157–206) that this is not, in itself, a direct reference to the Jerusalem collection. But even if it was (as most commentators claim), Galatians would still seem likely to be written at an earlier stage than 1 Cor. 16:1, when the collection in Galatia is under way (contra Schnelle 2005, 271).

The earliest possible date for Galatians is implied by the notes of the three-year and fourteen-year gaps between Paul's revelation (or his leaving Damascus) and his visits to Jerusalem (Gal. 1:18; 2:1, although these periods could be reckoned by including the start and end years, so "three years" might be only slightly beyond twenty-four months). We then need to add further time after the second visit for the Antioch incident and whatever else happened between then and the writing of the letter. My initial mark of AD 46 came from the earliest likely date for the crucifixion (AD 30) and taking the three and fourteen years concurrently. Second Corinthians 11:32–33 offers a further chronological clue. Paul says he escaped by basket(!) when King Aretas was in charge at Damascus. We cannot be sure when Aretas took over there, but many scholars assume that it was when his friend Gaius Caligula became emperor in AD 37. Aretas died in 39, so Paul probably left Damascus between 37 and 39. If this is right, the earliest scenario is that Paul went to Jerusalem, for his first visit, directly from Damascus in 37, with the second visit ten or eleven years later, in 47 or 48 (de Boer 2011, 7–9). We then need to allow time for the Antioch incident and any other events between the second Jerusalem trip and the letter. It would be difficult to place Galatians earlier than AD 50. The composition of the letter appears to be some time in the early fifties, after 1 Thessalonians (and possibly 2 Thessalonians, if by Paul) but before 1 Corinthians.

The Structure of Galatians

One key to understanding a text is to look at its structure. This can be done in several ways. The reader can consult good examples in many commentaries (esp. Betz 1979, 14–25; R. Longenecker 1990, c–cxix; Martyn 1997a, 20–27; de Boer 2011, 11–15). The variety seen in these is partly an indication that texts have a complexity that means that no single structural scheme can show everything of structural interest.

In this section we will investigate structure at three levels. The most basic level will be discussed in epistolary terms: as opening, body, and closing of a Greek letter. We will see how these basic sections are marked, how the opening and closing relate to each other, and how they might help in interpretation of the body. The second level involves sections of the letter body. This will primarily be done by looking for indicators of genre, especially grammatical ones (this only works because of the specific shape of Galatians; the body of another text might be best seen as a series of sections differentiated by topic). We will also consider discourse markers signaling beginnings and ends of sections. Our conclusion will be to read the body in three sections: narrative, argument, and instructions with argument. The third level of analysis will be to consider the main structure of each of these three sections. In each case we will consider subsections relating to the genre of the section. We will conclude that each of the three sections can helpfully be seen as comprising three parts. Finally, we will consider the extent to which this structure ought to be seen in terms of specific "rhetorical" genres, as quite a number of scholars have suggested.

The Basic Level of Epistolary Structure

Galatians presents itself as an ancient Greek letter. At the basic level this has three sections:

Letter Opening (1:1–10)	"Paul ... to the assemblies of Galatia ..."
Letter Body (1:11–6:10)	"I want you to know ... that ..."
Letter Closing (6:11–18)	"See with what large letters I write to you in my own hand ..."

The genres of the first and third sections as opening and closing are marked by a range of formulas known from various letters. It would be possible to see the opening as stopping at 1:5 (Betz 1979, 16). The key choice is whether to see the expression of astonishment at 1:6 as the sudden beginning of the body of the letter, or to see the rebuke in 1:6–10 as an inverted replacement for the thanksgiving section that we usually find in Paul's Letters. There are two advantages to making the second choice. One is that it then enables the letter body to begin at 1:11 with a "disclosure formula," "*I want you to know ...*" We see such a formula at the start of the body of Philippians (1:12) and many other Greek letters (e.g., Hunt and Edgar 1932, no. 113). The second is that it allows for an inclusio (a matching between start and end) between 1:1 and 1:10 (see below).

Both the opening and closing of Galatians are rather limited in the amount of formulaic material used. There are, for instance, no greetings at the end of the letter. However, the opening does include naming and description of the sender (1:1), naming of cosenders and recipients (1:2), and a grace wish (1:3). The closing includes a formula of Paul taking over use of the pen from the scribe who has written the rest of the letter (6:11), a blessing (6:16), and again a grace wish (6:18). Apart from the opening of the letter body, there is little in the body of Galatians that fits with formulaic elements in Greek letter bodies (e.g., common phrases recommending the bearer of the letter). As usual in Paul, there is no section giving general news about his current situation (Phil. 1:12–26 is an exception proving this rule by aiming at something different). One standard element that does occur in Galatians is an expression of desire to be with the Galatians (4:20). However, the tone of this is very different from that in most Greek letters.

How do the opening and closing of Galatians relate to each other (for the significance of such relationships, see Robbins 2013)? They do not have a close lexical relationship, but they do have a close semantic relationship. The only significant Greek word fairly frequent in both is *Christos* (5x in 1:1–10; 3x in 6:11–18). The key semantic link comes from a contrast between the realm of the current world and the realm of God and Christ. This contrast is most strongly highlighted in the case of Paul. The opening is framed by an inclusio (1:1, 10) in which Paul's identity and actions are emphatically asserted not to be linked to the realm of the *anthrōpos* (human, 2x in v. 1; 3x in v. 10) but to the authorization of God and Christ. (Some might reasonably extend this inclusio to cover 1:11–12. However, it seems better to see these verses as beginning the letter body by resuming the topic of 1:1.) In the letter closing, the same contrast about Paul is made, but in different words. He will not boast in the flesh (*sarx*), as his opponents do, but only in the cross of Christ (6:13–14). Through Christ's cross the world (*kosmos*) has been crucified to Paul, and Paul to the world (6:14; cf. 6:17). Paul effectively presents himself here as an example of someone who has been taken out of "this present evil age" through Christ's rescue mission described in 1:4. In contrast, Paul's opponents are still wholly devoted to the realm of the flesh. They want to be able to boast in that realm and to avoid persecution on account of the cross (6:12–13).

In terms of progression from the opening to the closing of the letter, a notable feature is that Paul has shifted the weight of his attack. In the opening, he rebukes his audience (1:6) and is fairly unspecific as to the nature of the opponents and the issues they raise (1:7–9). In the closing, his fire is directed just at the opponents and focuses on their specific interest in circumcision (6:12–13). As a second element of progression, the closing presents motifs of persecution and the cross (6:12, 14, 17). A third is the lexical shift, noted above, in the terms used to denote the realm of "the present evil age."

The relationships between opening and closing put a focus on a number of issues as possible guides for reading the body of the letter. The first is the contrast between things attributed to the realm of "the world" and those attributed to the realm of God and Christ. A second is the role of Paul as a paradigm for this contrast. A third is the shifting of terminology for this contrast, moving from the relatively neutral *anthrōpos* to more loaded terms, especially *sarx* ("flesh"). A fourth is the progression of Paul's rhetoric in repositioning the Galatians onto his side and away from the increasingly criticized opponents.

The Structure of the Body of the Letter (1:11–6:10)

Like Galatians as a whole, if we divide the letter body according to genre, it falls reasonably well into three parts:

Narrative (1:11–2:21)	"For you have heard about…"
Argument (3:1–4:11)	"For it is written that…"
Instructions with Argument (4:12–6:10)	"Be like me."

The three sections of the body are fairly clearly distinguished from one another grammatically. For instance, the main narrative section is sharply marked by temporal indicators governing verbs describing past events (e.g., "then I went," 1:21; "when Peter came," 2:11). On my reckoning, these occur 13 times in the 27.5 verses of 1:11–2:14a (1 per 2.1 verses) and only 6 times in the 121.5 verses of the rest of the letter (1 per 20.3 verses). Of course, this grammatical clue only enables us to detect narrative up to 2:14a. From 2:14b–21 (or part of it), what we see is narrated argument: quotation or description of what Paul remembers arguing in speaking to Peter. In most grammatical terms, it looks like argument rather than narrative. To look unambiguously like narrated argument, it would need more expressions such as "I said" (2:14). One clue to it being narrated argument is that Paul uses "we" to link himself to Peter rather than to his gentile Galatian hearers, "We, who are by nature Jews . . ." (2:15).

Grammatically, one way of looking for sections that we could characterize as "argument" is to look at the frequency of conjunctions and adverbs that act as logical connectives (such as "therefore," "because"). On my count, there are 5 of these in the 7.5 verses of 2:14b–21 (1 per 1.5 verses), 23 in the 40 verses of 3:1–4:11 (1 per 1.7 verses), and 28 in the 56 verses of 4:12–6:10 (1 per 2 verses). In contrast, there are only 12 (possibly 13) in the 45.5 verses other than 2:14b–6:10 (1 per 3.8 verses). The main directly narrative section of the letter, 1:13b–2:14a, only includes 3 (possibly 4) in 26 verses (1 per 8.7 verses). Although the frequency of logical connectives does not offer an overwhelming distinction between genres, it does help us characterize the sections.

The description of the third section of the body as "Instructions with Argument" is indicative of the overlap in genre between this and the argument section. However, there is a clear grammatical change at 4:12 with the introduction of the first Greek imperative that calls for action, "Be like me" (*ginesthe hōs egō*). There are no such imperatives prior to 4:12, but ten or eleven appear between 4:12 and 6:10 (with a further one or two after that). The only imperatives before 4:12 are probably *performative* ones; that is, they bring something about in the very writing and reading of them: "Let him be accursed!" (1:8, 9); "Know then that . . ." (3:7). These are probably not calling the Galatians to particular actions. In contrast, the imperatives from 4:12 onward give the Galatians a series of instructions, mixed in with elements of argument.

There are, of course, some complications apart from 2:14b–21 in the pattern of genres in the letter. There is a narrative aspect to several of the arguments. This includes some of those from Scripture: for instance, on Abraham in 3:6–8, and especially on his partners and sons in 4:21–31. This passage could also be put under another genre label as allegory (cf. 4:24). There is also a narrative aspect to the argument from the Galatians' experience (3:2–5; 4:12–20). Another genre that dominates a subsection of the letter is listing of vices or virtues (5:19–23). However, this still fits under the overall section genre of Instructions with Argument.

As well as the three sections of the letter body being marked by a change of genre, they are signaled fairly well by discourse markers that indicate beginnings or endings. The break from 2:21 to 3:1 is strongly marked, with 2:21 giving a rhetorical flourish, an emphatic maxim that caps the argument. Then 3:1 changes gear sharply into an expression of despair or bewilderment. Moreover, this is a key transition in the text because Paul now turns directly to his hearers and addresses them. (In contrast, there are no clear discourse markers signaling a section break between 2:14a and 2:14b: despite Paul's shifting into argument, the text flows directly on from 2:14a into 2:14b–21.)

In chapters 3–4 are several places with sufficient rhetorical flourish to mark an ending. However, the break between 4:11 and 4:12 is particularly strongly marked. Here 4:11 forms an inclusio with 3:1, as Paul again expresses some despair over the Galatians. Then 4:12 shifts sharply by changing mode of address to the imperative and by switching topic from theological argument to issues of personal relationship between Paul and the Galatians. Having said that, this break is not as strongly marked as that at 3:1. One could instead see a break later. For instance, 4:19–20 is also an expression of despair about the Galatians and could be seen as forming an inclusio with 3:1. Alternatively, one could break the later part of the letter into more sections. For instance, Gal. 5:13 is frequently seen as the start of a new major section. However, in genre terms, it is 4:12 that sees the main change. From there to the end of the body, the letter centers on instructions to the Galatians.

The Structure of Each Section of the Letter Body

The three sections of the body of Galatians can each be seen as consisting of three subsections.

In the case of the narrative section (1:11–2:21), the subsections are three narrated sets of events. In 1:11–24, Paul tells of the origin of his gospel message. He uses a narrative of the events around his Damascus-road experience to demonstrate the nonhuman origin of what he teaches. In 2:1–10, rather surprisingly, he writes about a visit to Jerusalem to consult with Christian leaders there about his gospel. He narrates their acceptance of his message and their unity with him. However, in 2:11–21, a third set of events disrupt the unity, both between him and the Jerusalem leaders and between Christian Jews and Christian gentiles. He narrates the disruptive events at Antioch and his vigorous challenge to Peter.

The argument section (3:1–4:11) splits into three smaller arguments. After an initial exclamation (3:1), in 3:2–14 Paul builds an argument about how the Galatians have received the Spirit. He interprets their experience (esp. 3:2) as equating to the blessing of Abraham, conferred by God on gentiles in Christ on the basis of trust (esp. 3:14). A complex series of exegetical arguments carries Paul's case. In 3:15–29, he looks at this process from another angle, in which time becomes a significant factor. He sets up God's promise to Abraham as being both for a single descendant, who is Christ (3:16) and, in due time, for all those made one in Christ (3:28–29). Paul uses the factor of time to present a valuable but limited role for the law (3:19–25). In 4:1–11, he again uses an argument based on time. He portrays a progress from slavery into freedom, which he turns around to use as an argument against current Galatian behavior, seen as a reversing of progress in a return to slavery.

The "Instructions with Argument" section (4:12–6:10) can be seen as centering on three instructions. In 4:12–20 Paul calls the Galatians to "be like me" (4:12) and to act in a way consistent with their first welcome of him (4:13–16). More discursively, in 4:21–5:13a he calls them to stand firm in their freedom (5:1). Paul makes his point from the contrast between the sons of the free and enslaved women who were mothers to Abraham's children (4:21–31). Then Paul makes it clear that the Galatians' danger of reenslavement lies in circumcision (5:2). After attacking those urging this (5:7–12), he reminds the Galatians again of their calling to freedom (5:13a). More loosely, in 5:13b–6:10—although we could arguably subdivide this further—Paul gives a series of instructions centered on love (5:13b–14, 22; 6:2, 10) and consequently against disunity (5:15, 20, 26). This loving behavior is seen as characteristic of the Spirit (5:16–18, 22–23) and in contrast to the "works of the flesh" (5:16–17, 19–21, 24). There are also some instructions without an obvious link to the topic of love.

Structure and Ancient Rhetoric

We have analyzed the body of Galatians mainly in terms of genre, understood as a broad analytical category. Beginning with the classic work of Hans Dieter Betz, quite a number of scholars look at the genre issue in a more specific way, by considering how the sections of the letter might fit patterns of expression used at different stages of speech delivery by a Greek or Roman orator (i.e., these scholars analyze the structure in terms of Greco-Roman rhetoric). Betz reads Galatians as an *apologetic* speech, primarily defending Paul and his gospel against accusations. This produces a structure for the body of the letter that is expressed in rhetorical terms: *exordium* (1:6–11), *narratio* (1:12–2:14), *propositio* (2:15–21), *probatio* (3:1–4:31), *exhortatio* (5:1–6:10), with the letter ending functioning as a *conclusio* (Betz 1979, 15–23). The shape is fairly similar to ours (*probatio* means a section of arguments proving the proposition expressed in the *propositio*), but the headings flag similarities to steps in Greco-Roman oratory in particular, rather than general genre terms such as "argument."

Most scholars who analyze Galatians in formal rhetorical terms now do so not as *apologetic* rhetoric, as Betz did, but instead prefer to see it as *deliberative* rhetoric: a speech given in order to persuade a group (e.g., a citizen assembly) to a particular course of action. However, this difference in *species* of rhetoric tends not to cause a radical change in the suggested structure. Many of the sections essentially remain the same, although sometimes under a different Latin term (e.g., the proof section being called *confirmatio* rather than *probatio*). The most significant difference between various suggested rhetorical structures tends to be in which passage is viewed as the *propositio* (or equivalent) of the letter. For instance, Betz sees it as 2:15–21, but Robert Hall (2002) sees it as 1:6–9, producing a structure that reads: Salutation/*exordium* (1:1–5); Proposition (1:6–9); Proof (1:10–6:10), consisting of Narration (1:10–2:21) and Further Headings (3:1–6:10); Epilogue (6:11–18). One of Hall's arguments for Galatians being deliberative rather than apologetic rhetoric is that Galatians includes much exhortation, which is not something to be expected in the apologetic rhetoric used for defense speeches in court.

How valuable the formal rhetorical approach to structure is depends on the extent to which it sheds light on Paul's discourse in ways that would not be seen by analyzing it in more general terms. Debate continues to go back and forth on this. My conclusion so far has been that we need to be aware of specific rhetorical moves that ancient orators tend to make, according to rhetorical handbooks and recorded speeches, but that there is not enough evidence to distinguish the structures of Paul's letters as being ones specifically seen in rhetorical handbooks. We can spot grammatical evidence to show that Paul is narrating, and we can see that he is using the narration as a form of argument, but it is more difficult to see the specific evidence that this is *narratio* as such, that he is constructing the passage using the kind of specific techniques drawn from ancient rhetorical handbooks rather than general techniques of narratives intended to persuade. We must give attention to known ancient modes of persuasion, but it is not clear that the rhetorical handbooks give us enough to set out the whole structure of Galatians.

Issues in the Reception of Galatians

For surveys and collections of texts, see John Riches (2008, for all periods), Martin Meiser (2007, for antiquity), and Ian Levy (2011, for medieval times). The following simply offers a basic orientation to a few key topics.

The first is that of Jews, gentiles, and Jewish law. Marcion, as reported by Tertullian and others, splits the God of Jesus from the God of the OT. For Marcion, in Gal. 3:13 Christ's cross frees us from the curse imposed by the bloodthirsty creator (Jerome, *Galatians* [Migne 1800–1875, 26:434]; Riches 2008, 13; Meiser 2007, 19). Other readers of Galatians have not gone to that extreme in dividing Paul from his Jewish roots, but the Lutheran tradition in particular has seen a very sharp disjunction between Paul's gospel and ideas of salvation centered on Jewish law. In the nineteenth century, F. C. Baur and the Tübingen school saw Paul's "law-free" gospel pitched against a Petrine and more conservatively Jewish gospel in a struggle that defined the shape of earliest Christianity (Riches 1993, 2–3). In the twentieth century, Ernst

Käsemann's reading of Paul saw "the devout Jew" as typifying the "religious" person, who misunderstands the law "as a means to a righteousness of one's own" (1969, 184–85). For Hans Hübner (1984), Galatians saw Paul at his most negative about the law, a view that Paul modified in later letters. For Heikki Räisänen (1983, 12–14, 264–65), Paul's view of the current redundancy of God's own law produced an inner tension that left Paul's writings riddled with inconsistencies.

Much post-Holocaust Pauline scholarship has seen extensive reevaluation of Paul's view of the law. E. P. Sanders (1977, 441–43, 489–90) presents first-century Judaism as a religion of grace and offers a rereading of Paul in which Gal. 2:21 is prominent: Paul has discovered that salvation comes through Christ's cross; it is essentially this, rather than something wrong with the law, that leaves Paul skeptical about any other potential source of salvation. James Dunn (1993, 135–37) endows Sanders's position with the name "the New Perspective on Paul" and nuances it by arguing that Paul opposes not the law itself but "works of the law," identity-marking actions (such as circumcision) that divide Jews from gentiles. Michael Bachmann (2010, 100–108) also considers this issue, arguing, for instance, that "works of the law" refers not to deeds done to fulfill the law but to the law's regulations themselves. Writers such as Stephen Westerholm (2004, 443) seek to push back toward the Lutheran line. He responds to Sanders's point—that first-century Jews did not see their religion as one of dependence on works—by arguing that in Galatians and elsewhere, we see Paul's specifically Christian analysis

---

Martin Luther on Galatians 2:16

"God sent his only-begotten Son into the world that we may live through his merit. He was crucified and killed for us. By sacrificing his Son for us, God revealed Himself to us as a merciful Father who donates remission of sins, righteousness, and life everlasting for Christ's sake. . . ."

". . . faith apprehends Jesus Christ. Christian faith is not an inactive quality in the heart. If it is true faith, it will surely take Christ for its object. Christ, apprehended by faith and dwelling in the heart, constitutes Christian righteousness, for which God gives eternal life."

". . . these three things, faith, Christ, and imputation of righteousness, are to be joined together. Faith takes hold of Christ. God accounts this faith for righteousness."

". . . A Christian is not somebody who has no sin but somebody against whom God no longer chalks sin, because of his faith in Christ."

Luther 1949/1535, on Gal. 2:16, trans. T. Graebner 1949

of Judaism, rather than the view Paul would have had prior to Damascus. Others, such as Mark Nanos (2002, 77–85), push Paul further into the ongoing life of first-century Jews, relocating Paul's Jesus-following communities within the life of synagogues.

The other great Lutheran concern has been with "justification." Luther's commentary on Galatians has been a most influential expression of this. His formulations have then been subject to refinement (and modification) by followers of this tradition, which many scholars continue to defend today (e.g., Schreiner 2010, 155–57). However, in the twentieth century this idea of justification, seen as the key component of Paul's soteriology (ideas about salvation), repeatedly came under attack. Albert Schweitzer (1931, 225) relegated justification to being merely a "subsidiary crater" in Paul's soteriological thought, which centered instead on mystical union with Christ. Sanders and other New Perspective scholars (see above) in effect question aspects of Lutheran ideas on justification, as does work by J. Louis Martyn and by Richard Hays (see below).

Douglas Campbell (2009) raised the temperature of the debate with an excoriating attack on what he sees as the negative effects of "Justification Theory" (renamed "Forward Theory" in 2011, 165). For Campbell, "forwardness" takes the idea of salvation as proceeding from an objective, evident problem to a solution (found in Christ). Campbell (2011, 168, 170) claims that this requires implausible history (e.g., first-century Judaism reckoned as evidently inadequate) and produces destructive theology. He sees Paul as primarily constructing his theology in a "backward" rather than "forward" manner: Paul begins from the revelation of Christ; Paul's descriptions of the world are effects of that revelation, rather than objective assertions. An exegetical feature of Campbell's reading is that at key points he takes negative assertions in the text as being about the teaching of Paul's opponents: for instance, in Gal. 2:16 justification by works of the law is *their* idea, rather than a description of Judaism (2011, 173).

In 1985, J. Louis Martyn published a paper that switched the soteriology of Galatians, turning from a Lutheran focus on the cross as enabling the individual's process of coming to salvation to the idea that the cross objectively changed the world. This event, which Martyn describes as being "apocalyptic," produced a new set of circumstances for existence. In particular, the cross did away with the dualities of the old world, which Martyn calls "antinomies." Martyn takes this a long way: the cross brings "the end of all religious differentiations such as the differentiation of holy, circumcised people from profane and uncircumcised people" (1997a, 561). The cross abolishes all these, although it does introduce some new antinomies, such as that between flesh and Spirit. Martyn sees Paul as arguing that if gentiles follow the way of circumcision, they misunderstand the realities of this new world (Martyn 1985, 412–21). Martyn's view has had wide influence (including beyond NT studies), although it has also attracted vigorous criticism (e.g., Wright 2012, 372–74). The major commentary on Galatians by Martinus de Boer (2011) offers a vigorous defense of an "apocalyptic" reading very close to that of Martyn.

Also in the 1980s, Richard Hays challenged the Lutheran reading of Galatians from another direction. He argues for an increased sensitivity to narrative elements in Paul's theology and to poetic aspects of the way in which he presents it. Most prominently, Hays reconsiders Paul's use of the phrase *pistis Christou*, suggesting that it means not "faith in Christ" but "faith of Christ." Hays particularly means the "faithfulness of Christ" to God, especially as seen in Christ's obedient death on the cross (2002, xxx). He sees this as reorienting the soteriology of the letter. Instead of primarily focusing on what people did—believing in Christ—it focuses on what God did, in Christ. Having said this, Hays is some distance from seeking to entirely overthrow Lutheran soteriology. He sees human faith as a response by which people participate in the faithfulness of Christ (2002, 211). Various scholars have further developed his ideas or suggested alternatives (e.g., Williams 1997). However, his reading has come under attack from scholars such as James Dunn (2002) and Barry Matlock (2000). Among Dunn's arguments, a prominent strand involves analysis of uses of *pistis* without *Christou*, taking that to refer to human faith, and discussion of how that relates to what *pistis* means when with *Christou* (Dunn 2008). One radical counterresponse to this line of analysis comes from de Boer (2011, 192–93), who argues that almost all of the uses of *pistis* in Galatians refer primarily to the faithfulness of Christ.

One final broad scholarly approach that we will consider here is the use of Galatians in relation to various issues of social justice. This has centered on Gal. 3:28, "There is no Jew nor Greek. There is no slave nor free. There is no male and female." Elizabeth Schüssler Fiorenza (1984, 205) made this programmatic for her vision of a gender-inclusive early Christianity. Among further gender-related work is the study by Tatha Wiley (2005) and analyses of Paul's rhetoric by Beverly Roberts Gaventa (2007) and Susan Eastman (2007), who makes the Sarah-and-Hagar passage central to the letter. Brigitte Kahl (2010, 275, 281–84) argues more broadly that Paul's message in Galatians is a call to unity in diversity. She sees this as particularly critiquing the structures of the Roman Empire. Indeed, she sees Paul's opponents' call to circumcision as subservient to an imperial strategy for keeping groups in order (Kahl 2010, 274). She is not alone in interpreting the letter in relation to the empire. Thomas Witulski (2000) interprets 4:8–20 as a response to the imperial cult. Justin Hardin (2008) goes further and sees this as the key issue in the letter as a whole.

Many other significant scholars cry out for attention. Some have been mentioned above in relation to the context of the letter or the structure of the letter. Others whose work relates to particular sections of the letter will be discussed at the appropriate point.

Outline of Galatians

Letter opening (1:1–10)

Paul's divine authorization (1:1–2)

Rescue from the present evil age (1:3–5)

Deserting the one who called them and the only gospel (1:6–10)

Letter body (1:11–6:10)

Narrative 1: Of a gospel revealed by God, not people (1:11–24)

Assertion of nonhuman origin of Paul's gospel (1:11–12)

Paul's previous behavior in Judaism (1:13–14)

Revelation to Paul and his avoidance of most contact with Jerusalem (1:15–22)

An effect of the change in Paul's behavior (1:23–24)

Narrative 2: Of a gospel affirmed by unity at Jerusalem (2:1–10)

Timing, origin, and purpose of a visit to Jerusalem (2:1–2)

Successful resistance to Titus being compelled to be circumcised (2:3–5)

God's lack of regard for people's reputation (2:6a–b)

Acceptance of Paul's gospel for the uncircumcised (2:6c–10)

Narrative 3: Of a gospel betrayed by division at Antioch (2:11–21)

Paul's opposition to Peter's withdrawal from table fellowship (2:11–14)

Paul to Peter about what Christian Jews know and have done (2:15–17)

Paul's dying and living (2:18–21)

Argument 1: For blessing in Christ through trust (3:1–14)

Paul's bemusement about the Galatians (3:1)

From the absurdity of not learning from experience of the Spirit (3:2–5)

From Abraham's receiving of righteousness by trust (3:6–9)

From texts about law, curse, righteousness, trust, and life (3:10–13)

The result: Abraham's blessing and the Spirit come to gentiles (3:14)

Argument 2: For unity in Christ (3:15–29)

From the nature of covenants and the wording of this one (3:15–18)

From the nature of the law (3:19–25)

From the nature of being in Christ (3:26–29)

Argument 3: Against returning to slavery (4:1–11)

From the slave-like nature of childhood and the liberating action of God (4:1–7)

From the absurdity of the Galatians returning to former slavery (4:8–10)

Paul's fear about the Galatians (4:11)

Instructions with argument 1: "Be like me" (4:12–20)

"Be like me, as I am like you" (4:12a)

Contrast between the Galatians' previous and current attitudes toward Paul (4:12b–16)

Contrast between the aims of Paul's opponents and his own (4:17–20)

Instructions with argument 2: "Do not be subject again to . . . slavery" (4:21–5:13a)

Allegory of freedom and call to stand firm in it (4:21–5:1)

Law and the danger of falling from grace (5:2–6)

"The one harassing you will bear the judgment" (5:7–13a)

Instructions with argument 3: "Through love be slaves to one another" (5:13b–6:10)

Call to make freedom an opportunity not for the flesh but to love, which fulfills the law (5:13b–15)

The effects of Spirit and flesh (5:16–26)

Doing good (6:1–10)

Letter closing (6:11–18)

Paul's handwriting (6:11)

Contrast between the opponents and Paul about circumcision and the cross (6:12–15)

Final blessing, plea, and grace wish (6:16–18)

Galatians 1:1–10

Letter Opening

Introductory Matters

Paul begins his letter in a strange and striking way. To us, its strangeness partly lies in the fact that it is an ancient Greek letter, and such letters were written rather differently from our own. However, there is also a strangeness that would have struck the first hearers even more forcefully than it strikes us.

With today's letter-writing conventions, and with the typical rhetoric of letters between people who know each other, we might expect something like this:

> Dear brothers and sisters in Galatia,
>   I hope you are all in good health. It seems so long since I was there, enjoying your generous hospitality. I have been keeping well, except for the usual ailments that you know about. The progress of the mission here has been encouraging. You may not know that, last month, Timothy went to . . .
>   . . . with best wishes,
>   Paul

Instead, as you can see from the opening of Galatians, the structure and tone are different. Most obviously, the names of sender and recipients are the other way around, with sender named first: "Paul, an emissary . . . , and all the brothers and sisters with me, to the assemblies of Galatia." Other NT letters follow the same pattern, which is typical of ancient Greek letters (Stirewalt 1993; Stowers 1986; White 1986). It gives the opportunity for the sender to characterize both sender ("Paul, an emissary") and recipients ("the assemblies of Galatia"). In Paul's other letters, he describes himself and his recipients in

Rylands Greek Papyrus 243, Letter of Demarion and Irene

"Demarion and Irene to their dearest Syrus, very many greetings. We know that you are distressed about the deficiency of water; this has happened not to us only but to many, and we know that nothing has occurred through any fault of yours. We now know your zeal and attentiveness to the work of the holding, and we hope that with God's help the field will be sown. Put down to our account everything you expend on the cultivation of the holding. Receive from Ninnarus for Irene's account the share belonging to her, and similarly from Hatres for Demarion's account the share belonging to her. We pray for your health."

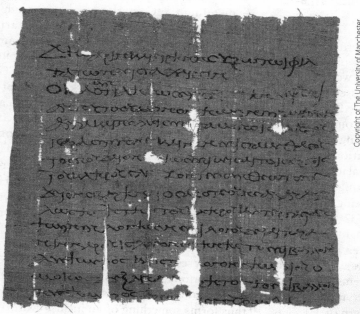

Copyright of The University of Manchester

Figure 4. Letter of Demarion and Irene. Rylands Greek Papyrus 243, second century AD (image number: JRL022778tr). By permission of the John Rylands Library.

On reverse:

"To Syrus from Irene and Demarion"

trans. from Bagnall and Cribiore 2006, §350

a range of ways. These can help set the tone of the letter or relate to its main agenda. In opening Galatians, Paul emphasizes his divine commissioning and characterizes his hearers in the most unvarnished way possible, without

**Galatians 1:1–10
in the Rhetorical Flow**

▶Letter opening (1:1–10)

Paul's divine authorization (1:1–2)

Rescue from the present evil age (1:3–5)

Deserting the one who called them and the only gospel (1:6–10)

positive terms such as "holy." Grace wishes such as Gal. 1:3 are standard in Christian letters, but Paul unexpectedly expands this with a reference to Christ as rescuing Christians from "the present evil age."

Even more unexpected is what happens in verse 6. One thing ancient and modern letters have in common is that, however problematic the issues to be addressed in the letter, the opening is almost always full of polite expressions. First Corinthians is a good example. In 1:1–9, Paul is warm in commending the Corinthians, even though later he will have severe things to say. (He starts subtly by setting up some of the difficult issues, even in his warm comments: "I thank my God . . . because you have been enriched in every way in him, in every word and all knowledge" [1 Cor. 1:5–6; cf. 2:1–4; 4:8; 8:1].) Galatians bypasses politeness with the shocking verse 6 (shocking but not unprecedented: the "angry letter" was, unsurprisingly, a form known in antiquity [see comments on 1:6]). Something has made Paul desperately concerned and angry. He wants to shock his hearers into a radical reevaluation of their situation and actions.

Galatians 1:1–10 clearly falls into two halves. The structured sender-receiver-greetings section is 1:1–5. Paul then launches his attack in 1:6–9. His denial of being a flatterer (1:10) is somewhat freestanding. J. Louis Martyn (1997a, 136–37) sees it as a transition, attaching it to verses 11–12 and separating it from 1:1–9. Hans Dieter Betz (1979, 46) links 1:10 to 1:11, seeing them together as a transition that forms the end of the *exordium* (see introduction above). We will take 1:10 with verses 1–9. This is partly because, stylistically, it forms part of a series of emotional outbursts from 1:6 onward. Also, as Martyn (1997a, 140) in fact argues, 1:10 mirrors the "not people but God" pattern of 1:1. Verse 10 thus forms something of an inclusio with 1:1 (as the end of a passage corresponds to the beginning). Although 1:11 echoes the "not people but God" pattern, that verse begins with a *disclosure formula* ("I declare to you"). This works well as the opening of the narrative that follows, and disclosure formulas are used in a similar way to begin the main body of the letter in other correspondence from Paul (e.g., Phil. 1:12).

Tracing the Train of Thought

Three arguments are forcefully made in verses 1–10: Paul's authority is of divine origin; salvation involves Christ's self-sacrificial rescue from this evil age; and the Galatians are abandoning their founder and the only gospel.

Paul's Divine Authorization (1:1–2)

1:1–2. Paul makes full use of the opportunity provided by the standard Christian letter-opening pattern, "A to B, grace," to describe A (himself) and to expand, theologically, on the "grace." In contrast, he barely describes B (the Galatians) at all. In itself this somewhat sets the tone of what is to follow.

First A, the sender. To some extent, Paul takes a risk here. **Paul, an emissary not from people, nor through a person, but through Jesus Christ and God the Father, who raised him from among the dead** (1:1). To argue that you do not have authority from other humans, but from God instead, is a high-risk strategy. Your hearers might just see it as wild assertion. However, Paul has an advantage. His hearers have become Christians as a result of his preaching. Their identity as individuals and as a group is consequently tied rather strongly to the validity of Paul and his message. It will be difficult for other teachers to challenge his authority. He can push his argument about his divine authority quite hard. Indeed, he does so through most of 1:1–2:10. Almost all of this largely narrative section brings home the divine origin and authority of Paul's calling and his message.

The Greek word that is here translated as "emissary" is *apostolos*. Of course, this gives us the term "apostle." The word was already being commonly used to designate a particular set of early leaders (see, e.g., 1 Cor. 15:9). This means that translating *apostolos* here as "apostle" would have the advantage of indicating, rightly, that by using the term Paul is making a claim to belong to this particular, authoritative group. However, the translation "apostle" does not convey what the function of an *apostolos* was, and as Martyn (1997a, 82–83) argues, the prepositional phrases that follow in the verse show that here Paul particularly has in mind the idea of the *apostolos* as a person who is sent: the noun is derived from the verb *apostellō*, "I send" (for a general discussion of the term, see R. Longenecker 1990, 2–4). Early Christians used the term to cover a range of types of people sent by churches (e.g., Epaphroditus in Phil. 2:25). In Gal. 1:1, the translation "emissary" is useful particularly because Paul's very first point is about his being sent: that he is not an emissary sent from a group of people—unlike, probably, the opponents whom he will attack in the letter.

Paul presumably implies that, instead, he is sent from God. However, he does not directly express this but instead jumps to the further point that not only was he not sent from people, neither was he sent "through a person." This probably refers to his sense of commissioning, that it was not done by a human person but by "Jesus Christ and God." Paul reinforces his divine commission in 1:15–16. God is the one who called Paul, by God's grace, to proclaim him among the gentiles. (If we compare this with Acts 9 and 22, we can see there the role of a human agent, Ananias. However, even in Acts there is a strong sense of fairly direct divine commissioning of Paul, most notably in 26:16–18.)

Jesus Christ and God are bracketed together in Gal. 1:1 in the action of commissioning Paul. This happens again in 1:3, where both are the source of grace and peace to the Galatians. On the other hand, it is only to God, not Christ, that glory is given in 1:5. In the earlier verses, the very naming of Jesus alongside God the Father both links them together and suggests that Paul sees their identities as distinct. We might also wonder whether there is implicit docetism in 1:1 (the idea that Jesus only appeared to be human but was not really so). If Paul was commissioned not through a person but through Jesus, it sounds as though Jesus is not a person. However, in the letter, Paul is very clear about Jesus Christ's human birth (4:4) and death (2:21), so the christological implication of 1:1 is very unlikely to be that Paul saw Jesus as nonhuman. Instead, he seems to see Jesus, whom he knew to be human, as also occupying a status much higher than that of humans—a status that enabled Jesus to act alongside God.

The description of God in Gal. 1:1 is twofold. He is "Father," and he is the one "who raised" Christ "from among the dead." In fact, God is described as Father three times in the first five verses. This is more than in the equivalent opening segment of any other Pauline letter. We should not make too much of this. However, in a letter that so strongly involves issues of obedience to authority, it could be that Paul is stressing God's role as a figure of authority, albeit a caring authority. The description of God as Father could also be beginning to lay the groundwork for the discussion of sonship later in the letter (3:26; 4:5–7; Hays 2000, 203).

More striking than the mention of God's fatherhood is the introduction, in the first sentence of the letter, of Christ's resurrection. Surprisingly, Christ's resurrection is not mentioned directly anywhere else in the letter. The closest Paul comes is to talk about the Christian life by using a pattern implicitly drawn from Christ's death and resurrection: "I have been crucified with Christ. I am no longer alive. Christ is alive in me" (2:19–20). The promise of Christian resurrection is also a key motivator at the end of the letter: "the one who sows to the Spirit will, from the Spirit, reap eternal life" (6:8). More broadly, the mention of the resurrection signals to us that this text has an apocalyptic worldview (although probably not Martyn's particular version [see on 6:15]). The dead are raised. Ages of the world can be good or evil (1:4). Angels speak (1:8). This text works with assumptions very different from those of most twenty-first-century Western discourse.

In the next verse, Paul broadens the pool of senders: **and all the brothers and sisters with me** (1:2). Many scholars view Paul as a somewhat isolated figure as he writes Galatians, rejected by his "home church" of Antioch and largely abandoned by his own converts in Galatia (e.g., Elmer 2009). Whether or not this is the case, Paul presents the letter as coming from a substantial group. This lends their authority to the letter.

The verse ends with the recipients: **to the assemblies of Galatia** (1:2). The Greek word *ekklēsia* is Paul's common designation of local Christian groups.

Translating *Adelphoi*

The inherent cultural difficulties of translation are neatly highlighted by the problem of handling *adelphoi*. The New Revised Standard Version renders *adelphoi* here as "members of God's family." In verse 11 it offers "brothers and sisters." For *pseudadelphoi* in 2:4 it gives "false believers." In 4:12, 28, 31, and 5:11 *adelphoi* is "friends." In 5:13 we are back to "brothers and sisters." Then 6:1 uses "friends," and 6:18 uses "brothers and sisters."

Traditionally, English translators have opted for "brothers." Most translators are aware that Paul uses the term to refer to all Christians, male and female. In past centuries, translators viewed "brothers" as being, in this kind of use, an inclusive term, encompassing women as well as men. In the twentieth century, feminist scholars argued that the presence in a language of such masculine "inclusive" terms encoded and reinforced patriarchal assumptions. At the same time, English usage was moving away from hearing these masculine terms as inclusive: many women perceived themselves as excluded from such categories. The result of these arguments was that translators have tended toward renderings of *adelphoi* such as "brothers and sisters," as in this commentary.

However, this does not entirely solve the problem. The word *adelphoi* is actually one of the masculine "inclusive" terms in question. Rendering it as "brothers and sisters" could, to an extent, mask a real patriarchal tendency in ancient Greek culture or in the Bible. Moreover, *adelphoi* may carry connotations of the activities of particular kinds of male groups, such as clubs or elite philosophical gatherings. It may also be that it was actually quite radical for Paul to use this term to designate the members of a gender-mixed and socially mixed group. He may effectively have been ascribing heightened status to some members who would not normally have moved in circles where they would have been addressed as *adelphoi* (see Oakes 2009, 107–10).

He also uses it of Christians more broadly in 1:13. Our "ecclesiastical" words derive from this term, and it has traditionally been translated as "church." However, the word can be used of other kinds of assembly, such as meetings of town citizens (Acts 19:32; Louw and Nida 1988, 11.78). Translating the word as "church" is also potentially misleading. It suggests a degree of institutional organization, and of similarity to modern Christian groups, that is not warranted at this period.

In other letters, Paul uses the singular, "assembly," in the address. That is because he is writing to Christians in a single town. Here he is addressing all the groups in a wide area, probably the Roman province (see introduction). In other letters, Paul always elaborates somewhat on the identity of the recipients. Their assembly is "in God" (1 Thess. 1:1), they are "made holy in Christ Jesus" (1 Cor. 1:2), and so forth. The Galatians just receive the unvarnished title "assemblies"—a sign of things to come.

Rescue from the Present Evil Age (1:3–5)

1:3–5. Grace to you and peace from God our Father and the Lord Jesus Christ, who gave himself for our sins, to rescue us from the present evil age, according to the will of our God and Father, to whom be the glory through all ages, amen. After a standard wish for grace and peace, Paul adds a surprising description of Christian salvation.

The description begins in a relatively common Pauline way. Christ "gave himself for our sins" (the Greek manuscripts are divided on whether Christ gave himself *hyper* [on behalf of] or *peri* [concerning] our sins, but the sense is similar in either case). Christ's initiative in self-giving is also expressed in Gal. 2:20, "the Son of God, . . . who . . . gave himself for me," which is in a context that speaks of Christ's death (2:21; cf. 2:19). Christ's death for our sins is an important point in Paul's ideas about salvation (see, e.g., 1 Cor. 15:3). The ways in which it comes into the argument of Galatians are, as we shall see, interesting and varied.

Christ's giving of himself for our sins is an idea based on the OT practice of animal sacrifice for sins. For instance, on the annual Day of Atonement of Lev. 16 (in view esp. in Rom. 3:25), various animals represented the priests and people of Israel, with the animal's death (or in one case, banishment) dealing in some way with consequences of people's sins. In talking about Christ's self-giving "for our sins," Paul is presenting Christ's death as an act of what theologians might call substitutionary atonement. This is not the only way in which Paul presents Christ's death, but it is one of the most prominent ways in which he does so.

Hans Dieter Betz argues that the self-sacrificial element of Gal. 1:4 shows that the precedent for Paul's view here is the idea that the death of righteous people, such as the Maccabean martyrs, could provide atonement for the sins of Israel (1979, 41–42, citing 2 Macc. 7:32, 37–38; etc.). Betz is right that this is a likely precedent. However, he sees self-sacrificial texts such as Gal. 1:4 as very distinct from those, such as Rom. 8:32, in which God gives Jesus over. It seems more likely that both kinds of text express a composite view held by Paul, modeled on the OT sacrificial system but adapted to the event of Christ's death, in which both Christ sacrificed himself and God gave him over. For instance, the purposive "for our sins" in Gal. 1:4 suggests the OT sacrificial system, even though the OT animal victims did not act voluntarily. Moreover, as Martyn (1997a, 91) points out, Paul's addition of the clause "according to the will of our God and Father" shows this to have been "a sacrifice enacted both by [Christ] and God." In any case, the atoning aspect of Maccabean martyrdom suggests that the ideas of those texts were themselves based on the OT sacrificial system.

The description of salvation then turns in an unexpected direction. Where we might be expecting Paul to write that Christ's self-giving for our sins was to reconcile us to God, he writes that it is "to rescue us from the present evil

The Golden Age of Nero

Seneca, Nero's adviser during the early part of his reign, wrote, at around the time when Galatians was composed, about the world as it had become under Nero's rule.

"Today your subjects one and all are constrained to confess that they are happy, and, too, that nothing further can be added to their blessings, except that these may last. Many facts force them to this confession, which more than any other a man is loath to make: a security deep and abounding, and justice enthroned above all injustice; before their eyes hovers the fairest vision of a state which lacks no element of complete liberty except the license of self-destruction."

Seneca, *Clem.* 1.1.8, trans. J. W. Basore 1928

age." Instead of salvation in terms of dealing with individual guilt, or dealing with a person's relationship with God, this verse presents a group salvation related to a particular view of the world. With the state of the world being viewed as evil, Paul sees Christ as having acted to take a group out of the bad situation. This clearly raises some difficult theological issues (see discussion below). It also implies a stark critique of society. This contrasted particularly with the view of the Mediterranean world held by its Roman rulers. For them, the current age was a golden one of peace and prosperity, brought about by the interethnic harmony enforced by Roman power. Scholars are divided on the extent to which Paul's gospel should be described as anti-imperial. For such as James R. Harrison (2002; writing on 1 Thessalonians), Paul's very un-Roman eschatology (ideas about the end) constitutes a challenge to the empire.

For many other scholars, Paul's eschatology has nothing to do with Rome. In Gal. 1:4, any anti-imperial message would be, at most, a relatively muted one. Paul's immediate aims lie elsewhere. However, whatever the aim of this particular text, we cannot avoid the conclusion that early Christians lived with an eschatology sharply different from the standard Roman one (Oakes 2005, 318). Non-Christian Jews also lived with an un-Roman eschatology, but they had always done so. Here Paul's mission was radical in drawing gentiles away from their traditional views of the progress of time and the nature of the ages.

Having said all this, F. F. Bruce's observation on this text makes a sharper point and plunges us into the heart of the letter's argument: it will turn out that "the present evil age" involves the Jewish law (Bruce 1982, 76). This astonishing idea is brought home in 4:1–10. In 4:9, Paul worries that the Galatians are returning "again to the weak and poor elements," to be reenslaved by them (4:9). They are doing so by observing "days and months" and so forth (4:10). This probably relates to Paul's main fear in the letter, that the Galatians are accepting circumcision and other aspects of practice of torah (the Jewish law) (5:3; 6:12). Paul thinks that if the Galatian gentile Christians take on torah practice, this means a return to a slavery to the elements of the world from which Jesus has freed them, as expressed in 1:4.

More radically than this (and here we enter a very highly charged scholarly field), Paul sees Christ's self-giving as for "our" sins, to rescue "us," ostensibly including himself and fellow Jews. Similarly, in 4:3 Paul writes that "we . . . were enslaved under the elements of the world." Paul's pronouns are often hard to interpret, but although the "we" alone would not automatically indicate that Paul included himself and other Jews in this slavery to "the elements," 4:5 is explicit: God's Son was born "to redeem those under law." Christ came to set free (redeem) law-observant Israelites from slavery. Being under the law was equivalent to being enslaved to the elements of the world. In 1:4 we should take the "we" as including all people, Jew and gentile. All needed to be rescued from "the present evil age." Jesus's death for sins brought this about.

For many scholars, the inclusion of Jews in this need for salvation in Jesus is somewhat anathema (e.g., Stendahl 1976). This is understandable, given the way in which Paul's Letters have been co-opted by many Christians to support some appalling acts of oppression of Jews by Christians down through the centuries. Let there be no doubt. Paul would be horrified by such acts. In Galatians, however, he undoubtedly argues that Christ brings salvation to Jew and gentile, not just to gentile. It is true, as (e.g.) Lloyd Gaston (1987, 23) points out, that Galatians is written specifically for gentile Christians and that the key issue at stake is that they should not adopt circumcision and torah-practice. Yet in his argument to the Galatians, one of Paul's key moves is to evoke the figure of Peter and to present his challenge to Peter that even Christian Jews have found righteousness through faith in Jesus, not through works of torah: "We, Jews by nature . . . trusted in Christ Jesus, so that we would be considered righteous on the basis of trust in Christ and not on the basis of works of law" (2:15–16). Paul's challenge to Peter is that, if even Christian Jews are justified in this way, how can Christian Jews compel Christian gentiles to adopt Jewish practice (2:14)? There seems to be no reason in Galatians to exclude Jews from Paul's "our" and "us" in 1:4.

When does Jesus's rescue of people take place? Does Paul intend the Galatians to think of it as a past, present, or future event? Galatians offers precedents for any of these (e.g., 5:1; cf. 5:5), as do other Pauline texts. One exegetical factor to consider is the experience of Pauline house churches. In the model house church that we are using in this commentary (see introduction), there usually are enslaved persons. Their continuing enslavement makes it unlikely that they would consider Jesus's rescue to be complete. On the other hand, substantive changes that would probably have come about for slaves as they joined (or formed) Christian groups, such as change of religious practice or changes of social relationships (at least for the duration of assembly meetings), mean that they would probably see a certain degree of rescuing from "the present evil age" as having already taken place. Paul's understanding of the timing of rescue would probably have related, to some extent, to that of assembly members. He too would have had the experience of some change but with some hopes not yet fulfilled (cf. 5:5).

Deserting the One Who Called Them and the Only Gospel (1:6–10)

1:6–7. I am astonished that so rapidly you are turning away from the one who called you in the grace of Christ, to a different gospel (1:6). As explained above, this sharp break from the polite conventions of letter writing would have shocked the hearers, a shock reinforced by Paul's use of the word "astonished," drawn from the repertoire of either angry letter writing or courtroom speeches in which the lawyer needs to bring about a radical change of attitude from an unsympathetic jury (Mullins 1972, 385; Betz 1979, 45, citing Cicero, *Inv.* 1.17.25).

Paul reinforces this effect by immediately charging the Galatians with flouting an important Greco-Roman moral convention, that of loyalty to a founding figure. Reverence for founders of a community was an extremely powerful motivator in the Greco-Roman world. Archaeological and literary evidence for this is widespread. Greek cities had cults devoted to their (usually mythical) founders (Spawforth 1996, 608). Roman colonies erected statues of their founding general or emperor and established cults to the founder's patron deity. At Pompeii, for instance, a temple was erected to Sulla's patron deity, Venus. Philosophical movements expressed reverence for founders—for instance, Zeno for the Stoics. In fact, the participle form (*ho metathemenos*) of the Greek verb translated here as "turning away" was a pejorative term used most famously of Dionysius of Heraclea, who deserted Stoic teaching in favor of Epicureanism (Athenaeus, *Deipn.* 7.281 D–E; Betz 1979, 47). Irrespective of any other considerations, the Galatians should feel guilty about moving away from the teaching of their founder.

But which founder is Paul referring to here? In the context of the letter as a whole, the founder whom the Galatians are most obviously in danger of deserting is Paul. If Paul is referring to himself here, then "in the grace of Christ" is probably a statement of modesty (in effect, "I didn't bring this about: Christ did") tinged with a claim to authority for the process ("Christ did it, so it is important"). Paul often described his ministry in terms of grace (Gal. 1:15; 2:9; 1 Cor. 3:10; esp. 15:10; 2 Cor. 1:12; Rom. 1:5; 12:3; 15:15).

However, most commentators focus on the word "call." Elsewhere, when Paul writes about conversion, it is always God who "calls." Paul never uses the word to describe his own evangelism. For this reason most commentators see Paul as accusing the Galatians of deserting God (e.g., R. Longenecker 1990, 15; Martyn 1997a, 48; Betz [1979, 46, 48] counts God as "the primary agent of calling" but sees the key issue here as desertion of Paul, who transmitted the calling). The argument about Paul's customary use of "call" is clearly strong. Yet it is not so easy to see how a reference to God fits the context, especially since the reference is only implicit. If Paul had wanted to shock the Galatians by characterizing their turning away from his message as a turning away from God himself, we might have expected a direct reference to "God" (*theos*) here.

A possible solution is to see the emphasis of the sentence as being on "grace," rather than on the caller. The word "grace" gains a little emphasis by being repeated from verse 3. Certainly Paul sees the main issue of the letter as having a link to grace. When he finally speaks directly about circumcision, he writes that gentiles who get circumcised, who "are being considered righteous by means of law, . . . fell away from grace" (5:4). It is as he writes in Rom. 11:6 in relation to "the remnant": "If it is by grace, it is not by works; otherwise grace would no longer be grace." In Gal. 1:6, the Galatians are reminded that they have been called in "grace." In pursuing circumcision, they are turning to "another gospel," which is not of grace.

On a technical note, a number of early manuscripts (e.g., apparently $\mathfrak{P}^{46}$) and church writers (e.g., Tertullian) omit the word "Christ," leaving the verse referring to "the one who called in grace." This slightly opens up the possibility that Paul could be talking of Christ as "the one who called" (e.g., Luther 1949/1535, on 1:6). An accusation that the Galatians have been turning away from Christ would, like a stress on grace, fit Paul's rhetoric about circumcision in 5:4. However, the limited range of textual support for the omission and the strong possibility of a reference to God or Paul, even with the omission, mean that a direct reference to desertion from Christ is unlikely here—although in any case, if the "grace" is "of Christ," the Galatians are, in Paul's eyes, implicitly deserting Christ too.

. . . to a different gospel—which is not actually another gospel. But rather, there are some people who are harassing you and wanting to pervert the gospel of Christ (1:6–7). Not only are the Galatians committing the crime of showing disrespect for their founder; they also are doing so by turning to a gospel that is not actually a gospel. As Paul makes clear by the curses of verses 8–9 (see below), he really does not think that any gospel other than his should be preached to the Galatians. We should probably take quite seriously the definite article in 2:7: Paul saw himself as having been entrusted with *the* gospel for the uncircumcised. In other letters, Paul indicates that he did not think he was the only person who could preach to gentiles (e.g., 1 Cor. 3:6–8; implicitly Romans as a whole, contra Klein 1991). However, he clearly expected that, in key essentials such as the lack of need for gentile circumcision, anyone else's gospel should be in line with his.

These verses also give us Paul's first characterization of his opponents. They are "some people [perhaps a dismissive term] who are harassing you." No respect is shown to them. They are not called teachers (even "false" teachers).

No positive motive is ascribed to them. They are just disturbing the Galatians. This total lack of respect by Paul probably implies that they are not official representatives of the church in Jerusalem or Antioch (contra Elmer 2009). Negative as he is about "some people from James" in 2:12, they at least have some categorization in relation to the early Christian movement. In fact, even the "false brothers" of 2:4 are in some way characterized in relation to Christian life. Paul does not give his opponents in Galatia the dignity of anything positive. His rhetoric is of total dismissal. They have not an iota of positive contribution to make or any trace of validity (cf. Betz [1979, 44–45] on Paul discrediting them). All they do is "harass" and want "to pervert the gospel." Yet they can only *want* to do that. Paul may be implying that the gospel is somehow inherently immune to actual perversion.

1:8–9. Paul reinforces the uniqueness of the gospel by raining down curses on the head of any being, himself and angels included, who would come to the Galatians and preach the gospel differently. **But even if we or an angel from heaven proclaimed a gospel to you, contrary to the gospel we proclaimed to you, let them be accursed! As we have said before and I now say again, if someone proclaims a gospel to you contrary to what you received, let them be accursed!** (1:8–9). Curses were a common part of life in the first century (cf. on 3:10, 13). Lead tablets and other objects with curses written on them are a particularly common find from antiquity (see, e.g., Meyer and Smith 1999). A conditional self-curse, such as Paul's here, is one of the strongest possible forms of denial. Paul also powerfully makes the point that what matters is the message, not the identity of the messenger. Credentials are irrelevant. He may imply a similar point in 2:6, where he heavily qualifies the value of some leaders being regarded as "pillars"—none of this matters to God. Paul's opponents may be claiming credentials in terms of support from Jerusalem. Paul's total disrespect for them suggests that he would disbelieve any such claims. However, even if they were true, he argues that any such credentials are irrelevant. Only the message matters.

Hans Dieter Betz (1979, 53, cautiously) and J. Louis Martyn (1997a, 113, confidently) both suggest that Paul's reference to angels may (or does) relate to his opponents claiming revelations from such a source. However, the rhetoric of the main line of Paul's response to the actions of his opponents (1:1, 11, etc.) seems to make it more likely that they claimed their authority based on commissioning and teaching from authoritative human sources.

A small oddity is the note in verse 9, "as we have said before." This implies that Paul has had some engagement with the Galatians previously on the subject of false gospel preaching (Paul's phraseology here seems unlikely merely to refer back to verse 8: contra Bruce 1982, 84). Scholars tend to see Galatians as Paul's first response to the problems described in the letter. That may not be the case. As with the Corinthians, we might need to think in terms of a more complex history of interaction (see on 4:15–16, below).

1:10. Finally, Paul in verse 10 denies, with some vehement elaboration, that he is a flatterer (R. Longenecker 1990, 18). **Am I now seeking to win favor from people or from God? Or am I seeking to please people? If I were still trying to please people, I would not be a slave of Christ** (1:10). The flatterer was a stock character of Greco-Roman rhetoric. The flatterer was a type of hypocrite. They acted to please people rather than acting out of conviction. They were not sincere. This also meant that they would act one way when in a person's presence, then differently when apart (Glad 1996, 55). Paul denies that he is a hypocrite of that kind (see on 2:13).

The phraseology of Paul's first question is strange. Translated literally, it reads, "For am I now persuading [*peithō*] people or God?" Betz (1979, 54–55) argues that Plato provides possible explanations as he uses "persuading people" in a definition of rhetoric (*Gorg.* 352E) and "persuading gods" (to serve the persuaders themselves) as an activity of magicians (*Rep.* 364C). For Betz, Paul denies both. However, Martinus de Boer is probably right in seeing the whole verse as rebutting the charge of people-pleasing, and that Paul's answer to the second half of his first question is yes, with "persuading . . . God" amounting to "trying to seek the approval . . . of God" (2011, 64–65; Schreiner 2010, 88–89). De Boer's view fits the context better unless one accepts Betz's general theory that the letter has a substantial magical aspect (1979, 25).

The charge against Paul was possibly that of relaxing the demands of law observance in order to please gentiles, who would dislike such observance (de Boer 2011, 64). Again, the possibility of Paul hearing of such a charge suggests that there may be a more complex backstory of interaction between the Galatians and Paul than scholars tend to expect. Another possible rhetorical aim of Paul's prominent denial of flattery and hence hypocrisy is that he could be setting up his later move of using hypocrisy as a key charge against Peter (2:13) and ultimately against Paul's opponents (6:12–13). Finally, we also need to recall that Paul's orientation toward the "people"/"God" pairing of 1:10 recalls that in 1:1 (Martyn 1997a, 139). As we see elsewhere in the letter, both Paul and his gospel are oriented toward God and the new creation, rather than to the flesh and the present world. In this, there is something paradigmatic, as well as Paul defending himself against an accusation.

Theological Issues

The Theology of Authority

For some writers such as Elizabeth Castelli (1991) and Joseph Marchal (2006), much of the positive value of what Paul writes in his letters is offset or even outweighed by the negative effects of his introducing into the church a theology and practice based on domination: what Marchal calls *kyriarchy* (rule by a lord). In this pattern, God is a dominating figure, and in unison with this, Paul and other church leaders are also dominating figures. For Castelli, Marchal, and others, a Pauline theology of authority, both divine and human, is problematic for the church and the world.

For the members of first-century house churches, the world was a complex network of authority. Slaves were dominated by their owners. The poor were dominated by the wealthy. Children were dominated by parents. Women were normally dominated by men. In Galatia, the patterns of civic authority varied somewhat, according to type of location. In the Roman colonies, such as Pisidian Antioch, the local non-Roman population would have been under the rule of Roman colonial authorities. This meant the local Roman elite, supplemented by any Greek elite landowners who had gained Roman citizenship (for the influence of some Greeks in the Roman colonies of Galatia, see Mitchell 1993a, 90). These elites were, in turn, lent authority by the distant power of Rome. In noncolonial parts of the province, other elites exercised control, but again, it was underwritten by Rome, whose grip on the empire was largely maintained by supporting local elites and broadly letting them control the rest of the local people, under the overall eye of the provincial Roman governor.

Paul's authority cut across the authority of family, town, or province. Such crosscutting authority figures can have important roles. Coming from outside the normal structures of a hearer's life, they can challenge existing patterns and open up new possibilities. Such people are central to religious innovation. The charismatic itinerant prophet, philosopher, or sage is a key agent of change. An essential element of the potential for effectiveness of change is the prophet's claim to have authority directly from God or the gods, rather than via the existing human religious or social structures, which are the very things that the prophet may be challenging in God's name (cf., more broadly, Brad Braxton's argument about the value of claims to revelation among people otherwise subject to oppressive control by other groups [2002, 61]).

For Christian theology, Paul occupies a specific kind of position with his claim to authority direct from Christ and God the Father. The early church, in accepting his claim, placed Paul as an apostle in the fullest sense, alongside Peter, Andrew, and the others who had their commission directly from Christ. Paul's claim to unmediated authority is essential to his stance in Galatians. This puts his message in a different category from that of other Christian teachers who were humanly commissioned, as the rival teachers who came to Galatia probably claimed to be. This also puts Paul's teaching in a different category from that of any later generation of Christian teachers, commissioned by people rather than directly by God. One implication of this is a theology of authority in which no present-day Christian teachers can claim an absolute authority on a level with the early apostles. This means that, paradoxically, a Pauline theology of authority limits the authority claims of any present-day leader.

Rescue from the Present Evil Age

Many Christians today have a very reasonable aversion to excessive dualism, such as a view that polarizes the world into a sphere of goodness, inhabited by Christians, and a sphere of wickedness, inhabited by everyone else. Such dualism has often led Christians to an intolerant detachment from the common life of society. It also seems to be a deeply unrealistic view. There clearly are many good things outside the church and many bad things within. The experience of conversion to Christianity is not one of sudden, sustained perfection.

And yet, many Christians who would vehemently oppose such dualism are also particularly aware that the present world needs to be subject to serious critique. The idea that the world is a benign place, ruled constructively for the benefit of the whole global population, is a rose-tinted myth that no one with access to a television or the streets of a city center could reasonably sustain. Our own present age is clearly full of trouble and unjust actions. Despite much goodness at work, the age has so many faults as to be undoubtedly worthy of some sort of negative evaluation.

The first century too was a place of structural injustice and cruelty. Many in the population were slaves, the property of other people. From Paul's Jewish-Christian perspective, there were many other widespread practices that struck him forcibly, such as idolatry, drunkenness, and sexual behavior contrary to Jewish norms. The members of Galatian house churches, who will have been mostly at the lower end of the socioeconomic spectrum, were no doubt particularly aware of all kinds of structural injustice.

Paul announces that Christ's giving of himself for our sins results in rescue from the present evil age (1:4). At first sight this is mad, apparently denying the reality of the continuing experience of evil, injustice, and suffering. To some degree the resolution of this paradox lies in the rescue being, to an extent, proleptic: the idea that Christ's rescue is real but is only fully brought to fruition at some future time. This pattern is seen in Paul's adoption language in Rom. 8. Christians have been adopted by God (8:15–17), and yet adoption still requires future fulfillment (8:23).

However, Paul undoubtedly also thinks that, in Christ's rescue, something has happened that has actual, current effects on the Christian. Part of that presumably has to do with the socioreligious change that the convert has undergone. The convert has changed religious affiliation away from the Greco-Roman gods to the God of Israel. The convert has also become part of a group that is a house church and part of the wider network of such churches. That means a change in social identity and behavior (Crook 2004). There has been some movement of the convert out from what Paul would have seen as malevolent aspects of the social structures and behavior of his day. One of the key underlying arguments of Galatians is the startling one that Paul sees gentile Christian adoption of Jewish law as a move back in the direction of rejoining "the present evil age."

In the present day, although Christian groups are still, to quite an extent, caught up in the structures of "the present evil age," again and again there are evidences, in many Christian communities, of ways in which some measure of freeing from these structures has taken place and is being lived out.

How Uniform Should the Gospel Be?

Does the gospel require adult baptism? Does it require papal authority? Does it require belief in scriptural inerrancy? At what points should Paul's horror at people "perverting the gospel of Christ" be echoed today? As with the issue of dualism, many Christians are reasonably skeptical about attempts to draw boundaries around the gospel, with the consequent anathematizing of others who also claim that label for their message. However, the same Christians would be particularly critical of the claims of some kinds of messages to be representations of the gospel. The most obvious twentieth-century case was anti-Jewish church preaching during the Nazi era. Boundaries to the gospel do exist.

In Gal. 1:1–10, Paul does not tell us enough to show at what points he thinks boundaries to the gospel lie. As we go through the letter, he will make it progressively clearer.

Galatians 1:11–24

Narrative 1: Of a Gospel Revealed by God, Not People

Introductory Matters

Having castigated the Galatians for turning away to another (unreal) gospel, Paul now begins the first major argument of the letter. It is conveyed by means of a narrative. He seeks to demonstrate that his gospel came not from a human source but directly from God. As with his claim to divine authority in 1:1, Paul has an unstated advantage in his argument. The Galatians were converted through Paul's gospel, so they are not going to dismiss it as fantasy. To them it is substantial and valuable. Paul's opponents have presumably acknowledged its value to some extent, but then went on to present a further message, which they saw as carrying a higher authority than that of Paul, and which called for some modification to the behavior that the Galatians had learned from him. Paul counters that his gospel came by revelation from God. It could not be trumped by a message backed by even the highest human authority.

The passage begins with a disclosure formula, "I declare to you." The information Paul gives this way in his letters tends to become the basis for persuading the hearers to some action or attitude (cf. 2 Cor. 1:8; Phil. 1:12). Galatians 1:11–12 also echoes verse 1. Paul's commission, and now his gospel message, are not from a human source but from God, through Christ. Verses 11–12 set the agenda. However, the outworking of the agenda has a rather unexpected shape. Instead of moving directly to recounting the revelation (1:16) and Paul's lack of early contact with other Christian leaders (1:16–22), he spends time first on his life "in Judaism" and his persecution of the church (1:13–14). His change from persecutor to preacher is celebrated in 1:23–24. This unexpected arrangement of the passage allows Paul to speak not only of the fact of the revelation but also of the degree of impact that the revelation had on him. This adds strength to his argument for the validity of the revelation.

Tracing the Train of Thought

Assertion of Nonhuman Origin of Paul's Gospel (1:11–12)

1:11–12. For I declare to you, brothers and sisters, that the gospel proclaimed by me is not a human opinion. For neither did I receive it from a person, nor was I taught it, but I received it through a revelation of Jesus Christ. Paul sets up his narrative with a preamble that asserts his key point, then backs it up by three further assertions.

> ### Galatians 1:11–24 in the Rhetorical Flow
>
> **Letter opening (1:1–10)**
>
> **Letter body (1:11–6:10)**
>
> ▶ **Narrative 1: Of a gospel revealed by God, not people (1:11–24)**
>
> > Assertion of nonhuman origin of Paul's gospel (1:11–12)
> >
> > Paul's previous behavior in Judaism (1:13–14)
> >
> > Revelation to Paul and his avoidance of most contact with Jerusalem (1:15–22)
> >
> > An effect of the change in Paul's behavior (1:23–24)

Here his rhetoric softens slightly as he addresses the Galatians with a relational term for the first time, "brothers and sisters." However, his point is the same one he has been emphasizing in 1:1–10: the message that they are turning away from is not a human message from a humanly commissioned messenger; it is the one and only gospel from God. Paul asserts that his gospel is not *kata anthrōpon*, literally, "according to a person." This is part of a key duality that Paul sets up in the letter, a duality between the human, fleshly realm of the present world and the realm of God, Christ, and the Spirit. By dying with Christ, Paul has died to the world (6:14) and lives to God (2:19). His message too is of the divine realm. As he will make clear, his opponents' message, despite talking about the law of God, is actually of the fleshly realm of this age (e.g., 3:3).

Martinus de Boer (2011, 76) argues that *kata anthrōpon* should be understood as "of human origin," because in 1:12 Paul uses points about origin to back up 1:11. However, it seems more likely that Paul would be using points about the nonhuman origin of his gospel to support a broader point: that his gospel had a nonhuman nature (Betz 1979, 56, 62). That also better fits Paul's use of *kata* elsewhere in Galatians (e.g., 3:15).[1]

---

1. On a more detailed point, some manuscripts (e.g., revised Sinaiticus [ℵ¹] and original Vaticanus [B]) begin 1:11 *gnōrizō gar* ("for I declare"), but others (e.g., 𝔓⁴⁶, original Sinaiticus [ℵ], Majority Text [𝔐]) have *gnōrizō de*, which can be read as "but I declare" or simply "I declare." The issue is fairly balanced, but *gnōrizō de* has the earlier support and is more Pauline in style (cf. 1 Cor. 15:1; Phil. 1:12), whereas a scribal change to *gnōrizō gar* could be explained by assimilation to the instances of

As Richard N. Longenecker (1990, 23) points out, the curious double denial—"neither did I receive it . . . nor was I taught it" (1:12)—echoes the "not from people, nor through a person" of 1:1. Paul repeatedly emphasizes both lack of human origin and lack of human agency in his commissioning and message. Of course, Paul is not doing this in order to say that his gospel is alien to human concerns. It is highly relevant to them, but it comes from God and carries God's wisdom. More specifically, it came *di' apokalypseōs Iēsou Christou*, "through a revelation of/from Jesus Christ" (the Greek allows either meaning, but the proximity of 1:16 suggests "of" rather than "from" is the correct sense here). In 1:16, God is the revealer and "his Son" is what is revealed. However, a point that we may need to be wary about is seeing "Jesus Christ" as being only a piece of information, as though Paul is saying in 1:12 that God just told him some things about Jesus. As the book of Acts vividly portrays, the "revelation of Jesus Christ" to Paul was the sudden presence of a person, breaking into his life. De Boer (2011, 81–82), following J. Louis Martyn (1997a, 98–99), sees it in broader apocalyptic terms, as the presence of God breaking into the world in Christ. For discussion, see below, on 1:16.

Paul's Previous Behavior in Judaism (1:13–14)

1:13–14. For you heard about my behavior previously in Judaism, that to the utmost extent I used to persecute the assembly of God and was destroying it. And I was making progress in Judaism beyond many of the same age in my race, being exceedingly zealous on behalf of the traditions of my ancestors. Having made his programmatic assertions, Paul backs them up by beginning his actual narrative.

This passage sets up a contrast that will show how powerful were the effects of his receiving his revelation from God. This is most clear in the report of Christian reaction to his change (1:23–24), which picks up specific terms from 1:13–14, "persecute" and "destroy," and comments on how far Paul has moved from this. However, the contrast is actually presented from 1:16 onward, at which point Paul clearly undergoes a radical change from his attitudes and actions as described in 1:13–14.

"Judaism" is not really a good translation of *Ioudaïsmos* (1:13, 14). Judaism is a religion. Many of its key texts date from the rabbinic period, well after Paul wrote. Its ideas and practices are, among other things, affected by centuries of experience of persecution by Christians and others. These points make "Judaism" a problematic translation of Paul's term here, a problem made even sharper because modern concepts of "religion" tend to be alien to first-century experience. In fact, *Ioudaïsmos* is an extremely rare word in this period, which makes it strange that the English word derived from it is

---

gar in 1:10, 12, 13. The reading with *gar* implies a closer logical connection to the preceding passage than does the reading with *de*.

Ioudaïsmos in Maccabean Literature

"...and the appearances that came from heaven to those who fought bravely for [Ioudaïsmos]..." (2 Macc. 2:21 NRSV)

"...and enlisted those who had continued [memenēkotas] in [Ioudaïsmos]..." (2 Macc. 8:1 NRSV)

"A certain Razis, one of the elders of Jerusalem, was denounced to Nicanor as a man who loved his compatriots and was very well thought of and for his goodwill was called father of the Jews [Ioudaiōn]. In former times, when there was no mingling with the Gentiles, he had been accused of [Ioudaïsmos], and he had most zealously risked body and life for [Ioudaïsmos]." (2 Macc. 14:37–38 NRSV)

"He himself through torture tried to compel each person in the nation to renounce [Ioudaïsmos], eating defiling foods [ēnankazen miarōn apogeuomenous trophōn exomnysthai ton Ioudaïsmon]." (4 Macc. 4:26 AT)

the most common term used by modern writers to denote whatever it is supposed to denote about the life of ancient Jews (Mason 2007, 461). The only occurrences in early texts other than Galatians are in 2 Macc. 2:21; 8:1; 14:38 (2x); and 4 Macc. 4:26.

Consideration of these texts shows that *Ioudaïsmos* was not a racial group: it was something that people could "continue in" or "renounce." It sounds more like a set of practices or, more broadly, a way of life. In particular, it is a set of practices followed by Jews but not by their Seleucid Greek rulers at the time of the Maccabean revolt. These practices included circumcision (e.g., 4 Macc. 4:25) and avoiding eating defiling foods such as pork and food sacrificed to idols (e.g., 4 Macc. 5:2). More generally, 4 Maccabees describes these practices as *eunomia*, a word that combines terms for "well" and "law" (3:20; 18:4). The word *Ioudaïsmos* really needs a paraphrase rather than a one-word translation: probably something like, "a way of life characterized by practices that Jews generally saw as being proper." Often the focus would fall on *distinctive* Jewish practices, but there seems no reason to suppose that adherence to other aspects of the law, such as almsgiving, should not also be part of it.

Steve Mason (2007, 467) argues that *Ioudaïsmos* denoted the actions of those who encouraged people *Ioudaïzein* ("to Judaize"), that is, those who sought to restore adherence to the law. He appeals to similar usage of some other terms of the form *-ismos* (2007, 462–64). However, the Maccabees texts appear to read more naturally if *Ioudaïsmos* is the practice that expresses adherence to the law. This makes *Ioudaïsmos* the practices that, for instance, would result from successfully encouraging people "to Judaize," rather than the actions of people who do the encouraging. In Galatians, if Paul's opponents succeeded in persuading the gentiles "to Judaize," those gentiles would adopt *Ioudaïsmos*.

Paul sets up his early life as being behavior according to *Ioudaïsmos*. He even presents it as exceptional progress in *Ioudaïsmos* and expresses this in terms of the core values of *Ioudaïsmos* (and, in fact, of any respected first-century system of practice), namely, zeal for ancestral tradition. But Paul has already undermined the value of all this, because he has described the primary content of his behavior as persecution of "the assembly of God."

One conceivable subtle aim of this passage is to somehow set going the issue of persecution, which becomes unexpectedly prominent in the latter part of the letter. As well as the ambiguous references to Paul's suffering in 4:12–20 (cf. Goddard and Cummins 1993; Eastman 2007), persecution is directly mentioned at 4:29 (Ishmael persecuting Isaac, with a current equivalent); 5:11 (Paul still being persecuted, showing that he does not still preach circumcision); 6:12 (the opponents compelling circumcision in order to avoid themselves being persecuted). There is also Paul's bearing of "the marks of Jesus" (6:17).

A remarkable expression in this passage is "the assembly of God" (1:13). Paul generally uses the term "assembly" (*ekklēsia*) to refer either to an individual house church (Rom. 16:5) or to the Christians gathered in a particular city (1 Cor. 1:2). The latter text is interesting because the phrase used is "the assembly of God that is in Corinth." Galatians 1:2 refers to "the assemblies of Galatia." For Paul to use "the assembly of God" in 1:13 to refer to all the earlier targets of his persecution implies that he had an idea of an overall, single Christian community. Martinus de Boer (2011, 87) argues the opposite case: that Paul's customary usage of "assembly" shows that he must have had just one city in mind as the target of persecution in 1:13, namely, Jerusalem. James D. G. Dunn's argument seems more likely, that Paul is here using an OT phrase (Neh. 13:1; also cf. Deut. 23:1–8 [23:2–9 MT]) to express his shock at discovering that "each group of believers" that he had persecuted was "in direct continuity with the congregation of Israel" (1993, 59). However, in Galatians there are at least theological grounds for going further. These lie especially in the theology of Gal. 3:28 in the context of the argument of 3:15–29: "For you are all 'one' in Christ Jesus. . . . You are Abraham's seed" (3:28–29). Paul's argument has been that the promises go to the single seed of Abraham (3:16). In Christ, the unified Christians are the single seed and hence "heirs according to the promise" (3:29). This must refer to all Christians, not just the Galatians. It therefore implies a concept of a single, overall Christian community. This strong ecclesiology makes the expression "the assembly of God" a natural one for Paul to use in 1:13. Paul could well see himself as having persecuted the Jesus movement as a whole, which was largely within Paul's geographical reach (cf. the same point in 1 Cor. 15:9, again with the singular). Dunn's argument could then be modified in a way that removes the awkwardness of trying to map a singular concept, the assembly of Israel, onto multiple Christian assemblies. Paul could, unusually, describe the whole Jesus movement as a single assembly, in order to evoke its continuity with the Israelite assembly. Of course, whether we read "assembly" universally or locally, seeing an allusion to OT concepts raises issues to consider later in the letter, most obviously at 6:16.

Revelation to Paul and His Avoidance of Most Contact with Jerusalem (1:15–22)

1:15–16b. But when God—who set me apart when I was in my mother's womb and called me, through his grace—was pleased to reveal his Son to me, so that I might proclaim him among the gentiles, then straightaway I did not go to get advice from flesh and blood. . . . This rather literal translation reflects the unexpected sentence structure of the Greek. Most notably, the sentence does not head toward the revelation of Christ as its climax. That amazing revelation is only in a subordinate clause, preparing for the main verbs (in the Greek indicative mood), namely, "I did not go to get advice," and the subsequent verbs about not going to Jerusalem, and so on (Schlier 1989, 53). Moreover, this unexpected sentence structure is reinforced by the emphatic "straightaway" (1:16c), which is made even more prominent by the oddness of being linked with Paul *not* doing a certain action.

This sentence structure may be unexpected in general. However, it is perfectly natural in the flow of the narrative of 1:13–24, seen as support for the assertions of 1:11–12, which like 1:1 are at their most emphatic on Paul's independence of human sources, rather than on his dependence on God. The point that he wants to really hammer home in 1:15–24 is that his movements and contacts were such that he could not have learned his gospel from earlier Christian teachers. Any other points are subordinate to that.

Having said that, some of the subordinate points are very significant, both for Galatians and for understanding Paul. First, Paul puts himself into the line of people who have received a classic calling to mission, according to Jewish tradition. However stark a change is about to be presented, Paul's calling, and the categories he uses to describe it, stem from the very tradition that his negative account in 1:13–14 challenges—although also the tradition from which 1:13 draws the term "assembly of God." Matthew S. Harmon (2010) explores in detail the strong links between 1:15–16 and Isa. 49:1–6 LXX. The unusual vocabulary of Gal. 1:15 and Isa. 49:1 makes an allusion between them rather definite. Isaiah 49:1 LXX reads *ek koilias mētros mou ekalesen to onoma mou*, "from my mother's womb he called my name [named me]." Galatians 1:15 uses the same expression for the womb and follows it with *kaleō* ("call"; Harmon 2010, 79; de Boer 2011, 90). Reinforcing this is the summons in Isa. 49:6 for this called servant to be a "light to the nations" (*ethnōn*), as Paul is effectively called to be in Gal. 1:16, using another characteristically Isaianic term, *euangelizomai*, "preach the gospel" (Isa. 40:9 [2x]; 52:7; 60:6; 61:1).

The other element of 1:15 is the "setting apart" of Paul in the womb. This is strongly reminiscent of the call of Jeremiah: "Before forming you in the womb, I knew you, and before you emerged from the womb, I sanctified [*hēgiaka*] you. I have appointed you a prophet to nations [*ethnē*]" (Jer. 1:5 LXX, AT). The Greek term indicating Jeremiah being set apart is not the same as Paul's term in Gal. 1:15 (*aphorisas*), but the combination of the womb, the setting apart, and the call to speak to the nations forms a strong link between the passages (and Paul could have had in mind the Hebrew of Jeremiah). Both the Isaiah and Jeremiah passages are significant here, particularly because, being more than one text, they show a scriptural *pattern* into which Paul sees his ministry fitting—a pattern of people being set apart by God from birth to carry his message to the nations, the gentiles.

"God . . . was pleased to reveal [*apokalypsai*] his son to me [*en emoi*]" (1:15–16). Scholars are seriously divided on whether this is the correct translation. There are two key issues: the forcefulness with which *apokalypsai* should be rendered, and what *en emoi* means.

J. Louis Martyn (1997a, 152) and Martinus de Boer (2011, 75) would strengthen the word "reveal" to indicate that *apokalypsai* is a technical term for the great event of God breaking into the world in Christ. These scholars prefer "apocalyptically to reveal."

The Greek noun *apokalypsis* and verb *apokalyptō* are something of a trap for readers of the Bible in Greek. We easily read them as expressions of our technical term "apocalyptic," which comes to us via the language of the book of Revelation and represents a highly debated scholarly field. In fact, the scriptural use of the Greek words is largely nontechnical. In the Septuagint it runs from Noah "uncovering" the top of the ark (Gen. 8:13), via numerous levitical references to "uncovering" nakedness (e.g., Lev. 18:6), to Ben Sira's warnings against "revealing" a friend's secrets (Sir. 27:16). When God "reveals" something, for instance to the prophet Samuel, this is not "apocalyptic" in an eschatological sense (1 Sam. 3:7, 21; 9:15). Such noneschatological usage continues into the NT. For instance, 1 Pet. 1:12 speaks of matters being "revealed" to OT prophets. Even Paul uses the verb *apokalyptō* to describe the common experience of revelation to people in the early house-church meetings (1 Cor. 14:30).

Martyn and de Boer see apocalyptic texts as bound up with a Jewish eschatological system that sharply distinguishes between the present age—a time of sin and suffering, under the domination of evil cosmic forces—and a new age, to be brought about by a decisive intervention by God. In this view, Paul's key theological idea is that God's eschatological intervention has been initiated in Christ. These two scholars see all of Paul's *apokalyptō* language (except 2 Cor. 12:1) as expressing some aspect of this idea. (For a valuable summary, see de Boer 2011, 31–35, 79–82.) However, our brief survey of biblical evidence shows that the presence of the term *apokalyptō* in a text, in this case Gal. 1:16, does not of itself imply that Paul sees the event as "apocalyptic" in any eschatological sense. In fact, another school of thought defines "apocalyptic" texts as those that recount revelations from God (Rowland 1982, 14). In this sense, Gal. 1:15–16 is an apocalyptic text, but it is the mention of God in 1:15 that is decisive in making it apocalyptic, rather than Paul's use of *apokalyptō* in 1:16 instead of some synonym.

As we saw in Gal. 1:4, Paul's thinking in Galatians does include some aspects of what Martyn and de Boer see as apocalyptic thought (whether or not they are right in seeing such a systematized scheme in a wide range of Jewish texts). In general terms, the revelation of Jesus to Paul was, in Paul's view, an aspect of God's action that followed from God's initiation, in the arrival of Christ, of the end-time events. However, translating *apokalyptō* in 1:16 as "apocalyptically reveal" goes too far. De Boer explains it as "God invaded Paul's life with Jesus Christ, his Son" (de Boer 2011, 82). For Paul, the revealing of Christ to him was not the same type of action as Christ's coming into the world. Paul sees the world as having changed decisively when Christ arrived. Paul's Damascus experience was just part of the aftermath. The point that Paul is trying to make in 1:16 by use of the term *apokalyptō* is about how he received his gospel: directly from God.

The other issue is whether *en emoi* is really equivalent to a simple Greek dative, as translated above, "to me" (Becker and Luz 1998, 29; Martyn 1997a, 152; Schreiner 2010, 100), or is better read as "in me," indicating either an all-pervasive experience (Dunn 1993, 64) or the effect of Paul's mission. In this last option, the revelation in question is not to Paul (certainly not Paul alone) but is to the gentiles, who come to see the Son of God "in" Paul or "through" Paul (an "instrumental" use of *en*; Harmon 2010, 82; Hays 2000, 215).

In the great majority of biblical and pseudepigraphical uses of *apokalyptō*, the person or people to whom a revelation is given are indicated simply by the Greek dative case (e.g., *emoi*). It is quite common in the Greek of the NT period for the word *en* to be added after a verb that takes the dative, without making any significant difference. A good example from Paul is 1 Cor. 14:11 (NRSV), "I will be a foreigner to the speaker and the speaker will be a foreigner to me [*esomai tō lalounti barbaros kai ho lalōn en emoi barbaros*]." A redundant *en* could have been included before the *emoi* in 1:16 for a minor reason, such as highlighting the *emoi* to emphasize the fact that the revelation was, surprisingly, to Paul. Thus we may well conclude that *en* + dative in Gal. 1:16 "stands for the customary dat[ive] proper" (BDF §220.1), that is, that *en emoi* is equivalent to *emoi* and should therefore be read as "to me."

Harmon disagrees and is particularly clear in setting out the counterevidence: *apokalyptō* with *en* "is a rare construction; there are only eight comparable examples in the LXX and NT," none of which uses *en* as simply the dative giving an indirect object. "When it is necessary to specify the 'indirect object' of [*apokalyptō*], either the simple dative (Isa. 53:1) or the preposition [*pros*] (Jer. 11:20) is used" (Harmon 2010, 82n122). This is a useful argument. However, to become really compelling it would need a broader statistical analysis, including moves such as establishing, from a large sample of Koine Greek texts, how frequently *en* + dative was simply equivalent to a dative. That would help us decide how significant an argument from nonoccurrence of a particular type of use of *en* in eight texts would be.

Other things being equal, we might well accept Harmon's argument that *en emoi* in 1:16 means "through me" and relates to the gentile mission. However, Paul's gentile mission is indeed the topic of the next clause, "so that I might proclaim him among the gentiles," but it does not relate to the revelation of Christ in the way Harmon proposes. De Boer (2011, 92) attacks the "through me" interpretation decisively by appealing to the syntax of 1:16: the revelation was a *past* event ("God . . . was pleased"); the preaching is a present activity (*euangelizōmai*) that follows from the revelation. They are not the same event. The distinction between past revelation and present mission is made even clearer by the "straightaway" (*eutheōs*), which indicates what happened (or not) *after* the event of the revelation *en emoi*. In any case, the phrasing of 1:16 is a very improbable way of saying that God revealed his Son to the gentiles through Paul. To say that, it would be far easier to put "to the gentiles" into the clause with "to reveal."

It is harder to exclude James Dunn's idea that *en emoi* signals how the revelation of Jesus affected Paul in an all-pervasive way (cf. Christ living "in me" in 2:20). However, the general focus of 1:12–16 on the fact of divine revelation suggests that it is risky to read as much as Dunn does into the inclusion of the word *en*.

1:16c–22. Then straightaway I did not go to get advice from flesh and blood, nor did I go up to Jerusalem, to those who were emissaries before I was, but I went away into Arabia then returned again to Damascus. Then, after three years, I went up to Jerusalem to get to know Cephas, and I stayed with him for fifteen days. I did not see any of the other emissaries except James, the brother of the Lord. See, before God! I am not lying in the things I write to you! Then I went into the regions of Syria and Cilicia. I was unknown by sight to the assemblies of Judea that are in Christ.

This sketchy information is frustrating for us. It is Paul's fullest account of his early life as a Christian, but it tells us virtually nothing. This is because it is constructed to provide evidence for the assertion that he did not receive his gospel from others in the first place, and neither did he then undergo any significant period of instruction to broaden his understanding of the gospel. In particular, he did not get these from the leaders at Jerusalem.

There are a few interesting, albeit enigmatic, details. First, Paul heads to "Arabia." It is unclear quite where that is. The most prominent group called

Arabs at that period were the Nabateans, whose ruler, Aretas IV, controlled Damascus at the time of Paul's exit in a basket (2 Cor. 11:32–33). (This could be his first or his second departure from the city: Gal. 1:17 indicates that he was there twice.) The Nabatean kingdom was centered at Petra, southeast of the Dead Sea. Galatians has another reference to Arabia, as being the location of Mount Sinai (4:25). If Paul headed off to the place he thought to be Mount Sinai, that could be a replaying of programmatic visits made by two key scriptural figures, Moses (Exod. 3:1) and Elijah (1 Kings 19:8). Like Paul's earlier allusions to Isaiah and/or Jeremiah, this would put Paul in the scriptural tradition of messengers of God. However, here the absence of reference to Sinai itself (or even better, Horeb, the name used in the key scriptural texts) should make us cautious about seeing Paul as seeking to make a point of this comparison in Galatians (even though the scriptural precedent may have affected the actions of the younger Saul/Paul).

Second, we begin to find out about leaders in the Jerusalem assemblies. There was clearly prominence for Cephas (1:18). This is the Aramaic name that is equivalent to the Greek *Petros*, used in 2:7. Both mean something like "rock." The other named figure is James, who is described as "the brother of the Lord," meaning the brother of Jesus. Such a mention so soon after the unadorned name Cephas indicates that "brother" here is a literal term rather than some fictive kinship honorific title. Thus the earliest Christian groups did have prominent leaders. Even though there were egalitarian aspects to early Christian rhetoric, there is no evidence of democracy in leadership. Although we do not know exactly how prominent people such as Peter and James functioned in relation to leading the assemblies, it looks as though they were permanently in positions of some authority. As far as we can tell, the members of the Jerusalem assemblies did not, for instance, elect something like a pair of leaders, with different leaders each year (following the model of Roman republican government). The long-term role of prominent individuals in Christian assemblies undoubtedly had a significant influence in the development of later church leadership structures.

According to Gal. 1:21, Paul went to "the regions of Syria and Cilicia." Syria was a large province, but Paul was presumably at the capital, Antioch (cf. Acts 11:19–30; 13:1–3). By "Cilicia," Paul presumably means Cilicia Pedias, "Flat Cilicia," centered on Tarsus and just around the northeastern corner of the Mediterranean from Antioch. The other part of Cilicia, the mountainous Cilicia Tracheia, "Rugged Cilicia," was at this time largely part of the province of Galatia. In Gal. 1:22, Paul refers to "the assemblies of Judea that are in Christ." This is back to his normal, plural usage of "assemblies." These groups are described as "in Christ." Thus being "in Christ" is not only a situation that individuals can be in. Among the effects of this phrase is that it should probably make us cautious of taking "in Christ" in too mystical a sense. Being "in Christ" is not a state attained by an individual through, say, meditation.

It is an existence that can apply to a mixed bag of people who gather as an assembly. It is a status. Although there will be difficulties for us in defining the boundaries of the group, those who are in the group are in a group that is "in Christ." Some are not more "in Christ" than others. Paul can also talk of individuals as being "in Christ" (e.g., Rom. 16:7), but the communal dimension of such an identity is an important factor in understanding Paul's thought.

An Effect of the Change in Paul's Behavior (1:23–24)

1:23–24. Galatians 1:15–21 has already indicated that the revelation of Jesus to Paul has changed him radically from how he behaved previously. Now he drives this point home with an extra comment on the assemblies of Judea. **Only, they were hearing, "The person who was previously persecuting us is now proclaiming the faith that he was previously destroying." And on account of me they were praising God** (1:23–24).

Language is picked up from 1:13 and reused to make the contrast: "previously," "persecute," "destroy." This was a 180-degree turnaround: from persecutor to proclaimer. This shows how far-reaching an event the revelation to Paul was. It had a power to change him in the most radical way. This is testimony to the power and truth of the gospel given through that revelation—a gospel that the Galatians are in danger of abandoning.

A detail here that many commentators find awkward is that Paul mentions "the faith." J. Louis Martyn, for instance, writes that "composing on his own," Paul does not speak of preaching "the faith." Martyn (1997a, 177) draws the inference that the term is part of the report heard from the Judean assemblies. I am rather skeptical about any ancient writer being consistent enough for this kind of detailed argument. Galatians 1:23 is evidence that Paul can be more flexible in his use of *pistis* ("faith") than many scholars assume.

Paul had been destroying "the faith" and "is now proclaiming the faith" (*nyn euangelizetai tēn pistin*, 1:23), very much as 1:16 has Paul "proclaiming him," that is, Jesus. The first point to make here is the parallel with 1:16. This is the first pair of several texts in Galatians that make "the faith" and "Jesus" sound rather synonymous. Galatians 3:19 sets up the expectation of a key event, the coming of the seed of Abraham, which the reader has been told is Christ (3:16). What then actually comes is "the faith" (3:23, 25), though this is clearly tied up with Christ (3:24, 26; 4:4). Martinus de Boer goes as far as to say that in 1:23 "faith" (*pistis*) is a metonym for Christ (2011, 103), particularly in his faithful actions, seen especially on the cross. This is what Richard B. Hays (2002, xxx) sees as *pistis Christou* ("faithfulness of Christ"; see discussion on 2:16–21). Whether or not we go as far as de Boer and Hays, it is vital to take seriously Paul's paralleling of Christ and "the faith."

We must be cautious about putting the English definite article, "the," in front of "faith" in translating the Greek with the article, *hē pistis*. Greek uses articles very differently from English. In particular, abstract nouns generally have the article in Greek but not in English; for instance, *hē sophia* means "wisdom." There is usually no difference in meaning when abstract nouns do or do not have the article. What is more significant for understanding Paul is the syntax of the sentences in which *hē pistis* occurs in Galatians. In 3:14, "we receive" *dia tēs pisteōs*, "through the faith": probably the article makes no difference. In 3:23 and 3:25 "the faith" "comes" at a particular point in time. Galatians 3:23 also refers to "the coming faith" (using a different term for "coming"). Galatians 3:26 speaks of being "sons of God through the faith, in Christ Jesus" (see comments on 3:26). Galatians 6:10 refers to "the household of the faith." In 1:23, "the faith" is something proclaimed and that has been subject to attempted destruction.

From the sentence structure in these texts, the most significant points are that *hē pistis* can be seen as being something that arrives at a point in time, presumably not having been here until that time, and conversely as something that a person could seek to destroy, to make it go away. In 1:23, it is a particular *pistis* that is proclaimed: the *pistis* that was previously under attack. *Hē pistis* appears not to be "trust," in a general sense. That existed prior to the arrival of Christ. It also appears not to be a metonym for Christ in his faithful action. That is primarily a past event, so it becomes very convoluted to talk about the possibility of destroying it, as 1:23 does. However, the hearers do seem likely to understand *hē pistis* in 1:23 via the functional parallel in 1:16. I would suggest that here the most natural way to take *hē pistis* is as indicating the way of life made available through proclaiming the Son of God. As *pistis*, this way of life is characterized by trust in Christ and loyalty to Christ.

Theological Issues

A Message Based on a Revelation of Jesus Christ

It is easy to pass over 1:11–24 as being introductory narrative, making relatively straightforward points. Modern readers of Galatians tend to want to press on to the theological fireworks of the end of chapter 2 and in chapter 3. Yet we should pause. What Paul is arguing in this passage is utterly scandalous and sensational to many modern Western ears. Even though, in the UK, most people put themselves down on the government census form as "Christian," most British people would be highly skeptical about anyone who brought them a message that they claimed to be of divine, rather than human, origin. A message can be clever, interesting, moving, even inspiring, but not divine. For most people in northern Europe, and for many other people elsewhere, words are human, not divine. Claims to a divine origin for words are viewed as ridiculous and frequently dangerous.

It is easy for Christians to retreat into a gospel that effectively claims only human origins. Such a gospel can seem reasonable to our non-Christian peers as the gospel of an ethic based on love rather than law, as the gospel of freedom from perceived guilt about the past, as the gospel of shared community, as the gospel of joyful service. All these can be promoted on the basis of human argument. And all these are aspects of Paul's gospel. However, Paul's gospel is ultimately a divine call on human life. Otherwise, in Paul's eyes, it would be nothing.

Whether we translate the end of 1:12 as "revelation of Jesus Christ" or "revelation from Jesus Christ," there is no doubt in 1:16 that the crucial event for Paul was a revealing of Jesus Christ: "when God . . . was pleased to reveal his Son to me." Just as there is a temptation for Christianity to retreat into a message that can be justified on the basis of purely human argument, there is also a temptation for Christianity to retreat into being a system of ideas, rather than being based on a revealing of Jesus. This retreat can happen at any point on the theological spectrum, from conservative (e.g., in what N. T. Wright [1997, 159] would characterize as holding to justification by faith *in justification*, rather than justification by faith *in Christ*) to liberal (when the gospel becomes a message about liberation per se rather than a message about Christ the liberator).

The early house churches could never ultimately be philosophical schools. Philosophical groups did indeed revere their founders and tell stories about them, figures such as Zeno or Diogenes. However, the philosophical movements were movements about ideas, and in the end the founders were of value mainly because of their ideas. For Paul, Jesus was not primarily someone whose teaching was a source of ideas. Instead, Jesus's death and resurrection were the decisive events bringing salvation to the world. Jesus, as risen Lord, also had a continued existence, and thus the church's existence was in Christ, a part of Christ's life. The early house-church members were not primarily called by Paul to a set of beliefs and ideas. They were called to participation in Christ.

A Radically Changed Life

How radically can the gospel change a life? Paul was seen to have changed from persecutor to preacher. People joining these early house churches would generally have undergone a fairly radical resocialization as they changed with whom they met and adopted the practices and discourse of their new group. This inherently involved some changes with moral dimensions, such as beginning to eat with people of a wider range of social statuses than one would have eaten with previously. No doubt there were also many cases of striking changes of attitude and practice, even if few were quite as striking as that of Paul. Many Christians today also have testimonies of radical change brought about by the gospel. These can be very encouraging to the Christian group that the person belongs to. Through publishing and speaking, some of the most dramatic testimonies become more widely encouraging.

However, the converse of stories of personal change produces a difficult puzzle for churches: How far can accounts of personal change be trusted if the original behavior was seriously wrong? To take a case like Paul's: churches in situations of persecution will want to remain on their guard if a supposedly former persecutor joins them. Less dramatically, if someone convicted for fraud professes conversion in jail and joins a church on release, few churches would make that person church treasurer. Most pointedly in the current situation, few churches would want anyone in the congregation who professed conversion in jail and whose crime had been sexual abuse of children. What roles should faith and caution play in such a case? For church leaders, the basic answer is fairly clear. Neither church leaders looking at evidence of conversion nor a former offender giving testimony to conversion can ultimately be sure whether abusive behavior will recur, so church structures need to work to avoid presenting a risk of dangerous contact.

And yet, on a personal level, Paul's experience does provide testimony that even the most radical changes can be brought about by the power of the gospel. As John Newton, the writer of "Amazing Grace," went from slave trader to clergyman, so can the most radical of changes continue to happen in people's lives.

Galatians 2:1–10

Narrative 2: Of a Gospel Affirmed
by Unity at Jerusalem

Introductory Matters

Paul was not divisive—not intentionally, anyway. Despite, as he saw it, having received his gospel directly from God rather than from people, he felt led to go and affirm that there was unity between him and the Jerusalem apostles over the gospel. They affirmed that unity, but at Antioch they then, in Paul's view, broke unity.

Paul's gospel wins approval, both in the recognition of his mission by the Jerusalem Christian leaders and in the practical matter of a Greek, Titus, not being made to undergo circumcision, which Paul links to the situation of the Galatians. He also inserts some unexpectedly emphatic comments about God not being interested in reputation.

Galatians 2:3 sees the introduction of a key practical topic in Galatians: circumcision. In Genesis, God commanded Abraham to carry out circumcision, as a sign of the covenant between God and Abraham's family (Gen. 17:11).

As E. P. Sanders forcefully brought home, the pattern, here and throughout Judaism, is that circumcision is a sign that the covenant has already been initiated, rather than a deed that brings a Jew into the covenant (see 1977, 472, for his general pattern of "covenantal nomism"). Even though Jews were not unique in using circumcision, the practice became a key Jewish identity marker, as seen especially in the struggles of the Maccabean revolt (1 Macc. 1:60–61; 2:46; 2 Macc. 6:10; 4 Macc. 9:21 [א]). It also had an important role in the entry of gentile converts into Judaism. Among the texts

On Circumcision

"This is my covenant, which you shall keep, between me and you and your offspring after you: Every male among you shall be circumcised. You shall circumcise the flesh of your foreskins, and it shall be a sign of the covenant between me and you. Throughout your generations every male among you shall be circumcised when he is eight days old, including the slave born in your house and the one bought with your money from any foreigner who is not of your offspring." (Gen. 17:10–12 NRSV)

"If someone comes to you as a resident alien [prosēlytos] to do the passover to the Lord, you will circumcise all his males, and then he will come near [proseleusetai] to do it and he shall be as a native of the land." (Exod. 12:48 LXX, AT)

"And many of the gentiles were circumcised and adopted Jewish practice [perietemonto kai Ioudaïzon] on account of fear of the Jews." (Add. Esth. 8:17 = Esther 8:17 LXX, AT)

"When Achior saw all the things that the God of Israel had done, he believed in God [episteusen tō theō] greatly and circumcised the flesh of his foreskin, and joined the house of Israel." (Jdt. 14:10 LXX, AT)

in the sidebar, in Exod. 12:48 see the Greek term *prosēlytos*, "resident alien," the word later used for converts to Judaism. In Esther 8:17, circumcision is bracketed with *Ioudaïzein*, "to adopt Jewish practice," the term Paul uses in Gal. 2:14. Finally, note in Jdt. 14:10 that Achior comes to believe in God, and this faith is expressed in circumcision. Paul's opponents no doubt thought it strange that Paul could see gentile faith and gentile circumcision as somehow at odds.

Philip F. Esler (1998, 127–29) draws attention to another contextual feature significant for understanding Gal. 2:1–10. This is the sociocultural practice of *challenge-and-response* (or *riposte*), classically studied by Pierre Bourdieu (1965). In a society dominated by concern for honor, two men (not relatives) compete in public for honor. One acts or speaks in such a way as to attempt to enter the social space of the other. The second must respond appropriately or will lose honor. That response may trigger a counterresponse by the challenger, and so on.

In the above sense, Esler (1998, 130–40) sees Paul's arrival in Jerusalem, accompanied by the uncircumcised gentile, Titus, as a challenge to the Jerusalem Christian community, triggering actions that are played out in the rest of the passage. In the comments on 2:1–10 (below), we will accept the idea that challenge-and-response is a key issue here, but we will argue that the targets of Paul's challenge are the "false brothers," rather than the Jerusalem Christian community as a whole.

A Challenge-and-Response Encounter on a Wall in Pompeii

"Successus the weaver loves the inn-keeper's servant girl, whose name is Hiris. But she isn't bothered about him. Yet he propositions her. She pities him. A rival wrote it. Farewell."

"Jealous! Because you are bursting yourself, don't injure [?] the handsomer man, and who is the most wicked and beautiful."

"I said it. I wrote it. You love Hiris, who isn't bothered about you . . . [becomes largely unreadable but includes name Successus] . . . Severus"

Graffiti between doorways to houses 3 and 4 of
Region I, Insula 10 (trans. in Oakes 2009, 33)

Tracing the Train of Thought

Timing, Origin, and Purpose of a Visit to Jerusalem (2:1–2)

2:1–2. Then, after fourteen years, I again went up to Jerusalem with Barnabas, taking along Titus as well. I went up in accordance with a revelation and set out to them the gospel that I preach among the gentiles—privately, to those who seemed to be something—lest I am running, or have run, in vain. The timed sequence of events in 1:16–24 continues on into Gal. 2. However, Paul begins to aim at matters other than those in 1:16–24.

Having said that, he does still make a couple of points to back up his claim of not having learned his gospel from others (1:12). He notes that the substantial discussion in Jerusalem did not happen until fourteen (or seventeen) years after his initial revelation from God (2:1; see introduction). Even then, the visit was determined by a further revelation (2:2) rather than somehow expressing dependence on Jerusalem. Moreover, the Jerusalem leaders "added nothing to my message" (2:6): the message remained as it was when revealed to Paul by God.

The narrative of Acts suggests why Barnabas was a natural companion for Paul on the trip. But what of Titus? Richard N. Longenecker (1990, 47) sees him as just one of Paul's normal helpers (e.g., 2 Cor. 2:12–13), with the significance of his visit only being seen in retrospect. Martinus de Boer (2011, 108) sees him as an example of the fruit of Paul's gospel. Philip F. Esler goes further and argues that Paul's taking Titus along was a *challenge* (see above) to the Jerusalem Christian community. He was taking an uncircumcised Christian onto their turf. How would they react? In this scenario, the noncircumcision of Titus represents victory for Paul in the challenge-and-response encounter with the "false brothers" (Esler 1998, 130–32). This group then launched their *response* once Paul, Barnabas, and even Peter were out of the way, resulting in James sending a message to Peter in Antioch to break off table fellowship, effectively breaking the Jerusalem agreement (Esler 1998, 136).

Esler's view of the significance of Titus is probably broadly correct. In the competitive world of the first-century Mediterranean, a Jerusalem group that advocated circumcision of gentile Christians would inevitably regard the arrival of the uncircumcised Titus as a challenge. Again, as Esler notices, Paul does somewhat exult in his victory that Titus was not compelled to be circumcised (2:3). A difficulty for Esler's scenario is that the key encounter with the Jerusalem leaders took place "privately" (2:2), whereas the essence of an honor contest is that it should happen before a public *court of opinion*. However, this prob-

> ### Galatians 2:1–10 in the Rhetorical Flow
>
> **Letter opening (1:1–10)**
>
> **Letter body (1:11–6:10)**
>
> > **Narrative 1: Of a gospel revealed by God, not people (1:11–24)**
> >
> > ► **Narrative 2: Of a gospel affirmed by unity at Jerusalem (2:1–10)**
> >
> > > Timing, origin, and purpose of a visit to Jerusalem (2:1–2)
> > >
> > > Successful resistance to Titus being compelled to be circumcised (2:3–5)
> > >
> > > God's lack of regard for people's reputation (2:6a–b)
> > >
> > > Acceptance of Paul's gospel for the uncircumcised (2:6c–10)

ably gives us a key clue for sharpening Esler's idea. He writes that "Paul was challenging the Jerusalem community" (1998, 130). The pattern of events in 2:1–10 would better fit the idea that Paul was specifically challenging the "false brothers" opposing his idea of mission to the gentiles, about whom Paul had presumably heard. Paul was not concerned with his own public honor, so the challenge did not need to be in public as such. He does not boast in himself but in his gospel of the cross (6:14). If his honor is to be upheld, it is only for the sake of upholding the place of "the truth of the gospel" (2:5) in the court of opinion of the early Jesus movement, which in this case meant the court of opinion of the Jerusalem leaders. They were witnesses of the challenge, not the object of the challenge. Their positive impression is given in 2:3, 6, 9.

Many scholars see the "revelation" of 2:2 as being that of Acts 11:28, in which a prophet, Agabus, announces to the Antioch assembly that there will be a famine (e.g., Schreiner 2010, 120). In response to this, they organize a collection for Christians in Judea and send it there by the hand of Barnabas and Paul (Acts 11:28–30; 12:25). For understanding Galatians, this would be interesting particularly as offering a link to Paul and Barnabas already being keen to "remember the poor" (2:10). It suggests giving that phrase a particular link to gentile collections for Judean Christians (see on 2:10). However, the reader is likely to take the revelation of 2:2 as being directly to Paul, rather than via a prophet (Bruce 1982, 108), and to assume that it relates to the purpose of setting out his gospel, rather than to famine relief. In either case, a key point is that Paul operates according to revelation. The pattern seen in the initial revelation of Christ to him (1:12, 16) is characteristic of his continuing mission. He is a person who operates in the sphere of God, Christ, and the Spirit, rather than being directed by human opinion and the flesh. In this sense he is a paradigm of the radical commitment and transformation involved in the gospel.

Paul writes that he spoke *tois dokousin* (2:2), literally, "to those seeming." As Martinus de Boer argues, the term is neutral in itself, meaning something like "influential people," but Paul's repetition of it (2:2, 6a, 6b, 9) suggests an ironic edge to his use of it, especially in view of 2:6. De Boer (2011, 106–7) sees the term as one introduced by Paul's opponents. This may well be correct, given Paul's rather pointed use of the term.

The final phrases of 2:2 make the aim of the visit sound curiously lacking in Paul's usual confidence: he set out his gospel privately to the Jerusalem leaders lest his mission was in vain (2:2). How could it be in vain if Paul was so assured of God's revelation of Christ to him (1:16)? One answer is probably that Paul never saw his gospel as something maverick, at odds with the teaching of Jesus and his first followers, now mainly in Jerusalem. Paul saw himself as having independently received a revelation that fitted in with the beliefs of the earlier apostles (esp. 1 Cor. 15:8–10 in the context of the preceding verses). However independent his receiving of the revelation, his ideas would have come to grief if it turned out that they were irreconcilably at odds with those of the earlier apostolic tradition. Paul's was a gospel of unity. That would make little sense if it inherently meant disunity with the first Christian leaders.

Successful Resistance to Titus Being Compelled to Be Circumcised (2:3–5)

2:3–5. But not even Titus, who was with me, was compelled to be circumcised, despite being a Greek. This arose on account of the false brothers who had been brought in, who slipped in to spy on our freedom, which we have in Christ Jesus, so that they might enslave us. We did not give in to them for a moment in submission, so that the truth of the gospel would remain for you. Despite the action being in Jerusalem, we now reach the sharpest issue for Paul's hearers in Galatia. Titus was not circumcised. The reason Paul and Barnabas did not allow this was "so that the truth of the gospel would remain for you," the Galatians. Up to this point in the letter, the way in which the Galatians were "turning away . . . to a different gospel" (1:6) has been unspecified. Now it looks likely to involve circumcision, a conclusion that will be made certain by Gal. 5:2–3. Even more specific is 6:12, where Paul's opponents are described as "compelling you to be circumcised," using the same vocabulary as 2:3. Paul implies that if gentile Christians get circumcised, that removes "the truth of the gospel." Why is circumcision such a big issue? Many boys and men get circumcised, for many reasons, including purely medical ones.

To answer this, it is worth looking at the next occurrence of "compel" (*anankazō*), 2:14, where Peter is accused of compelling the gentiles "to Judaize"

(*Ioudaïzein*), that is, to adopt the way of life characteristic of Jews. For Paul, gentile circumcision is a central step in this process. He sees circumcision as entailing an obligation to carry out Jewish law: "I testify again to every man who gets circumcised that he is under obligation to do the whole law" (5:3). From Paul's theology, we could make various arguments for why he sees this as a problem. Specifically from Galatians, there are at least three lines of argument that could be followed. One is soteriological: "the truth of the gospel" is that pursuing the law as a means of salvation cannot work; instead, the effective salvation has been provided in Christ (e.g., 2:16–21). Another is eschatological: "the truth of the gospel" is that the age of the law's role has passed; it was a temporary *paidagōgos* ("child minder") until Christ and faith arrived, which has now happened (3:19–25).

A third is about the nature of human existence now that Christ has arrived. "The truth of the gospel" is that, since the arrival of Christ, "There is no Jew nor Greek. There is no slave nor free. There is no male and female. For you are all 'one' in Christ Jesus" (3:28). The effect on gentile circumcision of the disappearance (in some sense) of the first of these polarities is clear. If there is no Jew nor Greek, it is clearly nonsensical to insist that Greeks, representing gentiles, adopt Jewish identity. In trying to do this, the "false brothers," Paul's opponents, and Peter at Antioch (as Paul sees him) are clearly going against "the truth of the gospel." Equally, throughout church history it has been nonsensical for churches to insist that Jews who follow Jesus must adopt gentile identity by stopping the practice of circumcision and other aspects of Jewish life. That too is against "the truth of the gospel" as seen in Gal. 3:28.

More subtly, the erasure of the other two polarities named in Gal. 3:28 also means that insistence on circumcision is contrary to "the truth of the gospel." Circumcision is an action specific to men (cf. Schüssler Fiorenza 1983, 210; more extensively, see Wiley 2005). The ability to choose circumcision is specific to gentile, free men. A religious identity dependent on the ability to choose circumcision is a religious identity dependent on being free and male: for anyone else, such a religious identity cannot be fully adopted. This is true despite quite proper arguments that Judith Lieu (2002, 101–14) makes about the limited extent to which this issue has affected religious discourse. Tatha Wiley (2005, 78) would argue that the issue's absence is itself indicative of the androcentric nature of such discourse. An identity centered on actions performable only by males who have control over their bodies (i.e., are not slaves) embeds the distinctions, slave and free, male and female, in the world, just as it does with the distinction Jew and Greek. It therefore goes against "the truth of the gospel" in all three of these areas of identity. (For further discussion, see comments on 3:28.)

Within the first-century house church, this is a major issue. In our model house church (see introduction), far fewer than half the people are free gentile males. Paul's expected hearers, when they originally accepted his gospel, took on a religious identity that directly engaged with every social type, an identity based on faith in Christ. His opponents now insist on a religious identity, based on circumcision, that only engages directly with about a third of the house church. Most of the others would hold that identity at second hand (women) or through the decision of others (slaves, young boys). Not only that, but the religious identity would center on those who were, in terms of general first-century culture, the most powerful in the house church: the free males. This is indeed a denial of the truth of the gospel.

F. Crawford Burkitt (1924, 118) argues that Titus may well have been circumcised but that Paul's point is that this was not the result of compulsion. This does not fit the rhetoric of Galatians (de Boer 2011, 111n164). As we have seen, it is clear from the letter overall (esp. 5:2) that Paul would see gentile circumcision as a betrayal of the gospel, irrespective of whether it happened under compulsion. Burkitt's view also underplays the sharpness of Paul's polemic, both here and in talking of his opponents in Galatia. "False brothers," *pseudadelphoi* (2:4), is an extremely negative term. It implies that, to Paul, these people in Jerusalem presented themselves as Christians but were not. When we match his description of the opponents' actions in Galatia with those of the "false brothers," "compelling [gentile believers] . . . to be circumcised" (6:12), we gather the impression that Paul saw his opponents in the same way: as people who presented themselves as Christians but were not.

One further observation is that 2:4 introduces the freedom/slavery motif that will run through the letter (e.g., 4:3, 9; 4:21–5:1).

God's Lack of Regard for People's Reputation (2:6a–b)

2:6a–b. But from those who seemed to be something—whatever they were makes no difference to me: God does not have regard for a person's reputation. In 2:1–10 we keep expecting Paul to get on with saying what the Jerusalem leaders thought about his gospel, which was the agenda set in 2:2. However, after putting in the comment about Titus, Paul again delays giving the Jerusalem leaders' opinion, this time even stopping partway through a sentence. "But from those who seemed to be something—whatever they were makes no difference. . . ." It is not immediately clear why Paul makes this argument. It could be that Paul's opponents have reckoned the Jerusalem leaders as being above him in some way, so Paul needs to qualify what he says to guard against this impression. There may also be a more basic connection to the way in which Paul presents himself in Galatians in comparison with his opponents. The Greek translated here as "reputation" is, literally, "face." Bruce Winter (1994, 137–39) makes much of 6:12, in which Paul describes his opponents as wishing "to make a good face in flesh," as one might render it literally. This could connect with God not having regard for "face": the noun in 2:6 is closely related to the verb of 6:12. If God does not have regard for "face," then the attempts of Paul's opponents "to make a good face" are pointless.

More broadly, Paul's portrayal of himself as someone who does not regard status (nor does his God) would reinforce his overall presentation of himself as a person who operates in the realm of God, not the flesh: a person to whom "the world was crucified" (6:14).

Paul's interjection of this comment on God's disregard for reputation could also feed into the letter's announcement of, and call for, oneness in the house churches. Both the ontological oneness announced in 3:28 and the mutual love and support encouraged in 5:13–6:10 fit well with the church giving allegiance to a God who has no regard for status. Distinctions of wealth, gender, and so forth are not ones that this God will underwrite.

Acceptance of Paul's Gospel for the Uncircumcised (2:6c–10)

2:6c–10. But . . . those who seemed to be something . . . added nothing to my message. But rather, seeing that I had been entrusted with the gospel for the uncircumcised, just as Peter had for the circumcised—for the one at work in Peter for apostleship to the circumcised was also at work in me for the gentiles—and, knowing the grace that had been given to me, James and Cephas and John, those who seemed to be pillars, gave me and Barnabas the right hand of fellowship, that we might go to the gentiles, and they to the circumcised, only with the proviso that we should remember the poor, which very thing I too was keen to do.

Accepting the usual caveats on mirror reading, it does seem safe to infer that Paul's opponents probably questioned how acceptable to the Jerusalem leaders his gospel was. If so, Paul responds firmly. He also sets up James and Peter as being inconsistent in their subsequent influence and actions at Antioch. Paul also marks out his "turf." James and Peter had acknowledged that God had given Paul responsibility and insight for the gentile mission. It was therefore invalid if people from James or Peter had now come to Galatia and told the gentiles to act in ways contrary to Paul's message.

Philip F. Esler (1998, 133) argues that the "giving of the right" in 2:9 (the Greek does not include a word for "hand" here) is an act of condescension in which a more powerful party makes peace with a weaker one. He claims that Paul dissents from their expression of superiority by his comment that they only *seemed* to be pillars. Esler's key evidence is that most "givers of the right" in the eleven occurrences of the expression in 1–2 Maccabees are the superior parties. However, 2 Macc. 14:19 shows that the practice is, in itself, reciprocal, as emissaries in that text both "give and receive right [hands]." It is probably not the practice itself that is condescending. It is that the key decision to take part in the practice is made by the more powerful party. That makes their actions the ones generally to report. In Gal. 2:9, the giving of the right hand by "the pillars" rather than by Paul and Barnabas is probably reported not because the pillars were condescending but because the topic of the verse is their acceptance of Paul's message. It would not be relevant for Paul to say that he "gave the right hand to them." Martinus de Boer (2011, 124) is probably right that the fellowship (*koinōnia*) of 2:9 is partnership in the work of the gospel (cf. esp. Phil. 1:5) and that the Greek *hina* here should be taken as an explicative "that" rather than a purposive "so that." In favor of reading the *hina* that way is the related use of *hina* in 2:10, "that we should . . ."

The final comment in this passage is about "remember[ing] the poor." Bruce W. Longenecker (2010, 135–219) has argued *against* the common scholarly position that this has particularly in view the major collection for Jerusalem that Paul conducted in the final years of his main mission work. Instead, Longenecker insists that we should see the commitment as a key element of Paul's mission as a whole, with the support of the poor being a theme flowing through Paul's work. If we consider the date of the meeting in Gal. 2:1–10, in the early 50s or late 40s AD (see introduction), it is clearly timed about right as a possible trigger for the Jerusalem collection, organized in the mid-to-late 50s. On the other hand, there is no sense in Gal. 2 that Paul sees his acceptance by the Jerusalem leaders as the kind of conditional acceptance that could involve the Jerusalem leaders effectively asking for money. Moreover, in Greco-Roman culture, to do so would have radically undermined the quality of their offer of friendship. As Aristotle writes, "Those who love for the sake of utility love for the sake of what is good for themselves" (*Eth. Nic.* 8.3, trans. W. D. Ross 1954). In particular, this would seem unbelievably crass if "the poor" was, as many scholars argue (e.g., Betz 1979, 102), seen as an expression for the whole assembly there (cf. the later Ebionites, whose name comes from the Hebrew for "poor") rather than particularly poor people among them. In fact, as de Boer (2011, 127) comments, 2:10 refers to current activity on behalf of the poor, involving Barnabas and Paul in Antioch, rather than Paul's future collection, gathered from assemblies further west.

As Bruce Longenecker (2010, 140–56) argues, Paul's concern for the poor is seen at all sorts of points in his letters, not just in his collection for the poor in Jerusalem (citing 2 Cor. 8–9; Gal. 6:9–10; 1 Thess. 5:14; Rom. 12; 2 Thess. 3:6–12). I reinforce the point about Rom. 12 (Oakes 2009, 104–23) and add Phil. 2:1–4, where "considering the interests of each other" looks likely to have had a strong economic component (Oakes 2001, 89–102, 187). For Bruce Longenecker, the key dynamic of 2:10 is that the Christian Jewish leaders, while accepting that gentiles need not get circumcised, urge that they should take on the characteristically Jewish virtue of providing help for the poor. This Paul was already eager to implement (B. Longenecker 2010, 198). Longenecker (2010, 214–15) then links this to 4:12–15 and 6:9–10, viewed as the culmination of the description in 5:13–6:10 of the life brought by the gospel: sow "to the Spirit," "do good to all, especially to the household members of the faith"—the body of the letter ends with a reinforcement of 2:10. (B. Longenecker draws on Hurtado 1979, although the latter relates 2:10 and 6:9–10 to the Jerusalem collection.)

Bruce Longenecker's general argument is compelling. However, it draws on only a few texts in Galatians. It might be better to see these economic concerns within the broader theme of unity. In Gal. 2:1–10, Paul goes to Jerusalem seeking unity and finds it, along with encouragement to promote the sharpest end of practical unity, concern for the poor. Unity runs through the letter, finding its most practical expression in the ethic of love in 5:13–6:10. Serious love is practical, bearing one another's burdens (6:2), doing good in a way that often finds focus in giving to deal with the difficulties of those who are under economic stress.

Theological Issues

Acting in Response to a Revelation

Paul went up to Jerusalem "in accordance with a revelation" (2:2). What would it mean for present-day Christians to act in the same way? The first reaction that many would have is that the attempt to act this way is a common route to disaster and should be avoided. Victor Hugo expresses this eloquently in *Les misérables* in the story of Fantine's catastrophic decision to entrust Cosette to the Thénadiers in an epiphanic moment on her journey away from Paris. Many of us know instances of damaging events that have flowed from people acting on what they saw as a revelation from God.

And yet most, if not all, Christian denominations maintain ways in which they seek to allow fresh guidance from God. This can be a means of reinterpreting or even challenging tradition, or of provoking action in spheres that tradition has not encountered. The ways of doing this vary. In the Catholic tradition, God's guidance is mainly seen as given via the church and its ministers, with some scope for the role of other specially inspired individuals, sometimes related to monastic movements. In the Pentecostal and Brethren traditions, revelations are seen as coming to individual members, especially in the gathered assembly, with the revelations usually being seen as subject to discernment by other members, especially congregational leaders. In the Baptist tradition, guidance is especially seen as coming through the collective mind of the local church members, together in the "church meeting," a periodic gathering to decide on the courses of action that the church should take.

Interestingly, each of these three rather different models can appeal to the experiences of the early Christians. A classic case of revelation via church leaders is the outcome of the Jerusalem Council, as described in Acts 15, resulting in a decision sent around to the churches, "For it seemed right to the Holy Spirit and to us to impose no further burden" (Acts 15:28). Revelations to individual congregation members are frequent, Agabus's prophecy in Acts 11:28 being a good example and the broader idea being seen in 1 Cor. 14.

Again in Acts, we can see collective congregational decision making at work in the commissioning of Paul and Barnabas in 13:2–3.

Having said all this, churches will never ultimately be able to tame "revelation" and the willingness of individual Christians to pursue actions in response to what they see as messages from God. This charismatic anarchic/theocratic element is inherent in Christianity (and in other religions too). Tradition can never fully close down the possibility of potentially disruptive, sometimes positive, sometimes destructive innovation. Although for most Christians at most times, the essentially continuing role of revelation is probably wisely within structures that make revelation subject to some form of communal discernment, it would surely indicate that Christianity was dead if the possibility of maverick revelation disappeared entirely.

Not Having Regard for a Person's Reputation

What does it mean to be a Christian whose God can be described in this phrase from Gal. 2:6? In our first-century model house church, the great majority of members were probably encouraged by this, because their social situations made it almost impossible to acquire anything that, in the public's eyes, would be seen as a significant reputation. Their chances of this were hampered by gender, poverty, age, or servitude. A God who does not regard reputation is good news for most Christians, then and now. Belief in such a God also relieves the pressure to expend energy in seeking status and reputation.

It is a little trickier to work out how a Christian should regard the value of the reputations of other people (both Christian and non-Christian). The sixteenth-century Anabaptists faced trouble for refusing to accord high status to anyone. Ought a Christian to avoid addressing anyone by use of an honorific title?

Various answers could probably be given to this, in various contexts. The more substantive issue is in the dynamics of how people relate to one another, especially within churches. Galatians 2:6 suggests that there is something wrong with their vision of God if members of a church do not interact with one another as equals, if they do not resist carrying across into church life either the status ranking endemic in society or the new status ranking that easily grows up within a group that meets over a long period, such as a church. In the first century, this required avoiding both carrying Greco-Roman household hierarchies into assembly life and also inventing new hierarchies, such as the one relating to exercise of particular spiritual gifts, evidenced in 1 Cor. 12–14.

Galatians 2:11–21

Narrative 3: Of a Gospel Betrayed by Division at Antioch

Introductory Matters

Having presented narratives of the origin and approval of his gospel, Paul surprisingly turns to tell of a challenge to it (2:11–13). Again surprisingly, he does not then narrate the challenge as explicitly having been defeated. Instead, he narrates the giving of his argument in response to the challenge. The narration of this argument (2:14 onward) blends, rather imperceptibly, into the letter's presentation of the argument to the Galatians in their own situation. We should also notice that the argument of 2:15–21 itself includes narrative, both of what Christian Jews have done and are doing (2:16–17), and of what Paul as a particular—but probably paradigmatic—Christian Jew has done and is doing (2:19–21).

The most well-known issue in Galatians, Paul's argument about righteousness and faith (or "trust," as this commentary will generally render *pistis*), begins in 2:15. The argument runs on through various parts of the letter (e.g., 5:4–5). However, there is a particularly striking structure from 2:15–3:14. In broad terms, 2:15–21 presents the relationship between righteousness and trust for Christian Jews (as seen by Paul), then 3:1–14 presents the relationship between righteousness and trust for Christian gentiles. There are many indications that Paul is presenting these two discourses in parallel (overall, not line by line). On the other hand, there are obvious differences in the terms of the discourse focused on gentiles. The pair of discourses together offer an opportunity for us to understand something of what Paul means by the righteousness language that he introduces in 2:16. Although he frequently uses the vocabulary of righteousness in 3:1–14, the benefits gained by the gentiles are expressed more specifically as "the blessing of Abraham" (3:14), which is related to being "sons of Abraham" (3:7), all of which, most concretely, is expressed in the house churches' experience of the Spirit (3:2–5, 14). The overall structure is something like the accompanying table.

The Structure of Galatians 2:15–3:14

Righteousness and Trust for Christian Jews (2:15–21)		Righteousness and Trust for Christian Gentiles (3:1–14)	
2:15–16a	What Christian Jews know about righteousness, trust, Christ, and works of the law	3:1	Exclamation relating to the Cross
2:16b–c	How Christian Jews have acted on this knowledge	3:2–5	The Spirit came to gentiles through trust, not law
2:17–18	Why there is no going back	3:6–9	Christian gentiles who trust are considered righteous, linked to Abraham
2:19–21a	Paul's experience of law, Christ and trust as a paradigmatic Christian Jew	3:10–13	Christ/trust is the route to righteousness and deals with the curse of law
2:21b–c	Conclusion on law and righteousness in relation to the cross	3:14	So gentiles in Christ receive through trust the Spirit and the blessing of Abraham

Paul tackles his Galatian problem indirectly. In 2:15–21 he shows that Christian Jews obtain righteousness through trust in Christ, not by works of law. Having done this, he could just let his predominantly gentile audience draw the inference that, if this is true for Christian Jews, Christian gentiles certainly do not need to get drawn into feeling the need to follow Jewish law. However, Paul goes on to directly address the situation of the Christian gentiles. If they wonder how it all involves them, the clue is their experience of the Spirit (3:2–5). Paul relates that to trust (3:2, 5), then links trust to Abraham and righteousness (3:6–9). He then explains how trust and Christ remove the obstacle posed by gentile failure to keep Jewish law (3:10–13). This enables the Spirit-filled life that their communities experience (3:14). Paul's use of language of righteousness and trust in 3:6–12 sheds light on his use of such language in 2:16–21.

Tracing the Train of Thought

Paul's Opposition to Peter's Withdrawal from Table Fellowship (2:11–14)

2:11–14a. When Cephas came to Antioch, I opposed him to his face, because what he did condemned him. For, before certain people from James arrived, he used to eat together with the gentiles. But when they came, he used to draw back and to separate himself, fearing those of circumcision. And the rest of the Jews joined him in his hypocrisy, so that even Barnabas was led astray into their hypocrisy. But when I saw that they were not walking in line with the truth of the gospel, I said to Cephas, in front of everyone . . .

> ### Galatians 2:11–21 in the Rhetorical Flow
>
> **Letter opening (1:1–10)**
>
> **Letter body (1:11–6:10)**
>
> > **Narrative 1: Of a gospel revealed by God, not people (1:11–24)**
> >
> > **Narrative 2: Of a gospel affirmed by unity at Jerusalem (2:1–10)**
> >
> > ▶ **Narrative 3: Of a gospel betrayed by division at Antioch (2:11–21)**
> >
> > > Paul's opposition to Peter's withdrawal from table fellowship (2:11–14)
> > >
> > > Paul to Peter about what Christian Jews know and have done (2:15–17)
> > >
> > > Paul's dying and living (2:18–21)

At first sight, Peter's behavior sounds so outrageously inconsistent that it is hard to imagine him acting this way. However, if we think about it in its house-church context, it becomes clear that it could have arisen quite easily. Antioch was one of the largest centers of the first-century Jesus movement. There were probably more Christians, and more house churches, at Antioch than at Rome, which had several such groups, as indicated by Rom. 16. As well as probable house-church meetings, there were at least occasional gatherings of a wide group of Christians in Antioch: the kind of occasion at which Paul challenged Peter (Gal. 2:14).

Some house churches in Antioch probably had Jewish hosts, and some gentile. Peter initially accepted meal invitations in either context (2:12). When the people from James came, and presumably lodged with Christian Jews, no one would be surprised that Peter went to eat with his newly arrived friends. Nor would it be a surprise that Barnabas and other Christian Jews went to eat with them too, especially since Barnabas had been part of the Jerusalem assembly (Acts 4:36–37; 11:22). However, the pattern persisted. Maybe Peter turned down some meal invitations with the excuse that he was invited elsewhere. Barnabas too kept seeing the visitors rather than eating in his usual places. All the Christians were periodically meeting together, but generally the Christian Jews and gentiles were now living separate lives. Whether or not the periodic joint meetings also involved food (cf. 1 Cor. 11:17–34), it appears to have been at such a meeting that matters came to a head.

Paul categorizes this situation alongside the actions of the "false brothers" who had sought Titus's circumcision. Like theirs, Peter's actions are seen as threatening "the truth of the gospel" (2:14; cf. 2:5). Why does Paul do this, using this conflict about eating together as the route into his argument about works of law, especially circumcision? In Galatians, unity in Christ is a crucial element in the idea of salvation. The oneness of Jew and Greek (and other polar pairs) in Christ is at the climax of the argument (3:28). This oneness

© Janet Oakes 1999

Figure 5. Dining room of the association of builders at Ostia.

in Christ makes the Christians the single seed of Abraham and hence heirs, as promised (3:29). Breaking that unity amounts to breaking Christian salvation. For Christian Jews and Christian Greeks to stop eating together is a practical denial of that unity, a central form of practical denial of it. This is both because, in ancient Mediterranean society, deciding with whom one ate was a key issue in conferring honor on one another, and because, in the life of house churches, eating together was an absolutely core activity (on meals, see Klinghardt and Taussig 2012).

In 2:11, Paul says that he opposed Peter because "he was having been condemned," to render *kategnōsmenos ēn* literally. Paul cannot mean that the Christian leaders at Antioch condemned Peter. In that case, Paul would not have needed to confront him. However, presumably the gentile Christians at Antioch thought Peter's actions to be wrong. That would make Paul a Christian Jewish leader who was standing up for the interests of the (less powerful) Christian gentile church members against the actions of the rest of the Christian Jewish leaders. That would clearly make a positive contribution to the rhetoric of Galatians: Paul positions himself as the champion of gentile Christian interests against certain Christian Jews who were acting in ways detrimental to the gentiles. Anyhow, in 2:11, Paul does not specify who has condemned Peter. Martinus de Boer (2011, 131) appears correct in taking the main thought to be that Peter stood self-condemned by his actions. Another way of putting this would be that Paul saw Peter's actions as inherently condemning him in the court of all reasonable public opinion, in particular on the grounds of hypocrisy (2:13).

The charge of hypocrisy was powerful in a Greco-Roman context (Konstan 1996, 17). Even before Paul levels that charge, his hearers will have recognized how Peter's actions condemned him by falling into that category. Paul presents him as the waverer, the "flatterer," who instead of acting on principle, changes his actions to please different sets of people (Glad 1996, 55). There is also a structural hypocrisy evident, affecting both Peter and, implicitly, James, who one moment are giving Paul the right hand of fellowship, and the next moment are undermining his gospel to the uncircumcised, to which they had given approval.

2:14b. I said to Cephas, in front of everyone, "If you, being a Jew, live in a gentile manner and not a Jewish manner, how can you be compelling the gentiles to Judaize?" The importance of Philip F. Esler's insistence (2012) that *Ioudaios* ("Jew," although using the translation "Judean"; see the introduction) is an ethnic term becomes evident here. Contrary to Hans Dieter Betz (1979, 112), *Ioudaios* is not Peter's "present religious status" but is his ethnicity, a usually inseparable and central aspect of his identity. This ethnic identity includes expectations of normal behavior, especially religious behavior. However, the identity is ethnic rather than only religious. The paradox that Paul now proposes centers on Peter's departure from the norms of behavior expected of his ethnic group. Incidentally, here (and in 2:15) is a key element of the answer as to whether the revelatory event in 1:16 should be seen as involving Paul stopping being a Jew. The answer is no. He and Peter are still *Ioudaioi*. What has changed are aspects of their behavior: it no longer fits the norms usually expected in accordance with their Jewish ethnic identity. There are ways in which Paul (and Peter) is no longer living in *Ioudaïsmos* (1:13), the way of life typical of Jews. There are ways in which Peter (and Paul) is living in a manner expected of gentiles, not Jews.

David deSilva argues attractively that the use of *zaō*, "to live," even though here it refers to mode of behavior rather than existence, foreshadows the soteriological use of "life" in the coming verses, especially 2:19–20 (2011, 109–10). It would simplify the argument of 2:14 if we could take this soteriological sense of *zaō* as its main use in the verse, "If you . . . are alive on a gentile basis . . ." The most frequent usage of *zaō* does support this. However, that is not true of *zaō* when used with adverbs of manner. In those cases, *zaō* refers to a way of life. For instance, in Luke 15:13, the prodigal is *zōn asōtōs*, "living dissolutely" (cf. 2 Tim. 3:12). This being the case, what is Paul referring to when saying that Peter is living in a gentile rather than Jewish manner? As commentators generally indicate, it probably has to do with Peter eating with gentiles (e.g., Schlier 1989, 86). He seems to feel free to eat, or not eat, with gentile Christians, depending on whether there are Christian Jews around who will be upset by it. This is actually not far from Paul's position of adjusting one's behavior to be appropriate to the other believers present, as discussed at length in 1 Cor. 8–10 and Rom. 14–15. However, Paul clearly has a proviso that Christian gentiles and Jews must be willing to be united in eating. This is not directly stated in those texts, but it is implicit in the thrust of those texts toward enabling fellowship, as particularly brought home in 1 Cor. 10:17

(NRSV), "Because there is one bread, we who are many are one body." It is also probably implied by the call in Rom. 15:7–12 for gentiles and Jews to rejoice together, especially since eating has been a key topic in Rom. 14–15. Peter's surprisingly Pauline practice is certainly out of line with Jewish laws over avoidance of food potentially contaminated by gentiles who might have offered the food to idols or broken other purity rules.

Paul sees Peter's willingness to accommodate the sensitivities of some Christian Jews (whom Paul disparages as being the ones Peter fears; 2:12), by temporarily not eating with gentiles, as tantamount to "compelling" the gentiles "to Judaize." Contrary to decades of confusing scholarship that has called Paul's opponents "Judaizers," meaning people who encourage others to adopt Jewish practices, the Greek verb *Ioudaïzein* means "to live in a Jewish way" or "to adopt a Jewish lifestyle" (see, e.g., Add. Esth. 8:17 = Esther 8:17 LXX; Josephus, *J.W.* 2.454; Dunn 1993, 15, 129). Paul's assertion that Peter's actions add up to this is surprising. However, Gal. 3:28 can make sense of Paul's logic. Since salvation culminates in being one in Christ, any Christians who act in such a way as to exclude other Christians from fellowship with them are effectively asserting that the culmination of salvation, seen in practical oneness, can only be attained if the excluded Christians change to become like those who are excluding them. In this case, it means the gentile Christians "Judaiz(ing)."

Finally, notice the word "compelling" itself. Paul ties together the narratives of the "false brothers" who sought Titus's circumcision (2:3–4), and of Peter in Antioch, with the actions of Paul's opponents, who are "compelling" the Galatians to get circumcised (6:12).

Paul to Peter about What Christian Jews Know and Have Done (2:15–17)

2:15–16. **We, Jews by nature and not sinners from among the gentiles, knowing that a person is not considered righteous on the basis of works of law, except through trust in Jesus Christ, even we trusted in Christ Jesus, so that we would be considered righteous on the basis of trust in Christ and not on the basis of works of law, "because" on the basis of works of law "no flesh will be considered righteous."** The main argument of the letter opens with this statement by Paul to Peter. Paul uses the case of Christian Jews to argue that "righteousness" now depends not on keeping the Jewish law but on trust in Christ. The implicit point of all this is that, if this is the case "even" for Christian Jews, it must also be the case for Christian gentiles. Peter was therefore wrong to effectively "compel the gentiles to Judaize" (2:14), and especially the gentile Galatians would be wrong in accepting the call of Paul's opponents to adopt practice of the Jewish law.

Our consideration of Paul's and Peter's Jewish identity will involve thinking about Paul's quotation of Ps. 143:2 (142:2 LXX) at the end of Gal. 2:16. We will then return to deal with other key issues in the order in which they first occur in 2:16—namely, the words or phrases translated above as "considered righteous," "works of law," "except," and "trust in Jesus Christ."

Paul and Peter remained in the ethnic category of being "Jews by nature." They were not gentiles, outside Jewish law, "sinners." However, turning to trust in Jesus as *māšîaḥ* (Messiah, Christ), they were turning to a new way of understanding the place of the law, a new way of reading the law, exemplified for Paul in the new way in which he read Ps. 143:2 (142:2 LXX). Paul was not writing Galatians in order to stop Christian Jews from practicing the law (the only partial exception being 2:11–14, in which he effectively opposes some practices at times when they keep Christian Jews and Christian gentiles from eating together). However, he does think that Christian Jews have, in accepting Jesus as the Messiah (Christ), switched from dependence on law as a means of righteousness to dependence on trust in Christ for that. Moreover, he thinks that Christian Jews ought to be reading Scripture in a way that means they see "works of law" as being unable to put people in a position where they are considered righteous. The last clause of 2:16 probably quotes Ps. 143:2 (142:2 LXX), although switching the psalm's "all things living" to "all flesh" and, crucially, inserting "on the basis of works of law." As a quote, the last clause of 2:16 makes sense as an argument: Jews, such as Paul and Peter, know their Scripture, so they should know Ps. 142:2 LXX: "because, before you no living thing will be considered righteous" (*hoti ou dikaiōthēsetai enōpion sou pas zōn*). They therefore know that the law, which the writer of Ps. 143 (142 LXX) was living under, does not bring about a situation where a person is considered righteous.

Did non-Christian Jews of Paul's day read Ps. 143 in this way? Surely not. They surely read it as the psalmist's humble statement of unrighteousness, which emphasized the need to depend on God's mercy. Paul's interpretation is part of a pattern of early Christian reinterpretation of Scripture, gathering texts and developing ways of reading them that supported Christian beliefs. In fact, even within the Jesus movement (even in Paul's Letters!) there were differing uses of texts. The rhetoric of Gal. 2:16 could work either by Paul saying what he knows that he and Peter already agree on about this, or by Paul calling Peter to agree with Paul's way of seeing the situation, including his way of reading Ps. 143, which he brings into the argument because of its use of the unusual verb, *dikaioō*.

All this means that the pre-Christian Paul and Peter were not wandering around in despair about the ability of the law to bring righteousness: Paul has already described his prior devotion to ancestral traditions (1:14). What we see in 2:16 is a reevaluation of the law by the Christian Paul, one that he expects or encourages other Christian Jews to share. There is no evidence that Paul thought this to have been a general first-century Jewish view: he would have been crazy to have thought that way. Neither did Paul feel a particular calling to seek to persuade non-Christian Jews that their view of the law was wrong: he saw himself as called to gentiles. However, in Galatians, even though it is not the point that the letter is driving at, Paul does see Jews as facing a plight (the impossibility of being considered righteous on the basis of works of law) from which they can only be freed by trusting in Christ. This is what he sees Christian Jews, such as himself and Peter, as knowing, with the result that even they, who are not from among the habitually sinful gentiles (2:15), have trusted in Christ.

... **A person is not considered righteous** [*dikaioutai*] **on the basis of** ... (2:16a). We saw how Martin Luther read Gal. 2:16 (see introduction). Is that correct? Here most translations offer the word "justify," which is not used in its normal English sense ("to give an explanation as to why your actions were correct"). How could we express the idea of the word in Gal. 2:16 in terms of normal English usage? J. Louis Martyn reads the righteousness language in 2:16 very differently from Luther. Martyn (1997a, 246) offers the translation "rectify." Would that be better? Scholarly readings of righteousness language in 2:16 are effectively dominated by discussion drawn from consideration of the fuller evidence in Romans. How is righteousness language configured in Galatians itself?

There are two key questions. How does *dikaioutai*, which is a present passive form of the verb *dikaioō* in Galatians, relate to the adjective *dikaios* ("righteous") and the noun *dikaiosynē* ("righteousness")? What does "righteousness" mean in Galatians? This second question will occupy various parts of the commentary. In the absence of an immediately obvious answer, it looks wise to proceed by collecting the ideas that Paul relates to righteousness in Galatians, to try to compose a picture of what he means by the idea. (See discussions on Gal. 2:19b–20, 21; 3:6–9, 10–13; 5:5–6; 4:21–5:13a "Theological Issues.")

Turning to the first question, the correspondence in relations between the law, Christ, and *dikaio-* terminology in 2:16 and 2:21 suggests that the noun *dikaiosynē* (2:21) is the state of someone to whom *dikaioutai* (2:16–17) has occurred or is occurring. This point is reinforced by 3:6–8. The fact of righteousness being reckoned to Abraham (3:6) is made parallel to a process (3:8) in which God *dikaioi* (the same verb as in 2:16) the gentiles. Accompanying terminology reinforces the link: both 3:6 and 3:8 operate on the basis of trust. The link between noun and verb is also supported by comparing their use in 3:21 and 3:24, and in 5:4 and 5:5.

In Galatians, the only occurrence of the adjective *dikaios* ("righteous") is in 3:11. It is in parallel to the verb *dikaioutai*. "Because no one *dikaioutai* . . . by means of law, it is clear that the one who is righteous will live on the basis of trust" (or possibly "righteous on the basis of trust will live"). The attendant terms—"law" and "trust"—reinforce the link between verb and adjective by binding them into the patterns seen in 2:16 and elsewhere. The one who *dikaioutai* is *dikaios*, being characterized by *dikaiosynē*. This conclusion is reinforced if we broaden our focus to Paul's Letters as a whole. In Romans especially, we can see *dikaios* and *dikaiosynē* related to the process that he describes using the verb *dikaioō*. With a future reference, Rom. 5:19 asserts, "Through the obedience of the one man the many will be made righteous." With a past reference in Rom. 9:30, the gentiles "attained righteousness, the righteousness that is on the basis of trust."

What kind of link is there between the verb and the noun and adjective? Does *dikaioō* mean "to make (someone) righteous"? Is Martyn right in translating the verb as "to rectify," referring this to God's act in "making things right," "making right what has gone wrong" (1997a, 250, 263; 1997b, 143)? We will take a twin approach: first looking at the usage in 3:6–8 and asking how far that can govern our conclusions; then surveying Septuagint occurrences of the passive of *dikaioō*, to see the range of use there.

Among the texts in Galatians where the verb and either noun or adjective relate to each other, it is 3:6–8 that gives the most specific indication of how Paul is likely to see the verb functioning. It looks as though God's action in 3:8, as he *dikaioi* (verb) the gentiles "on the basis of trust," is equivalent to his action in 3:6, where he "reckoned" Abraham's trust in him (in believing God's promise) "as righteousness." The working assumption flowing from this is that the verb *dikaioi* (3:8) means something like "reckons as righteous." If we try this out in the other uses of the verb in Galatians (2:16 [3x], 17; 3:11, 24; 5:4), it fits reasonably. If we go beyond Galatians, it finds strong support in the account of Abraham in Rom. 4 (4:2–5).

More specifically, the expression in Gal. 3:6, "it was reckoned [*elogisthē*] to him as righteousness," uses a financial metaphor (on financial use of *logizomai*, see Burton 1921, 154–55). However, it does not look safe to make the jump to seeing all Paul's uses of the verb *dikaioō* as involving a financial metaphor. Although he can use financial metaphors (e.g., Rom. 6:23), they are far from dominating his ideas of salvation. The broader cultural use of *dikaioō* also suggests looking at other spheres. For instance, in the LXX it appears several times in a lawcourt setting (e.g., Isa. 1:17; 5:23), a point that has formed the predominant basis for interpretation of the term in Paul's Letters (e.g., Kertelge 1990, 331: "Every NT use of [*dikaioō*] has a forensic/juridical stamp: 'justification' and 'vindication' result from judgment"). However, the only points in Galatians that suggest lawcourt ideas for *dikaioō* are the unstated context of Ps. 143:2 (see sidebar below) and the hope of future righteousness in Gal. 5:5. Neither is very compelling, especially since—to bring us back to the case at hand—the tense of *dikaioutai* in 2:16a is present, not future, as we would expect if it were about acquittal before God at a future judgment. Moreover, Abraham in 3:6 has been central to our argument thus far, and there is no sign that "righteousness" there means something like "acquittal before a lawcourt."

In fact, if we look more broadly at the LXX evidence, we see frequent use outside law court settings. This is particularly clear if we survey the use of *dikaioō* in the passive, which is the voice in which Paul usually uses it (7 of the 8 uses in Galatians are passive, as are 18 of 25 uses in the undisputed letters overall). The evidence presented in the sidebar shows that the passive of *dikaioō* tends to carry meanings such as "be considered righteous," "be righteous." This also works with Paul's usage in Rom. 2:13; 3:4; 1 Cor. 4:4. The combination of general usage and the evidence of Gal. 3:6–8 suggests that we should be seeing *dikaioō* as meaning something like "consider righteous" (see also Barclay forthcoming).

. . . **A person is not considered righteous on the basis of works of law, except . . .** (2:16a). "Law" in 2:16 means the torah, the Jewish law found in Scripture. This makes most sense in the context, which is about what "we . . . Jews" are "knowing," and which is responding to what is essentially a disagreement about how Jewish laws on eating should apply in Christian meetings. It is also clear from texts such as 3:10, in which Deuteronomy describes itself as "the book of the law," and 3:17, in which "the law" arrives 430 years after the covenant with Abraham. Galatians 4:21 uses the term to include narrative from Genesis, rather than just legal material. Since it refers to Jewish law in this programmatic first appearance in 2:16, we will take it in that sense elsewhere, unless there are good reasons for thinking otherwise (questions could be asked about whether 5:18, 23 might use the word to include law in general, and about the phrase "law of Christ" in 6:2).

James D. G. Dunn (1993, 135–37) argues that "works of law" is a term most commonly referring to practices that were understood in the first century to characterize Jews, as distinct from gentiles, especially circumcision, food laws, and Sabbath keeping. Michael Bachmann (2010, 108) sharpens this by showing that use of comparable terminology in texts such as 4QMMT makes the term a likely one to designate the law's commands that are used to distinguish groups. The key issue at stake in Dunn's suggestion is that Paul could be opposing certain elements of law practice, those that distinguish Jews from gentiles, without opposing the law in a more general sense. To put it sharply: in Dunn's view Christ would be clarifying and bringing about the real meaning and use of the law rather than abolishing it (Dunn 1993, 289; cf. Bachmann 2008, 30 and Paul's positive comments about the law in Rom. 3:2, 7:12, 14).

On a technical level, it is unlikely that Galatians consistently distinguishes "works of law" from the unadorned term, "law" (e.g., cf. 2:21 with 2:16). Dunn would not deny that. He sees Paul in 2:21 (where the word "law" appears alone) as criticizing the "works of law" approach that keeps gentiles from the grace of God (1993, 149). Indeed Bachmann uses the terminological parallel to support his argument that "works of the law" are the law's commands, rather than actions taken by people to try to keep the law (Bachmann 2008, 12). However, in Galatians it is difficult to see Paul separating out certain types of law-based practices, those that distinguish Jews from gentiles, from others. Matters come to a head in 3:19–24. There Paul argues that the whole

Dikaioō in the Passive Voice in the Septuagint

Dikaioō occurs 22 times in the passive (and 26 times in the active). The following indicate most of the range of use.

The most common passive subject of the verb is God or his judgments.

"The judgments of the Lord are true, dedikaiōmena *altogether."* (Ps. 19:9 [18:10 LXX])

Dedikaiōmena must be somewhere in the area of indicating that they "are righteous" or "are seen to be righteous" (a statement of what is evident about them), possibly with an overtone of being vindicated. There is clearly no thought of them being "made righteous" or "acquitted." Other texts relating the verb to God are probably similar (Sir. 18:2; Pss. Sol. 8.23; 9.2; Isa. 42:21).

Some specific people are objects. Judah admits,

"Dedikaiōtai Tamar than I [am]." (Gen. 38:26)

Tamar "is more righteous" than Judah, or "is seen to be more righteous," or, consequently "is vindicated over against Judah." Again, the verb is not about "making righteous." This is not in a specifically courtroom setting. In Gen. 44:16 Judah (again!) does not know how he and his brothers *dikaiōthōmen* before Joseph. The meaning is presumably something like, "will be seen to be righteous," with possible connotations of being vindicated or acquitted.

Ben Sira writes of various people who tend to lack righteousness. For instance, the NRSV translates Sir. 26:29 as,

"A merchant can hardly keep from wrongdoing, nor is a tradesman innocent of sin [ou dikaiōthēsetai . . . apo hamartias*]."* (cf. 31:5)

NRSV looks reasonable in taking *ou dikaiōthēsetai,* although in the Greek future passive, as essentially indicating a current state of lacking righteousness.

None of the passive uses is in the context of a human lawcourt. The closest examples are in texts about divine action, which draw on the analogy of a court case. For instance, Ps. 142:2 LXX (143:2 MT) reads

"And do not enter into judgment with your servant, because no living creature dikaiōthēsetai *before you."*

Here *dikaiōthēsetai* could have meanings ranging from "is righteous" (cf. Sir. 26:29, above), to "will be seen as righteous," presumably to something like "will be acquitted." Other texts in something like a divine "courtroom" setting are Isa. 43:9, 26; 45:25.

Courtrooms are far from being the only setting for LXX use of *dikaioō* in the passive. Even in a text such as Ps. 142:2 LXX, which operates using a courtroom analogy, it is far from certain that *dikaiōthēsetai* carries a sense significantly beyond the general "is righteous." If we attempt to generalize, most passive uses of *dikaioō* could be fitted under the rubric of being evidently righteous, being acknowledged as righteous, being considered righteous, whether that is merely a value judgment or carries a practical effect such as acquittal.

law has now fulfilled its honorable but limited task. The effect is that the law no longer places any demand on those who are in Christ. That is not to say that Paul intends to stop Christian Jews from following the law: "Neither circumcision is anything, *nor is uncircumcision*" (6:15). But 2:16 is making an argument that encompasses all life under Jewish law. In Paul's view, Christian Jews know that life under the law cannot bring righteousness except where there is trust in Christ.

Where Dunn (1993, 137) is probably correct is in reading *ean mē* in 2:16 as "except": "a person is not considered righteous on the basis of works of law except through trust in Jesus Christ." Dunn went against the great weight of scholarly tradition, which took *ean mē* here as "but rather." Commentators argue that, even though Paul's consistent usage elsewhere is "except," "if not" (Rom. 10:15; 11:23; 1 Cor. 8:8; 9:16; 14:6, 9, 11, 28; 15:36; 2 Thess. 2:3), they know from many texts, not least the end of Gal. 2:16, that Paul sees no circumstances in which "works of law" bring righteousness, whereas translating *ean mē* as "except" makes it sound as though there are such circumstances. Such commentators assimilate *ean mē* to *ei mē* in 1:7 (Betz 1979, 117), which does mean "but rather," or they appeal to texts such as John 5:19 (Goodwin 1886, 124–25, cited in Das 2000, 531), where *ean mē* means "but," or they take "except" to refer back to the conditions for being considered righteous, rather than the conditions under which works of law might be a basis for righteousness (Lightfoot 1890, 115).

Andrew Das has forcefully made the case that we should indeed read *ean mē* as "except" and should see it as relating to works of law. He argues that the whole clause was an affirmation agreed among Christian Jews but ambiguous so that different groups could interpret it in different ways. Das (2000, 537–39; cf. de Boer 2011, 144–45) argues that in the rest of 2:16 Paul shows that he takes the need for trust in Christ as making the need for the law redundant. This is reasonable, although it does not seem necessary for Paul to be using a preexisting formula in 2:16a. It works well as a construction by Paul. He is arguing with Peter and is therefore seeking to express the logic of Jewish Christianity. In 2:16a Paul expresses what he sees as a basic idea that makes a Christian Jew Christian. He then argues that that view effectively does away with the need for the law as a source of salvation. He ends the verse by reinforcing his point through a Christian reading of Ps. 143:2 (142:2 LXX). Interpreters have probably been thrown off course by the fact that the order of Paul's argument is not what we would expect. He could have proved his case simply from his reading of Ps. 143, but he chooses to precede his use of that text with other arguments that appear not to be logically necessary. However, he does similar things elsewhere: for instance, on a large scale in 1 Cor. 8:1–11:1. In Gal. 2:16, by beginning from a premise that he thinks Peter must agree with, Paul's rhetoric stands more chance of carrying Peter with him.

Douglas Campbell (2011, 172) argues that "works of law" in 2:16 should be seen as a label for the false gospel of Paul's opponents, rather than any description of an aspect of Judaism. Campbell is probably right that the picture in 2:16, of the inability of "works of law" to lead to righteousness, is not one that non-Christian first-century Jews would recognize as true. However, he goes so far as to argue that we should "relocate the reference of 'works of law' away from Judaism per se" (2011, 170). This is deeply unpersuasive, especially since the reference in question is part of the flow of rhetoric in Galatians, during which Paul embeds this expression heavily in his account of the history of Israel up to the arrival of Christ (3:6–29). As a Christian operating on the basis of revelation, Paul clearly now sees Jewish law as, for instance, not bringing life (3:21). (On the theological "swamp" that Campbell sees Pauline scholarship as being in, see under "Theological Issues" below.)

. . . **A person is not considered righteous on the basis of works of law, except through trust in Jesus Christ** [*dia pisteōs Iēsou Christou*] (2:16a–b). Gerhard Barth (1993, 93) is sure that: "Gal. 2:16 shows unequivocally" that *pistis Iēsou Christou* means "*faith* in Jesus Christ." Barth calls this an "objective genitive" reading, seeing *Christou* as the grammatical object of *pistis*: Christ is the *object* of the faith. In contrast, Richard B. Hays (2002) holds a "subjective genitive" view of the term: Christ is the *subject* who has the faith(fulness). He "understands *pistis Iēsou Christou* to mean 'the faithfulness of Jesus Christ' as manifested in his self-sacrificial death" (2000, 240). For Hays and others this offers a theological reorientation of Paul's idea of salvation, putting the central focus on the action of God in Christ rather than on human belief (although Hays still sees that as important).

Despite Barth's confidence, although the arguments based on 2:16 are powerful, they are contested. For instance, in 2:16 *pistis Iēsou Christou* is contrasted with *erga nomou,* "works of law." To contrast "faith" with "works" sounds like discourse about two alternative modes of existence for the person who is seeking to be righteous, in which case *pistis Christou* is probably "faith in Christ." However, Hays argues that if Paul objects to dependence on works, the most effective response is "to juxtapose futile human activity to gracious divine initiative," namely, Christ's faithful death on the cross (Hays 2002, xlvii). Similarly, what Peter and Paul have done (according to Paul) is "trusted in Christ Jesus." Since this is described as the route to attaining righteousness through *pistis Christou*, that suggests that the *pistis* in question must be that of the people who have believed. However, Hays can mount the opposite argument, that the syntax of 2:16 means that reading *pistis Christou* as "trust in Christ" produces a strange appearance of redundancy: "We trusted in Christ Jesus so that we would be considered righteous on the basis of trust in Christ" (see, e.g., Williams 1997, 68).

The arguments based on 2:16 alone are not decisive, either in Barth's favor or Hays's (the redundancy argument underestimates the stylized heavy repetitiveness of the verse). General grammatical considerations do not decide the issue either. As well as obvious subjective genitives such as Rom. 4:16, on "the faith of Abraham," there are various objective genitive examples such as 2 Thess. 2:13, *pistei alētheias*, "by faith in the truth"; and Acts 3:16, *pistei tou onomatos autou*, "(by) faith in his name." In fact, the terms "subjective" and "objective" are a little questionable and mask a range of other possible ways of understanding the genitive *Christou* (for a range of these, see Bird and Sprinkle 2009). Three issues look particularly significant in trying to make progress: the meaning of *pistis*, the roles of Christ in the soteriology of Galatians, and the role of *pistis* in the soteriology of 3:6–14.

Hays (2000, 240) rightly notes that the Greek word *pistis* can be translated as "faith," "faithfulness," "fidelity," or "trust." He could have added financial terms such as "credit," or other words relating to trustworthiness (see, e.g., the entry in LSJ). As Zeba Crook (2004, 201–14) discusses in his study of conversion, *pistis* and the related Latin word, *fides*, encapsulated the attitudes and behaviors of trust and loyalty on which successful relationships in society depended, whether personal, or at civic or state level. In the view of this commentary, *pistis Christou* is, in terms of trust and fidelity, the way of life (cf. Williams 1997, 65) characteristic of those who are in a properly functioning relationship with Christ. If Paul chose to do so, it would also be a good way of characterizing Christ's mode of engagement in that relationship. He shows fidelity to those who entrust themselves to him.[1] As George Howard (1990, 57–58) and Hays (2002, xxx) argue, this would also express God's fidelity, seen in Christ's actions. The idea of reciprocal fidelity between the believer and Christ/God is a powerful one. However, the focus of Paul's emphasis in Galatians and the arguments below lead this commentary to opt for a relatively traditional rendering, "trust in Christ," although regretting that that hides the undoubted connotations of faithful allegiance to Christ and the conceivable subtler connotations of Christ's fidelity to his followers.

As Hays argues, it is the cross on which Christians are to depend (cf. Gal. 3:1). Like him, I would construe 2:16 precisely as speaking about that relationship of dependence on the cross (cf. 2:16 with 2:21; see Hays 2000, 240; and Martyn 1997a, 271). However, given the content and context of 2:16, it seems much more likely that *pistis Christou* expresses the relationship between Christians and Christ than between Christ and God. We can make this point more broadly by considering the roles of Christ in the soteriology of Galatians.

As Hays (2002, 6–8) argues, even though Galatians is not primarily a narrative text, there is a christological narrative that underlies the argument and makes itself evident at various points. Christ has an astonishing range of roles in the ideas of salvation in Galatians. If we run through them in chronological

---

1. The work of my PhD student Jonathan Tallon, who is exploring *pistis* in John Chrysostom's preaching, has encouraged me in reflection in this area.

order—the order of the underlying christological narrative—the list is as follows. As "the seed" of Abraham, Christ received the promise made to Abraham (3:15–16, 19). Christ was sent as God's Son into a life "from a woman" and "under law" (4:4). Christ acted to "redeem those under law," with the intended result of enabling "adoption" (4:5). Galatians repeatedly states that Christ experienced death, crucifixion (2:19, 21; 3:1, 13; 6:12, 14, 17). This death is described as a motivated action by Christ: he "gave himself" "for our sins" (1:4), "for me" (Paul, paradigmatically, 2:20; see below). In 1:4, this has a purpose, "to rescue us from the present evil age." We can link that with 5:1, Christ "set us free," and 3:13, in which redemption from the law's curse involves him becoming "a curse." The cross also acts as locus for identification with Christ (2:19–20) and a changed relationship to the world (6:14). Christ experienced resurrection by God (1:1). Christ "lives" in Paul and, by implication, in other Christians (2:20). God sends "the Spirit of his Son" into Christians' hearts (4:6). Conversely, Christians are "baptized into Christ" and "put on Christ" (3:27). They are "in Christ Jesus" (3:28) and share Christ's identity as "seed of Abraham" (3:29) and as "sons of God" (3:26; 4:6).

God acts in relation to Christ (and in relation to people). Christ acts in relation to people. In Galatians, the blessings of God generally come to Christians through Christ. Christ has the central role in the soteriology of Galatians, a role that relates to people (see also discussion, below, on Martyn's reading of 6:14, in which he sees Christ as primarily acting in relation to the world).

Putting this negatively, in Galatians, Christ is not described as acting toward God. There is nothing in Galatians like the teaching about Christ's obedience in Rom. 5 or, more briefly, Phil. 2. Although there is a great theological attractiveness in Hays's reading of Christ's obedience to God as the center point of the soteriology of Galatians, that does not fit the shape of Paul's christological narrative in the soteriology of the letter.

Also theologically attractive is Sam K. Williams's idea that *pistis Christou* is so called because it "bears the character of Christ's own steadfastness . . . grounded in [Christ's] absolute confidence in, and reliance upon, God" (1997, 69). However, again, the christological narrative of Galatians does not draw any attention to Christ's trust in God. What Galatians draws attention to is Christ's love for us (2:20) and his many-faceted action on our behalf. To sum up, this argument about the roles of Christ in the soteriology of Galatians does not, in itself, prove that *pistis Christou* means "trust in Christ." It does show that a reading of *pistis Christou* that fits with the soteriology of Galatians as a whole is likely to be one that places the expression in the interface between people and Christ (in one direction, or the other, or both), rather than in the interface between Christ and God as Hays and, partially, Williams do.

Finally, discussion of *pistis Christou* in 2:16 needs at least a brief comment on how this relates to use of *pistis* language in the soteriology of 3:6–14. In the introduction to this section, we saw how discourse about righteousness, *pistis*, and Christ in relation to Christian Jews in 2:15–21 is followed by discourse on these topics in relation to Christian gentiles in 3:1–14. It is hard to avoid the conclusion that the Christian gentiles' *pistis*—seen in 3:7–9, 14 and related by Paul to Abraham's *episteusen*, "trusted," in 3:6—is somehow congruent with the Christian Jews' act of believing and their dependence on *pistis Christou* in 2:16. This congruence is made especially pointed by the use both of *ek pisteōs* ("of/on the basis of trust") in 2:16; 3:7, 8, 9, 11 and of *dia (tēs) pisteōs* ("through trust") in 2:16; 3:14. Also, Gal. 3:11a looks like a recapitulation of 2:16c (see below). Various scholars have fairly forcefully argued points such as these (e.g., Dunn 2008). A logical alternative position is that of Martinus de Boer, who argues that every use of *pistis* in Galatians except in 5:22 refers "primarily" to "the faith of Christ himself: his faithful death on the cross" (2011, 192). This goes beyond Hays (2000, 256) and is very difficult to sustain, especially given the relationship between 3:7 and 3:6 (see below).

To conclude, the general flow of ideas about Christ in the soteriology of Galatians suggests that *pistis Christou* is probably located in the sphere of the relationship between Christians and Christ (see also on 3:22). The comparison between 2:16 and the closely linked texts in 3:2–14 suggests that, within that relationship, *pistis Christou* is likely, in the rhetoric of 2:16, to be focused more on the human side of that relationship than on Christ's side.

. . . Even we trusted in Christ Jesus, so that we would be considered righteous on the basis of trust in Christ and not on the basis of works of law, "because" on the basis of works of law "no flesh will be considered righteous" (2:16c). Our translation of *ek* as "on the basis of" becomes rather cumbersome here. However, it is important. The old translations, "justified by works" and "justified by faith," gave the impression that "works" and "faith" are the entities that carry out the justification. Paul never meant that. It is always God who is "justifying," "declaring righteous," "considering righteous." "Works of law" and "trust" are conditions, on the basis of which God was thought to be ascribing righteousness. A limitation on our translation of *ek* will become evident at 3:7, where it is probably best rendered differently.

Paul gives an interpretation of the characteristic actions of Christian Jews. Since they knew there was no righteousness via the law except through trust in Christ, "even" they (Christian *Jews*—so also Christian gentiles certainly should not rely on the law!) came into a relationship with Christ based on *pistis*, "so that" they could be righteous through that. As Margaret Sim argues (although not specifically on 2:16), *hina* ("so that") is not a term that requires the Christian Jews to agree with, or even be aware of, this being their motivation. It is Paul's interpretation of their motivation (cf. 6:13, where he brands his opponents as acting "so that [*hina*] they may boast"; Sim 2010, 44–45). For Paul, although they might not realize it, the logic of the action of Christian Jews in trusting in Christ was that they were no longer trusting in the law for righteousness. He then caps his argument with a Christian rereading of Ps. 143:2 (142:2 LXX), as we have discussed above. It is not necessary to read Paul as making the argument of 2:16b *on the basis of* the psalm in 2:16c. The argument of 2:16a–b is effective in itself. The psalm then backs it up by drawing Peter's attention to what any Christian Jew should know on the basis of the Psalter.

2:17. If, while seeking to be considered righteous in Christ, we too have been found to be sinners, does that make Christ a servant of sin? Not at all! In 2:15, Paul has pointed out to Peter that his situation-dependent practice over eating meals means that he is actually living in a gentile, rather than a Jewish, manner. Now he brings up a potentially problematic corollary of this: Jews such as Peter and Paul, who have turned to Christ as a route to righteousness, discover that living as Christians means, in some ways, living like gentiles—who, as Paul has indicated in 2:15, are thought of by Jews as inherently being "sinners." Does this mean that Christ serves sin? To answer this question, Paul switches from "we" to "I." He explains what has happened to him in relation to the law.

Paul's Dying and Living (2:18–21)

2:18–19a. For if I build up again the things I tore down, I prove myself to be a transgressor. For I, through law, died to law, so I might live for God. Here Paul produces an astonishing theological tour de force. He, a Jew, says that living for God has, for Paul, involved "dying" to God's law. This sounds outrageous.

In practical terms, in the context of 2:11–21, there is an extent to which it makes some fairly obvious sense. Eating with gentiles is contrary to the law. Life in Christ demands that all Christians eat together (Wright 2000). Paul sees life in Christ as the way for him to live for God. Paul has therefore "died" to the demands of the food laws. This also makes sense of 2:18 as an answer to the problem in 2:17. Paul's mission has torn down the barrier between Jews and gentiles: Christians of both kinds eat together. If Paul reerected that barrier, that is what would really make Paul a transgressor (2:18; cf. Martyn 1997a, 256). In the context of that, any breaking of food laws evoked in 2:17 is not only insignificant but not sin at all. (As we shall observe later in the letter, Paul sees a new time as having arrived, in which the unity of Jews and Greeks in Christ is a decisive norm, whereas the law is not—especially any law that would once have kept the groups apart.)

How much further than food laws does Paul's "dying to law" go? And does he also expect it to apply to other people? We take the second question first: he presumably wants Peter to apply it to himself, in order to end his periodic withdrawal from eating with gentiles. This would make sense of the rhetoric of Paul's switch from first-person plural to first-person singular at 2:18. Up to 2:17, "you and I are doing this." Then 2:18 says, "I am actually doing this," implying "you should too." Paul would presumably also apply this to Barnabas and indeed any Christian Jews inclined not to eat with Christian gentiles. The first question is trickier. As we have commented already, Galatians does not urge Jews to abandon practice of the law. Uncircumcision is just as insignificant as circumcision (5:6; 6:15). Christian Jews are no more required to abandon circumcision than gentiles are required to adopt it. However, Galatians does call Christian Jews to a different *attitude* toward the law. It is clearly subordinated to the effects of existence in Christ. The law is also no longer seen as providing the route to righteousness. That comes through trusting in Christ. We will also see, later in the letter, that moral life comes through the action of the Spirit, which fulfills the law but is not based on doing works of the law. Does all that add up to "dying to law"? Paul's former Pharisaic colleagues would presumably have thought so. His opponents in Galatia would undoubtedly have thought so.

In a further surprise, Paul says that this dying to law happened "through law." We can see one example in 2:16 of how Paul understands this mechanism, in his use of Ps. 143, which Paul would think of as part of the law in a broad sense (cf. 1 Cor. 14:21). Paul sees Ps. 143:2 as evidence for the gospel because the psalm denies the ability of life under law to bring righteousness. In Gal. 4:21, explicitly under the heading "law," Paul sees the story of Hagar and Sarah as firmly pointing to the gospel. Paul sees many texts, from the Pentateuch and elsewhere, as acting in the same way (see, e.g., most of 3:6–13).

A difficulty comes with this picture: it is hard to make it work as an account of the sequence in Paul's life. He clearly only arrived at this new reading of the law after turning to Christ. There is positive evidence against the idea that he reread the law in gospel terms before Christ was revealed to him on the Damascus road (1:14; Phil. 3:6). To make the process of dying via rereading fit the biographical sequence, "dying to the law" would need to be something after he became a Christian. "Dying to the law" would then be a description not of what happened at the point of first believing in Christ, but of Paul's subsequent process of arriving at his particular stance on the law. The difficulty with this solution is that Paul's idea of his "death" appears more sudden, absolute, and linked with his turning to Christ. Paul has been "crucified with Christ" (2:19). "The world was crucified" to Paul, "and I to the world" (6:14).

A different approach is taken when scholars such as F. F. Bruce suggest that one clue to understanding 2:19 is that it was Paul's zeal for the law that led him to persecute the Christians. This led to the encounter on the road to Damascus, after which he knew that the path of zeal for the law had been wrong (Bruce 1982, 143; de Boer [2011, 160] puts it more forcefully: that the persecution produced "a collision between the law and Christ"). This would work well as biographical sequence, but it probably underplays the significance of Paul's process of coming to reinterpret scriptural texts. More seriously, despite the emphatic "*I* . . . died to law" (with person and number expressed by the verb's ending, Greek generally does not need to use the pronoun *egō*, but Paul does so here), Paul sees his dying to the law as paradigmatic, rather than something relating only to the specific circumstances of his persecuting. The saying is set here at the end of a response to Peter. Paul thinks that Peter should take the same view as him.

Hans Dieter Betz links the instrumental role of the law in 2:19 with the extensive discussion of the role of the law in 3:19–25: "the law was our *paidagōgos* until Christ so that we would be considered righteous on the basis of trust." In leading people to trust, the law led away from dependence on law. Paul sees this as having been a process at work in the world until the arrival of Christ and thus the possibility of trust in him. For Betz, Paul's experience in 2:19 reflects what he sees as a general function of the law (1979, 122; R. Longenecker 1990, 91). However, appeal to 3:19–25 makes the "through law" of 2:19 a process prior to the Damascus road—in fact, before the arrival of Christ. This would be a process of which Paul at the time was unaware but which he now thinks of as having been happening. It is difficult to see this as representing the dynamic of 2:19.

We may do best by returning to the first idea, that of Paul's reinterpreted Scripture as now pointing away from law. However, we would need to tie this more firmly to the moment of the Damascus-road event. Paul seems unlikely to have viewed his reinterpretation of Scripture as something that he gradually arrived at in the years following. Instead, he may have viewed the reinterpretation as coming about, entire, in the moment when God revealed the risen Christ to him. As Seyoon Kim argues in his classic study, much of Paul's theology can be linked, one way or another, to that event (Kim 1981). That includes Paul's understanding of the law. As he writes Galatians, Paul probably sees the vision of the risen Christ as having opened his eyes to the true reading of the Scriptures, a reading that pointed to faith in Christ and away from dependence on works of law.

2:19b–20. I have been crucified with Christ. I am no longer alive. Christ is alive in me. For the life I now live in the flesh, I live by trust in the Son of God, who loved me and gave himself for me. Paul "died." Socially, we can see a sense in which that happened. His social persona, his status in society, the perception of his honor in the court of Judean public opinion—all disappeared. By choosing Christ, Paul gave up everything that made up the fabric of his honor. As he put it in Philippians, "I lost everything" (Phil. 3:8). In Gal. 2:20, Paul's description of himself as undergoing crucifixion deepens the idea of loss of honor because crucifixion was the most dishonorable public death. Paul may have further dimensions of "death" in mind too. Ben Witherington III sees a reference to Paul "being conformed to the sufferings of Christ . . . when he is persecuted for Christ's sake" (1998, 190). Again in the key passage in Philippians, Paul's turning to Christ meant that he no longer had "my own righteousness, which was on the basis of law" (Phil. 3:9). In Galatians, Paul does not build his argument on the basis that "works of law" are specifically a person's own works. However, in Gal. 2:20, there probably is some idea of giving up self-reliance, to replace it with reliance on Christ. A further strand that could relate to the "dying" in 2:20 is something like a willingness to be possessed by a spirit. Paul appears to see himself as having given up strategic direction of his own actions in favor of Christ taking over such action. Some effects of this are seen in the discussion of the Spirit in 5:13–26.

Paul's process of dying is a sharing in Christ's crucifixion. He also ends the letter on this point, boasting in "the cross of our Lord Jesus Christ, through which the world was crucified to me and I to the world" (6:14). Paul bears "the marks of Jesus" (6:17). Galatians 2:19 is the first explicit occurrence of the cross in the letter. The cross's function here is not as a place of atonement (although Paul believes in that, as 1:4 indicates). Here the cross functions as the place of radical identification between the believer and Christ. In some sense the believer undergoes the crucifixion alongside Christ. In coming to trust in Christ, the believer "dies" (in senses something like those discussed above) and, in doing so, becomes identified with Christ—linked with Christ in such a close sense that Paul can say that "Christ is alive in" the believer (2:20) and the believer is "in Christ" (e.g., 3:28).

Above, we resisted reading *zaō* ("I live") in 2:14 as part of the argument in Galatians about being alive. However, 2:19 firmly launches this theme. Following Paul's "death" in 2:19, he does "live for God." Paul's crucifixion in 2:20 is followed by living (in various expressions). Discourse about life is then a key component in the discussion of righteousness, faith, and law in 3:11–12. The link between being considered righteous and life is also implicitly present already in 2:19–21. Paul's elaborately made points about "living" (the verb *zaō*, "I live," comes five times in two verses) are the climax of his response to Peter, a response that centers on the issue of being considered righteous. The vocabulary of righteousness breaks off after 2:17, gives way to "life" vocabulary in 2:19–20, then returns for the punch line in 2:21 (Harvey 2012, 64). This point can be reinforced by glancing ahead to 3:21: "For if a law was given that was able to make alive, righteousness would actually have come by law [*ek nomou an ēn hē dikaiosynē*]." In some sense "righteousness" is language of life from death (Boakye 2014). As Douglas Campbell (2009, 686) argues, there is a clear link between Paul's language of "righteousness" and life.

From the above reading, it follows that Paul is offering his own salvation experience as a paradigm. In the first instance, it is a paradigm for other Christian Jews such as Peter, who, as Paul sees it, have not recognized the full implications of identifying with the cross of Christ and in consequence have not sufficiently "died to law," as shown by their unwillingness to eat with gentiles when there are other Jews present. This is not a call for Christian Jews to abandon the law as a whole, but Paul does appear to want a recognition that, since they are now seeking righteousness by *pistis Christou* rather than by works of the law, the demands of living in Christ must take priority over commands of the law where the two conflict. Later in the letter he will tangentially address the difficulty that this engenders. In Gal. 5–6 he will provide an idea of life by the Spirit, which fulfills the law without being based on obedience to all its commands. The life of loving unity, as exemplified by Jews and gentiles eating together, is far from being a breach of the law and is recognized as its fulfillment.

More broadly, Paul's salvation provides a paradigm for all his readers, even (esp.) the gentile Galatians who do not have a prior relationship to Jewish law that they could die to. An argument *a maiore ad minus* (from greater to lesser) is probably implicit. If Paul went so far as to die to the law, the gentile Christians (who had never had Paul's heavy stake in the law) should not be adopting it. On a larger point, Paul is also presenting himself as a paradigm of the person who has been (or is being) rescued from the present evil age by Christ, who gave himself for him (2:20; cf. 1:4). Paul has died. Paul has been crucified to the world (6:14). Paul is the person radically connected to God and Christ, not to this age and the world. This is seen in everything from his commissioning (1:1) onward. Paul links the views of his opponents to the sphere of the world, to the "flesh" (e.g., 6:12). The Galatians should imitate Paul and adhere to his message, not that of his opponents.

This brings us to "the flesh." The fact that Paul says he continues to live "in flesh" (2:20) prevents us from seeing "flesh" (*sarx*) in Galatians as synonymous with sin. The 1984 edition of the New International Version had great difficulty over this, rendering *sarx* as a general term for a person (2:16; it contributes to a negative, rendered as "no one"), "the body" (2:20), "human effort" (3:3), "sinful nature" (5:19), and "outwardly" (6:12; for "in flesh").[2] However, it is quite possible to give *sarx* a fairly consistent meaning throughout Galatians. It appears to denote bodily human existence, with a connotation that such existence is inherently weak and limited. This connotation seems present even in 2:16 and 2:20. The inability of "all flesh" (*pasa sarx*) to be considered righteous "on the basis of works of law" (2:16c) probably has its rhetorical effect partly through the idea of the limitations of flesh, as Paul explicitly says in Rom. 8:3: "the inability of the law in that it was weakened through the flesh." In 2:20, Paul's comment that he lives "in flesh" sounds like a description of being in a less-than-ideal situation.

2:21. I do not set aside the grace of God, for if there is righteousness through law, then Christ died for nothing. This verse is central in E. P. Sanders's construction of Paul's thought. In his reading, Paul is perfectly aware of the normal first-century Jewish view of the law: that it provides a normative way of life for those who are part of God's people by birth, by grace. For

---

2. The 2011 edition of the NIV seeks to avoid the problem by simply using the word "flesh" to render most of these occurrences.

Sanders, Paul does not think that there is an inherent problem in the law's ability to guide a life of righteousness. Paul does not see the Jewish view of the law as an incoherent view. He simply sees it as a non-Christian view. Paul has discovered the solution to the problem of finding righteousness: that solution is Christ's death. Since Paul now knows that to be the solution, he knows that nothing else is so. He has therefore concluded that those who depend on the law for righteousness are in a serious plight. For Sanders, Paul's thought has gone from solution to plight, not the other way around (1977, 443, 489–90; 1983, 152).

Leaving aside Sanders's general point about the structure of Paul's thought—which involves consideration of all his letters and is not actually a necessary corollary of his interpretation of 2:21—Sanders's reading in exegeting this verse ties 2:21 in well with 2:20b, where Paul praises the love and self-giving of Christ; this can represent the grace of God and be a reference to Christ's death. Galatians 2:20–21 then forms a tight argument from the necessity of Christ's self-giving death, a point on which all Christians presumably agree, to the impossibility of there being an alternative sufficient route to righteousness, namely, the law. This reading is logical, fits the text well, and seems a quite possible type of argument for Paul to have used. It backs up the case in 2:16 through a subtle broadening of terminology from "works of law" to "law" as nonroutes to "righteousness." Of course, even more so than the Christian reinterpretation of Ps. 143 in 2:16, the argument in 2:21 is a specifically Christian argument, not one that would be acknowledged by non-Christian Jews of Paul's day.

James D. G. Dunn follows a different route from Sanders, arguing effectively that 2:21, as the conclusion to the letter thus far, should be interpreted against its broader themes and in relation to the Antioch incident. So, for Dunn, "the grace of God" is that manifested in the calling and mission of Paul (1:15; 2:9), and the point of Christ's death here is to break the boundary between Jew and gentile and, hence, the law's role in defining boundaries. The main thrust of Paul's argument in 2:21 is that "any retreat back into a Judaism, or Jewish Christianity, which insisted that Jew and Gentile should eat separately, was to render invalid the whole gospel" (Dunn 1993, 147–49; see also Wright 2000). Like Sanders's view, this is a powerful argument. It is probably to be preferred to that of Sanders because Dunn's view ties better into the flow of the chapter's argument. One point that we might question in Dunn's reading is whether "grace" really does refer to Paul's calling and mission. Paul also uses it of the calling of the Galatians (1:6). God's grace in calling gentiles is threatened if the law that makes gentiles and Jews eat separately is the route to righteousness. It therefore makes good sense for Paul to conclude the argument of this section by asserting that he will stand firm in his position ("I do not set aside") because the grace that called the gentiles came at the expense of Christ's death.

Theological Issues

Is There an Exegetical Way out of the Pauline Theological Swamp?

Douglas Campbell (2009) passionately plots a range of theological, political, and social problems that he sees as stemming from misguided exegesis of Paul. He offers a series of exegetical routes out of this "swamp." These most prominently center on rereading the problematic aspects of Paul's Letters as descriptions of the views of Paul's opponents, who are advocating destructive distortions of the Christian gospel (Campbell 2011, 172, 188–89). Many scholars have responded that various of these reassignments of arguably problematic texts are very difficult to sustain linguistically and historically (in addition to the reviews of Campbell 2011 in *Journal for the Study of the New Testament* 34, there is copious further literature reviewing Campbell 2009). Campbell's most pervasive response to this is that those scholars have failed to appreciate the breadth or seriousness of the overall problem, to which he sees his set of textual exegeses as offering an effective, and hence likely, set of solutions (2011, 163, 174–76).

There is indeed a theological swamp, even if I would not describe it in Campbell's terms. As he argues, incorrect exegesis has indeed contributed to flooding the swamp. However, overwhelmingly the swamp has surely been created by the historical, and in some cases continuing, wrong behavior of churches and their members, and of governments purporting to act on behalf of Christianity. For the key issue in Gal. 2:16, the wrong behavior has been violence and discrimination against Jews, both by attacking non-Christian Jews and by demanding that Jews who accept Jesus as Messiah should renounce Jewish practices.

Campbell's attempt to make exegetical change contributes to solving some of the problems and is to be welcomed. However, the hearts of the problems lie elsewhere, in aspects of church teaching and behavior, much of which still needs repentance and change. I myself have tried to offer some suggestions toward hopefully more constructive and socially effective engagement with the text through attention to the range of expected hearers other than the "implied reader," which is a literary construct that has taken scholarship down very fixed tramlines (see introduction above; Oakes 2009). I suspect that Campbell's attempts to do this by radical revisionist approaches to specific passages will themselves become so mired in linguistic wrangles that they will not produce as substantial a move forward as he hopes. However, some of his more modest moves, such as seeking more accurately to discuss the various meanings of "righteousness" terminology in Paul's Letters, do look likely to offer positive exegetical help. This commentary's approach is sympathetic to his project: see the various discussions seeking to move toward an understanding of the "righteousness" language in Galatians by considering the other terms with which Paul associates it.

A problem with the approaches of Campbell, J. Louis Martyn, Martinus de Boer, and probably Richard B. Hays is that they try to avoid seeing Galatians as a text advocating a certain type of religion. From experience as a teacher in a department of religions and theology, it looks clear to me that Christianity is one religion among many, and that Pauline Christianity is one (key) version of that religion. Claiming otherwise is, in itself, a radical form of Christian exceptionalism. As a religious text, Galatians makes totalizing claims about the plight of humanity (gentile and Jew) and about the consequent necessity of adopting the text's prescriptions for belief and practice. As a Christian, I accept the religious claims of Christianity. I expect adherents of other religions to accept the claims of their religion, though I know they are not compatible with the claims of Christianity. This is how the world of religions is. Galatians is part of that world.

With Whom Do You Eat?

I eat with my family, friends, work colleagues, students, colleagues at conferences, and fellow members of the church to which I belong. Eating at church is a little different from the other types of eating. All the other groups have inherent factors tending toward social homogeneity. In principle, this should not be the case at church if it is following the pattern advocated in Galatians. There should be unity, represented by eating together, across an unlimited social range. I am not going to discuss the social dynamics of the church I attend, except to say that we do eat together quite frequently, including people from all corners of the globe, thus well representing one form of diversity.

For the first-century house churches, eating together was a radical social act. This can be seen in the very problems handled in 1 Cor. 11:17–34: the group needed to figure out how to organize social interaction between economically diverse people, who normally would not interact in that way. In the first century, eating together carried great social weight. It is socially important now too, but there is probably nothing quite akin to first-century slave owners and slaves eating together. This raises a further question. Although eating together is still very significant, are there also other types of current action that carry aspects of the significance that the early house-church meals had?

Galatians 3:1–14

Argument 1: For Blessing
in Christ through Trust

Introductory Matters

Having used narrative to defend the divine origin of his gospel and to set up the context in the Jesus movement, with the basic issues and arguments about people putting pressure on Christian gentiles to Judaize, Paul now turns to the Galatians, urging and presenting arguments to them directly. He begins with their experience, moving from a note of despair (3:1) to evoking the work of the Spirit among them (3:2–5). He relates this, and them, to Abraham's trust in God (3:6–9); delves further into Scripture with texts about curses, law, trust, and life (3:10–13); then emerges back at the blessing of Abraham and the Spirit coming to the gentiles (3:14).

The structure of 3:2–14 is chiastic:

A The Galatians received the Spirit through trust (3:2–5)
  B The gentiles are blessed children of Abraham on the basis of trust
    (3:6–9)
    C The law provides a curse (3:10)
      D Righteousness comes on the basis of trust (3:11)
      D′ The law is not on the basis of trust (3:12)
    C′ Christ on the cross redeemed us from the curse (3:13)
  B′ So the blessing of Abraham comes to the gentiles in Christ (3:14a)
A′ So we receive the Spirit through trust (3:14b)

As noted in the introduction to 2:11–21, the topics of righteousness, trust, and Christ, discussed in relation to Christian Jews in 2:15–21, are correspondingly dealt with for gentiles in 3:2–14. It was fairly obvious that the person whom Paul believed to be the Messiah should bring about good things for Jews, but why should he do such things for gentiles? Paul starts from the Galatians' experience that they have already received good things, in the form of the Spirit. Then, as Oda Wischmeyer (2010, 130, 135) argues, he offers a theological explanation of their current situation. This explanation underpins the value of standing firm with Paul's message about trust and their lack of need to turn to the law.

Tracing the Train of Thought

Paul's Bemusement about the Galatians (3:1)

3:1. **O foolish Galatians! Who has cast the evil eye on you—you to whom Jesus Christ was presented before your very eyes as having been crucified?!** If 3:1 is seen as the end of 1:11–2:21, it fits a pattern in which Paul ends sections of the letter with expressions of despair about the Galatians (cf. 4:11, 20). Thematically, 3:1 has much closer links to 2:19–21 than to 3:2–5. It is in 2:19–21 that we have references to Christ's crucifixion (2:19) and death (2:21). Moreover, in 2:21 Christ's death is an argument against law-based righteousness, and hence against the Galatians' behavior that Paul sees as foolish. It would be reasonable to see 3:1 as at least providing a rhetorical application to the Galatians of 2:21. If Paul intends a link that goes further, to 2:19–20, the point of reminding the Galatians in 3:1 of the portrayal of Christ crucified could be to urge them to become like the crucified Christ. In the light of the preceding verses, that would involve self-giving love (2:20) and an attitude to the law in line with Paul's death to the law that occurred in his being "crucified with Christ" (2:19; see Gorman 2008, 124–25). This reading of 3:1 would fit with some other key elements of the letter. One of these is the way in which,

---

**Galatians 3:1–14
in the Rhetorical Flow**

Letter opening (1:1–10)

Letter body (1:11–6:10)

Narrative 1: Of a gospel revealed by God, not people (1:11–24)

Narrative 2: Of a gospel affirmed by unity at Jerusalem (2:1–10)

Narrative 3: Of a gospel betrayed by division at Antioch (2:11–21)

▶Argument 1: For blessing in Christ through trust (3:1–14)

　Paul's bemusement about the Galatians (3:1)

　From the absurdity of not learning from experience of the Spirit (3:2–5)

　From Abraham's receiving of righteousness by trust (3:6–9)

　From texts about law, curse, righteousness, trust, and life (3:10–13)

　The result: Abraham's blessing and the Spirit come to gentiles (3:14)

---

when the language of love reappears in Gal. 5:13–22, it is the key virtue for the Galatians (*agap-*, "love," comes only in 2:20 prior to Gal. 5). A second is the call to be like Paul (4:12). Apart from his apostleship, his self-portrayal in Galatians centers on being identified with the suffering Christ (2:19–20; 4:13–15, 19; 5:11; 6:14, 17).

Having said all this, syntactically 3:1 is closely bound to 3:2–3. The "foolish Galatians" of 3:1 are the "you" of both 3:1 and 3:2. The "foolish" of 3:3 is also clearly a reference back to 3:1. The point above about ending sections with expressions of despair can also be turned around, seeing 3:1 as the opening of a section of argument framed by expressions of despair. Then 3:1 forms an inclusio with 4:11 or possibly with 4:19–20, where Paul both despairs and expresses his ambition for Christ to "be formed" in the Galatians.

What should we make of the question in 3:1? Heinrich Schlier argues that it implies a demonic force behind the preaching of the law to the Galatians: "The Galatians have not been humanly persuaded, but they are under a spell" (1989, 119, AT). More specifically, John H. Elliott and others argue that the Greek verb here, *baskainō*, refers to the culturally prominent practice of casting the evil eye on people, a point strengthened by the reference to eyes a few words later. Casting the evil eye is a practice in which harmful rays come from the eyes of a person, especially an envious person, and strike the target of their envy, causing harm such as illness (J. Elliott 2011; B. Longenecker 1999, 93–97). One textual piece of evidence for the prevalence of this idea in ancient Mediterranean culture is the frequency of the epithet *abaskantos*, "free of the evil eye," in papyrus letters mentioning people's children (e.g., P.Brem. 20.18). In this reading of Galatians, Paul's opponents, envying something about the Galatian Christians (cf. the language of envy in 4:17–18; 5:20–21, 26)—perhaps their freedom in Christ (Lightfoot 1890, 133)—cast the evil eye on them, resulting in derangement that has led them senselessly to turn away from the gospel.

Other scholars argue that *baskainō* was often used figuratively, and that that is the case here (e.g., Betz 1979, 131; Witherington 1998, 203; de Boer 2011, 170). However, the main figurative meaning of *baskainō* with the Greek accusative is to "disparage," as in Plutarch, *Per.* 12.1: "This, more than all the public measures of Pericles, his enemies maligned and slandered [*ebaskainon . . . kai dieballon*]" (trans. B. Perrin 1916). This is unlikely to be the sense in Gal. 3:1. In terms of *baskainō* as meaning something like "bewitch," Hans Dieter Betz and Martinus de Boer's asking whether it is literal or figurative is probably the wrong question. Anyone familiar with even modern Mediterranean culture will know how astonishingly pervasive is belief in the evil eye, with the use of amulets, various microrituals, and other behavior, all designed to avoid it. The pervasiveness of ancient apotropaia (protective devices) confirm the same for antiquity. In that context, it would be hard to find bewitch-type uses of *baskainō* that were truly figurative. Betz cites what he

© Janet Oakes 2005

Figure 6. Powerful eyes. This huge pair of eyes was brought down from the wall of the Greek city of Thasos. It is an *apotropaion* designed to ward off any evil eye that might emanate from the next town.

sees as a supporting example from Plato: "Do not be boastful, lest some evil eye [*baskania*] put to rout the argument" (*Phaedo* 95B, as cited in Betz 1979, 131n32). However, he would need a substantial discussion about Socrates and Plato to make the case for this being figurative, especially since it neatly fits the common pattern, in which boastfulness provokes the evil eye. The right question about *baskainō* in Gal. 3:1 is surely not whether it is figurative or literal but whether Paul thinks that it has or has not happened. Should we follow Schlier and see Paul thinking that the Galatians' waywardness is due to magical influence? Or is 3:1 the kind of rhetorical question that is based on counterfactual irony? In that case Paul would be saying to the Galatians that, in view of their awareness of Christ's crucifixion, their behavior is so irrational that it surely cannot be explained (he says, sarcastically) without the malign effect of the evil eye. In favor of this explanation, Paul's stress here is not on the nature of his opponents (as possessors of the evil eye; contra J. Elliott 2011) but on the stupidity of the Galatians.

Consideration of the evil eye opens a further possibility for the function of the reference in 3:1 to presentation of the cross. Looking to the cross could be seen as offering protection from the evil eye. Susan Elliott (2003, 339) suggests the cross here as having some apotropaic power. J. B. Lightfoot (1890, 134) more specifically suggests that this could have worked for the

Galatians by the cross acting as a focus, which should have kept their eyes from wandering.

From the Absurdity of Not Learning from Experience of the Spirit (3:2–5)

3:2–5. **Just this one thing I want to learn from you: Was it by works of law that you received the Spirit, or by a message of trust? Are you so foolish that, having begun in the Spirit, you are now ending in the flesh? Did you suffer such things for nothing?—if it was indeed for nothing. So, the one who provides the Spirit to you and works miracles among you, does he do it by works of law or by a message of trust?** While eating together was central to the *practice* of the house churches, charismatic phenomena were central to the *experience* of the house churches (cf. 1 Cor. 12–14). Paul has shown how people with views like his opponents behaved self-evidently badly in regard to eating together (Gal. 2:11–14). Charismatic experience now offers him a knockdown argument against his opponents. When did the house churches start experiencing these things? Was it after they started listening to Paul's opponents? Of course not. The Galatians had been experiencing these things much longer: in fact, since they heard Paul's message about trust in Christ. Having begun with all these spiritual experiences, were they going to end with something fleshly? Paul is presumably here at least partly alluding to the physicality of circumcision, as J. Louis Martyn argues (1997a, 285).

However, contrary to Martyn (1997a, 290–91), there is also likely to be a broader point based on Paul's view of flesh overall in the letter. In Gal. 5, as here, "flesh" is contrasted with "Spirit." In 3:2–5, receiving "by works of law" is paralleled to living "in flesh." The way of "works of the law" is the way of flesh, not Spirit. The way to which Paul's opponents call the Galatians leads them away from their experiences of the Spirit. Galatians 5 will argue that it also leads them away from the love-centered morality characteristic of the Spirit, back to the kind of impure and divisive life that they had before encountering Christ. Even though "flesh" in 3:3 probably has some reference to the physical matter of circumcision, there is already a contrast set up with "Spirit," in which Spirit is clearly the better entity.

A key rhetorical effect of 3:2–5 is to draw the language of "works of law" and "trust" from Paul's argument with Peter into the situation of the Galatians. The argument of 2:16, which is primarily about the experience of Christian Jews, also has an application to the lives of Galatian gentiles. What we don't yet have is the application of "righteousness" language to the gentiles (that will come in 3:8). Instead, we see "trust," as opposed to works of law, linked to receiving the Spirit, a new element in the discourse of Galatians. Also, *pistis* ("trust") is paired with *akoē*, in the expression *akoē pisteōs* (3:2). This could refer to "hearing" or to the content of what is heard, "a message." It is hard to decide between the options: for hearing, see as in Luke 7:1 (Williams 1997, 84); for content, see as in 1 Thess. 2:13 (R. Longenecker 1990, 103).

Either way, the effect is to tie trust specifically into Paul's proclamation: the trust that led to the Galatians' experience of the Spirit did not arrive from some other source but from the proclamation of the Pauline message. They therefore should stand firmly with Paul.

Returning to the *pistis* question from 2:16: Is *pistis* in 3:2, 5 human trust or Christ's faithfulness? Contextually, a reference to the faithfulness of Christ as seen in the crucifixion (3:1) would indeed work well. However, if here Paul were referring to a message about Christ as the faithful one, we would expect something like "message of the faithful one," *akoē tou pistou*. Also, if we cast our eye forward to what Paul is about to do with *pistis* language in 3:6–9, it looks even more likely that *akoē pisteōs* is a message about trust, or that brings trust, rather than being about Christ's faithfulness. Reading *akoē pisteōs* as "message of trust" also better fits the various arguments on *pistis Christou* that were discussed above.

The word *epathete* in 3:4 is a puzzle. It fits the argument neatly if we follow J. Louis Martyn in rendering it as "experienced": "Have you experienced such remarkable things . . . ?" (1997a, 285). However, all other Pauline usage suggests taking it as "suffered" (1 Cor. 12:26; 2 Cor. 1:6; Phil. 1:29; 1 Thess. 2:14; 2 Thess. 1:5; 2 Tim. 1:12). Suffering by the Galatians is not generally a topic in the letter. However, the call to imitate Paul, who suffers and is linked to the suffering Christ, does make a reference to the Galatians as suffering fit coherently into the letter. If we read the crucified Christ in 3:1 as paradigmatic, a reference to the Galatians as suffering in 3:4 would fit quite well and offer a further strand to Paul's case in 3:2–5. Suffering of one sort or another among early Christian groups is alluded to in many NT texts. It must have been quite a common experience.

From Abraham's Receiving of Righteousness by Trust (3:6–9)

3:6–9. As readers reach the expression "just as . . ." in 3:6, they inevitably hear it as introducing a point of comparison with what Paul has just said to the Galatians in 3:2–5. On the other hand, by normal syntactical rules, this "just as . . ." begins a sentence, "Just as Abraham . . . , know then that . . ." (3:6–7), with the "just as" setting up the context for the "know then. . . ." The overall rhetorical effect is that, rather irregularly, the "just as" begins by looking backward, linking 3:2–5 with 3:6 onward, but is then reused by Paul when his point in 3:7, about "those who are of trust" being sons of Abraham, in turn looks back to 3:6. However, this double use of 3:6 actually fits the structure of Paul's soteriology. God's considering the gentiles as righteous on the basis of trust turns out to be another way of talking about the gentiles' reception of the Spirit via the message of trust. And both of these are linked to what happened to Abraham and how he responded.

Just as Abraham "trusted God and it was reckoned to him as righteousness," know then that those who are of trust, these are sons of Abraham. The

Scripture, seeing beforehand that God considers the gentiles righteous on the basis of trust, proclaimed the gospel in advance to Abraham, "In you will all the gentiles be blessed." So those who are of trust are blessed along with the trusting Abraham (3:6–9). We might prefer Paul to have used gender-neutral language here: "children" or "sons and daughters," especially as he is undoubtedly including both women and men. Among the likely factors leading him to speak of "sons" (*huioi*) is the way his argument will relate to inheritance, which is not a gender-neutral practice. For further discussion, see on 3:26, below.

The argument of 3:6–9 is tightly constructed and rather surprising. It is built around word groups, "trust" (*pist-*, 5x in 3:6–9), "Abraham," "righteousness," "gentiles," and "blessing." The chain of argument is as follows:

Step 1: Genesis 15:6 shows that *Abraham* "*trusted* God and it was reckoned to him as *righteousness*" [Gal. 3:6]. Therefore, those of *trust* are sons of *Abraham*.

Step 2: Because those of *trust* are sons of *Abraham* (who was declared *righteous*), when Gen. 12:3//18:18 says that all the *gentiles* will be *blessed* as *Abraham's* sons ("in you"), this is Scripture seeing beforehand that God considers the *gentiles righteous* on the basis of *trust*.

Step 3: To sum up: those of *trust* are *blessed* along with the *trusting Abraham*.

In step 1, Paul draws on Scripture (which he could also call law: 3:21–22; 4:21, 30) to argue that, since Abraham "trusted," those "of trust" are his sons. Paul also mentions that Abraham's trust was reckoned as "righteousness." In step 2, Paul uses the repeated scriptural promise of Gen. 12:3 and 18:18 (unlike Gal. 3:8, the LXX of Gen. 18:18 is in the third person, "in *him*," etc.; Gen. 12:3 is in the second person, "in you," but has "tribes of the earth" instead of *ethnē*, "nations"/"gentiles"). The promise is that the gentiles will be "blessed" "in Abraham." Paul uses "in Abraham" synonymously with being a "son of Abraham" (see on 3:8). In 3:7, Paul has already concluded that people who are "of trust" are descendants of Abraham. Gentiles who are "of trust" therefore are sons of Abraham, thus "in Abraham," and therefore "blessed." Also, Paul takes "blessed" as equivalent to "considered righteous." The gentiles who are "blessed" in Abraham are "considered righteous." Since they are in Abraham (that is, sons of Abraham) because they are "of trust," this means they are considered righteous "on the basis of trust." This cements the argument because that was effectively what happened to Abraham himself in 3:6. This allows the summarizing step 3: those "of trust" are blessed (which could equally read "are considered righteous") along with Abraham, who also trusted.

Hoi ek pisteōs, "those of trust" (3:7), represents a common grammatical form in which the definite article is used with *ek* and a noun to specify a person, thing, or group. This can, for instance, be geographical, *hoi ex Enaton* ("those from Anathoth," 1 Esd. 5:18), or a matter of birth, *ho ek tēs*

Israēlitidos ("the son of the Israelite woman," Lev. 24:10). Paul greets *tous ek tōn Aristoboulou* ("those of the household of Aristobulus," Rom. 16:10). In all these, *ek* + noun acts as an adjectival phrase specifying the person, thing, or group by using a feature such as location or origin. In Gal. 3:8, God considers the gentiles righteous *ek pisteōs* ("on the basis of trust"): here *ek pisteōs* is *adverbial*, specifying the basis of the verb "to consider righteous." This makes it tempting to try to read *ek pisteōs* in 3:7 adverbially too, supplying an unspoken verb such as "to consider righteous," making 3:7 effectively read, "those (who are considered righteous) on the basis of trust." This would soften the theological difficulty of 3:7, where Paul, as elsewhere in Galatians, appears to make "trust" the sole property of Christians. However, the common usage of *hoi ek pisteōs* suggests taking it adjectivally: if an unspoken verb is supplied, it would be *ontes*, "being," making the phrase read "those who are of trust." It is a phrase specifying identity.

Martinus de Boer (2011, 191) is eager, if possible, to supply an implied *Christou*, to make 3:7 read *hoi ek pisteōs* (*Christou*), "those who are of faith (of Christ)." We will return to this in a moment, but we ought to notice that if we were to add an implied name in 3:7, a good candidate would actually be Abraham. Then 3:7 would implicitly read *hoi ek pisteōs* (*Abraam*), *houtoi huioi eisin Abraam* ("those of Abraham's faith, these are sons of Abraham"). This would be rather close to Rom. 4:16–17, *tō ek pisteōs Abraam, hos estin patēr pantōn hēmōn*, "the one who has Abraham's faith,[1] who is the father of us all." If *Abraam* is implicit after *hoi ek pisteōs* in Gal. 3:7, the relationship between "trust" in 3:7 and "trusted" in 3:6 is unambiguous: *hoi ek pisteōs* would be people who trust, just as Abraham trusted.

How easy is it to read an implicit *Christou* after *hoi ek pisteōs* in 3:7? It is fairly easy to do if *pistis Christou* is read objectively ("faith in Christ"). James D. G. Dunn takes it this way and uses it to attack Richard B. Hays's preference elsewhere for the subjective genitive reading of *pistis Christou* (Dunn 2008, 358–60). It is much harder to supply *Christou* in 3:7 if the genitive is read as subjective. It leaves the syntax of 3:7 very obscure. In the phrase "those who are of trust," trust would not be that of those people. Another problem is that a subjective *pistis Christou* in 3:7 can only really work if *pistis Christou* means "Christ's faith": the relationship between 3:6 and 3:7 only really works if *pistis* in 3:7 primarily means something closely related to the act of trusting, what Abraham was doing in 3:6. That is the basis for calling the people of *pistis* his sons. Paul never presents Christ as the subject of the verb *pisteuō* ("I trust"), so it is unlikely that Christ's believing is in view here.

Maybe the most problematic theological issue in Galatians is the question, who are "those of trust" in 3:7 and 3:9? It is problematic because it

---

1. Here and in some other places I use the word "faith" rather than "trust" because using "trust" would produce particularly awkward English or mean something different, as here.

is tied up with the absence of *pistis*, according to Gal. 3, between the time of Abraham and the arrival of Christ. We will discuss this under "Theological Issues" (below). Exegetically, the answer is that by "those of trust," Paul means Christians. He is especially thinking here of gentile Christians, although his argument against Peter in 2:16 shows that Paul could use similar language about Christian Jews. That Paul is thinking about Christian faith in particular in 3:7, 9 is reinforced by his hermeneutics in 3:8. "Scripture" was "seeing beforehand" the effect of the Christian mission to the gentiles. God "proclaimed the gospel in advance to Abraham." The texts in Genesis containing the promises to Abraham are read as very firmly being promises about the Christian gospel (esp. Gal. 3:16).

The relationship between 2:21 and the preceding argument from 2:16 suggested that "righteousness" (*dikaiosynē*, 2:21) was the outcome of being "considered righteous" (*dikaioō*, 2:16–17). This point is reinforced and further clarified by the relationship between 3:8 and 3:6. Those verses suggest that God's action in considering gentiles righteous on the basis of trust (3:8) is probably equivalent to him "reckoning" their trust as righteousness, as happened to Abraham. We are also building up quite a repertoire to help us understand what Paul's righteousness language entails. It involves receiving a blessing and being part of Abraham's family (3:7–9). The connection of 3:6 back to 3:2–5 suggests that being considered righteous also involves receiving the Spirit. In 2:18–20, we saw that being considered righteous is also closely linked to gaining life.

Matthew V. Novenson revived A. J. M. Wedderburn's suggestion that *en soi* (3:8) should be read instrumentally, "by means of you" (Wedderburn 1985, 89; Novenson [2012, 126] calls this "a figurative use of the locative"), rather than "in you." Wedderburn sharply points to the link with 3:14, *en Christō Iēsou*, suggesting that may well be drawing on Gen. 22:18 LXX, in which the nations are to be blessed *en tō spermati sou*, "in your seed," which for Wedderburn effectively signifies "by means of your seed" (1985, 88; Novenson [2012, 125] links this with Gal. 3:16: see on 3:16, below). Wedderburn's reading fits with what the Septuagint intends by the phrase and makes good sense in itself. However, as he notes, in Gal. 3:28 "You are all 'one' in Christ Jesus" suggests a "spatial metaphor," especially since it immediately follows 3:27, in which the baptized "put on Christ." The best he can say is that this and the instrumental idea of *en Christō* are not mutually exclusive and that the spatial idea need not necessarily apply in other texts (Wedderburn 1985, 95n37). This is, of course, true. However, once we allow that Paul is using, in some texts in Galatians, a spatial idea of being in Christ, it is clearly likely in other texts in the letter too. In particular, the strong link between 3:29 (where Christians are Abraham's seed) and 3:16 (where the Abrahamic promise is to Christ, the one seed) implies that Paul sees Christians as sharing in the promises because they are somehow incorporated into Christ. This makes it likely that this is already Paul's thought in 3:14. Also, the *en soi* ("in you") of 3:8 follows so quickly after the identification of Abraham's sons in 3:7 that *en soi* looks like a reference to being "in Abraham," as part of his family, especially given the logic of 3:8 as a whole.

One final point in 3:6–9 is that Abraham is described as *pistos*. This clearly refers back to his action of trusting God in 3:6. *Syn tō pistō Abraam* (3:9) should therefore be translated as "along with the trusting Abraham." However, as we saw earlier, *pistis* (the noun related to the adjective *pistos*) is capable of implying any of the positive trust-related aspects of a relationship. If Abraham was *pistos*, he not only trusted God but was faithful to God as well.

From Texts about Law, Curse, Righteousness, Trust, and Life (3:10–13)

3:10–13. **For as many as are of works of law are under a curse. For it is written, "Cursed is every person who does not remain in all the things written in the book of the law, to do them." Because no one is considered righteous before God by means of law, it is clear that "the righteous one will live on the basis of trust." The law is not on the basis of trust: instead, "The one who does these things will live by means of them." Christ redeemed us from the curse of the law, becoming a curse on our behalf, because it is written, "Cursed is everyone who hangs on a tree."**

Galatians 3:10–13 plunges the reader back into the, to us, bewildering world of thought and practice in which curses are common and deeply feared, a world in which a particular manner of death, on something wooden, can be thought to deal with a curse. This is the same world as that of the evil eye in 3:1. The world in which curses and the evil eye are significant is one in which official sanctions to control behavior are weak. For the daily life of most people, there is no very effective police force or judiciary. As a consequence, threats of punishment for wrongdoing tend to be

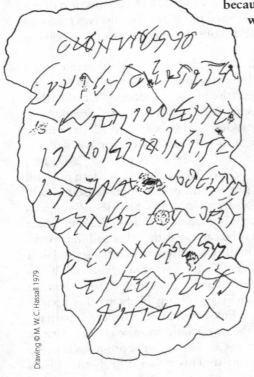

Drawing © M. W. C. Hassall 1979

Figure 7. Ancient curse tablet. Uley, Gloucestershire, second century AD; lead, 85 by 135 mm (Goodburn, Hassall, and Tomlin 1979, 340–42, no. 2, fig. 20). Used by kind permission of the artist.

Curse Tablet Complaining about a Stolen Animal

"Cenacus complains to the god Mercury about Vitalinus and Natalinus his son concerning the draught animal that was stolen. He begs the god Mercury that they may neither [one] have health before/unless they repay me promptly the animal they have stolen and (repay) the god the devotion which he himself has demanded from them." (trans. from Goodburn, Hassall, and Tomlin 1979, 342, no. 2)

---

transferred to the gods: they, rather than the state, are expected to avenge the wrong action that is in view. This is the world of Scripture. In the Septuagint, *epikataratos* ("cursed") and *kataraomai* ("I curse") occur 115 times between them, and there are other relevant terms too. The covenants between Israel and God were related in form to other covenants or treaties of the time. Blessings and curses on those who keep or break the covenant are a common feature. Even treaties on what we might (in fact inaccurately) call nonreligious matters, such as alliances between cities, could evoke divine punishments on potential treaty breakers. The curse of Deut. 27:26, cited in Gal. 3:10, is of this kind. A good example of a conditional curse comes from an inscription at Teos in Asia Minor (see sidebar).

All those who can be specified as people "of works of law" (see discussion, both above on *hoi ek*, of which this is a variant, and below on 3:14, on Gaston's view of this phrase relating specifically to gentiles) are ipso facto subject to this curse. This is not a value judgment, as though it makes scriptural law a bad thing. Scriptural law operated by using curses, as many ancient laws operated. The curse just means that if you break the law, the primary sanction is not that an official will put you into prison but that God will punish you.

A Conditional Curse from Teos, Ionia (ca. 475 BC)

"Anyone who prepares and administers poisonous potions to the Teians or to a single Teian, let him perish, himself and his descendants. Whoever obstructs the import of wheat to Teos with any means or method, at sea or on land, or refuses grain when it is imported, let him perish, himself and his descendants. . . . Those magistrates, who have not pronounced this curse during the festivals of Anthesteria, Herakleia and Dieia, shall be liable to this curse. Whoever writes on, breaks, defaces the stele [stone tablet] on which the curse is inscribed, let him perish, himself and his descendants." (trans. from Arnaoutoglou 1998, 63, no. 70; van Effenterre and Ruzé 1994, 104; for discussion of the Teos text in comparison with Deuteronomy, see Hagedorn 2005, 127–50)

That is not remarkable in a first-century context, and neither in its rhetorical context in Galatians since it follows immediately after talk in 3:9 of blessing, the converse of curse. What is remarkable is what Paul now does with his argument, both negatively in regard to the law and positively in regard to the cross. He essentially argues that the law is not able to provide freedom from the curse but that the cross does so.

Modern readers tend to expect Paul to make his case about this inability of the law by saying that no one keeps the whole law (for a strong argument that Paul intends this without stating it, see Matlock 2009). Instead, Paul mounts an apparently tangential exegetical argument. He first reminds his hearers of the point that 2:16 has argued (de Boer 2011, 203), that "no one is considered righteous" "by means of law" (3:11). This further broadens our awareness of the set of near synonyms and antonyms that he is using for righteousness language. We have seen this language linked with life (2:18–20), the Spirit (3:2–5), being in Abraham's family (3:7–8), and being blessed (3:8–9). We now have the state of not being considered righteous linked to being under a curse (3:10–11). (In fact, we could already have guessed this from the link made between righteousness and blessing in 3:6–9.)

Since "no one is considered righteous" "by means of law," people depending on works of law fall afoul of the curse that Deut. 27:26 utters against the unrighteous. By contrast, in 3:6–9 we have already seen that the blessing, which is linked to righteousness, comes to those "of trust." It is therefore clear that only this way of trust brings blessing and righteousness. In other words, it is clear to Paul that, as Habakkuk wrote, life comes to the righteous by trust. Reading the syntax of Gal. 3:11 this way around, with the sentiment of Hab. 2:4 being an expression of a conclusion that Paul has already reached, draws on a suggestion by Christopher Palmer, mentioned by N. T. Wright (1991, 149n42), adopted by Richard B. Hays (2000, 259) and Ben Witherington III (1998, 234), and affirmed by Martinus de Boer (2011, 202) and especially Andrew H. Wakefield (2003, 162–67, 207–14). Thomas Schreiner disagrees, arguing that Wakefield's case, based on frequency of Greek usage, is not decisive and that, in the rest of 3:10–13, scriptural texts follow, and act as proof for, Paul's assertions (2010, 210). However, this second point is not very compelling. Paul uses Scripture in many ways, not just as proofs to support assertions. Moreover, an argument from frequency of usage does point strongly in Wakefield's direction.

Having made the transposition from being under a curse to not being considered righteous, Paul now brings in "trust" and "life" by means of his well-known key text, Hab. 2:4 (cf. Rom. 1:17). The syntax of Paul's version of Hab. 2:4 is more ambiguous than the Septuagint, which in the main manuscripts (de Boer 2011, 203) reads *ho . . . dikaios ek pisteōs mou zēsetai*, "The righteous one will live on the basis of my [God's] faithfulness." But Paul writes, *ho dikaios ek pisteōs zēsetai*, "The one who is righteous on the basis

Dēlon in Early Jewish and Christian Texts

The impersonal form, *dēlon*, "(it is) clear," occurs nine times in total across the Septuagint, Pseudepigrapha, NT, and Apostolic Fathers. Seven texts have *hoti* ("that") following *dēlon*. Apart from Gal. 3:11, they appear here:

*"Unless it be clear that [*dēlon hoti*] reasoning..."* (4 Macc. 2:7, trans. Evans)

*"If you answer, ... it will be clear that [*dēlon hoti*] we..."* (T. Job 36.6, trans. Evans)

*"Everyone is in agreement that Alexander... Therefore it is clear that [*dēlon oun hoti*] our nation..."* (Pseudo-Hecateus 6.3, trans. Evans)

*"It is clear that [*dēlonoti*] it speaks..."* (Apocr. Ezek. 1.14 AT; cf. Evans; note the compound form)

*"For everyone whom the Master..., we must welcome.... It is obvious, therefore, that [*oun ... dēlonoti*] we must..."* (Ign. *Eph.* 6.1, trans. Holmes 2007)

*"When it says that [*hoti*] all things have been made subject, it is clear that [*dēlon hoti*] that does not..."* (1 Cor. 15:27)

One text lacks *hoti* but uses *hōs* ("how") to function similarly:

*"But if also fathers ... it is evident how [*dēlon hōs*] neither wives..."* (4 Ezra 7.103, trans. Evans)

The remaining text does not fit the pattern. *Hoti* is absent and the verb *esti* ("is") is supplied, rather than assumed.

*"You who speak are chosen ... for from the gleam of your eye it is clear [*dēlon esti*]."* (4 Bar. 7.3, trans. Evans)

Despite the limited number of instances, the evidence of usage speaks strongly in favor of reading *dēlon hoti* in Gal. 3:11 as "it is clear that."

of trust will live." "On the basis of trust" can be read adverbially with "will live," producing the translation, "The righteous one will live on the basis of trust." Alternatively, it can be read adjectivally with *ho dikaios*, making the phrase equivalent to "The one who is righteous on the basis of trust will live" (e.g., Bruce 1982, 161–62). However, the usual Greek word order for the latter translation would be *ho ek pisteōs dikaios zēsetai*, so the former rendering is probably to be preferred.

The difference between the translations is not very significant for Paul's argument. The main effect of using Hab. 2:4 is to bring together language of righteousness, trust, and life. This in turn offers him a way to reinforce the point of 2:16//3:11a. He does so by citing Lev. 18:5, "The one who does these things will live by means of them." The context in Leviticus shows that "these things" are all the commandments, as in Gal. 3:10 (de Boer 2011, 206), so Paul probably has that context in mind (despite, again, modifying the text slightly as he quotes Lev. 18:5). It is by "doing" (the commandments) that the person depending on the law gains life. Dependence on doing is not living "on the basis of trust." Law does not operate "on the basis of trust" (Gal. 3:12a).

Setting *pistis* in contrast to "doing" requires Paul's focus here to be on the "trust" side of *pistis*, rather than on "fidelity." In fact, taking *pistis* here to mean "fidelity" would be very insulting to the law. Moreover, Paul clearly has a specific relationship of *pistis* in mind, namely, to Christ. It is not that no Jew prior to Christ trusted God: we have already seen Abraham doing so. What Paul argues is that the way of life under Jewish law was life dependent on doing the law. The arrival of Christ opens the possibility of a new way to life based on trust in him and, in particular, as we will now see, on trust in what he achieved on the cross. The new way of trust brings righteousness in a way fitting the pattern of Hab. 2:4. It can bring righteousness because the trust that is involved binds the person into relationship with the action of Christ on the cross, which did away with the curse of the law.

In 3:13, Paul gets back to tackling the curse of 3:10. "Christ redeemed us from the curse of the law, becoming a curse on our behalf, because it is written, 'Cursed is everyone who hangs on a tree'" (3:13). This is from Deut. 21:23, amended slightly to highlight the match with Deut. 27:26, quoted in Gal. 3:10 (mainly Paul has changed the verbal *kekatēramenos* [Deut. 21:23] to the adjective *epikataratos* [Gal. 3:13] and removed a reference to God as the one cursing). In talking about the cross as bringing salvation, we might have expected Paul to refer to the scriptural system of sacrifices, as he does elsewhere (e.g., Rom. 3:25). However, this would not have made Paul's point. He wanted to show how God dealt with curse. None of the temple sacrifices deals with curse as such: that language is not used. However, the law does speak of one situation that produces a cursed dead body: death caused by, or followed by, hanging on a tree or something wooden. Deuteronomy mentions it because it fears pollution for the land if this cursed body is left exposed overnight. For Paul, it offers a way in which Christ, in his death, can absorb the curse on people's behalf. The curse is established in the law, but the law also provides a means of dealing with the curse, albeit one that was unlikely to be spotted except by early Christians searching the Scriptures for material relating to the cross.

Although Deut. 21:23 looks strange, a key idea behind it is actually a general social phenomenon, that convicted criminals are widely viewed as, in some sense, a focus of the problematic aspects of the nature of society. Criminals tend to bear the equivalent of curse. This focusing of "curse" onto the criminal is a way in which society copes with difficulties. The reality of the chain of causes behind a particular crime may be complex, involving much of society, but the blame is focused on one person (or a few), and society is able to move on. The crime has, in some sense, been dealt with.[2] Deuteronomy 21:23 represents a theological form of this phenomenon, combined with concern for consequent issues of impurity of the land. Galatians 3:13 represents a radical Christian theological appropriation of the general social phenomenon of the cursed criminal. Christ fulfills this role for the whole community, drawing all the curse onto himself, leaving the community free. They are "redeemed," that is, they have a freedom purchased at a price, the price of Christ's crucifixion. (For further discussion, see "Theological Issues.") Freedom will become a prominent theme in Galatians (see comments on 3:28; 5:1; etc.).

The Result: Abraham's Blessing and the Spirit Come to Gentiles (3:14)

3:14. . . . **So that the blessing of Abraham would come to the gentiles in Christ Jesus, so that we would receive the promise of the Spirit through trust.** This verse completes the "unwinding" of the chiastic structure of 3:2–14 (see "Introductory Matters"). In 3:6–9, Paul argued from Genesis to the conclusion that the gentiles who were "of trust" were "blessed" "in" and "along with" the trusting Abraham. In the first clause of 3:14, Paul reaches the conclusion that indeed this "blessing of Abraham" now takes place for the gentiles. However, it does so "in Christ Jesus." The reason for this is related to Christ's curse-bearing work in 3:13.

In fact, 3:14a clarifies the argument of 3:10–13 in two significant ways. First, it shows that gentiles were in view in 3:10–13. At 3:10, we might have thought that Paul had switched topic, from considering the gentiles in 3:1–9 to considering Jews, who would be the most natural referent for "those of works of law" (3:10) and who were the people we would think of as having been subject to instructions, threats, and promises of the law. Since Paul has already made an issue of Christian Jews being considered righteous on the basis of trust (2:16), he would presumably see them as indeed subject to the issues argued about in 3:10–13. However, he clearly has gentiles particularly in view right through 3:1–14. As Lloyd Gaston has suggested, gentiles who sought to be "of works of law" would clearly fall under the curse of Deut. 27:26, cited in Gal. 3:10 (Gaston 1987, 23, 75; cf. Eisenbaum 2012, 147). They clearly would not have done "all the things written in the book of the law" (cf. 2:15, which characterizes gentiles as "sinners"). However, just as with the scholarly view that Paul had an unexpressed minor premise (no one perfectly keeps the law) in the argument of 3:10, we must again observe that neither does Paul express in 3:10 the alternative minor premise that the hearers have

---

2. The literature is extensive. A major theoretical approach is that of René Girard (e.g., 1986), who relates it to handling what he calls mimetic violence. For a summary of this approach and one angle on its implications for criminal justice, see Redekop 1993.

not kept the law because they are gentiles. Instead, as we have seen above, Paul argues his case exegetically. There may also be complexities of the kind envisaged by Bruce Longenecker (1998, 91–93), who links 3:13–14 with 4:4–5 in order to argue that redemption of Jews and redemption of gentiles are woven together in these passages.

The second way in which 3:14a clarifies the argument of 3:10–13 is by the qualification "in Christ." It remains to be seen what light the later part of the chapter will shed on this expression. However, in some sense the redeeming, curse-bearing effect of the crucifixion is implemented through people being incorporated in Christ. Paul writes that he has "been crucified with Christ" (2:19). It could well be that in 3:13–14 he sees Christians generally sharing in crucifixion in the way that he does. Alternatively, he may be seeing them as incorporated in a postcrucifixion and postresurrection Christ, with Christ having taken on some sort of heightened nature that makes him into a sphere of which a community can become part. Either way, a probable implication is that Christ's curse bearing takes place not indiscriminately but for those who participate in him. The curse bearing takes effect through people coming into a relationship with Christ that could be described as incorporation.

In the second clause of 3:14, Paul brings the conclusion back to the agenda of 3:2–5. A consequence of receiving the blessing of Abraham in Christ is receiving "the promise of the Spirit," and doing so "through trust." This further ties 3:2–5 to 3:6–9, by confirming the link between Abrahamic blessing and the Spirit. It also sets going the argument of 3:15–29 by introducing the term "promise," which had been latent in 3:6–9 because Abraham's trust in God was in fact trust in specific promises. An innovative point in 3:14b is that the promise is "of the Spirit," a point not present in the Genesis texts. Paul's move here is probably a further expression of the rough synonymity that he is building up between "righteousness," "blessing," "Spirit," and "life." "Spirit" and "life" in fact do have an inherent link. The English word "Spirit" masks the way in which both the Greek pneuma and the Hebrew rûaḥ are words that primarily denote "breath" or "wind" and are thus a central component of life (see on 3:21 and 6:15). This is then taken up in a further link when Ezekiel sees God's Spirit/breath as the agent producing new life in Israel (Ezek. 37).

The second clause of 3:14 also helps us in relation to pistis, "trust." It reiterates the link between the Spirit and trust. Receiving the Spirit through trust is equivalent to receiving the Spirit "by a message of trust" (3:2). Also, the two clauses of 3:14 appear to be essentially in parallel: "the blessing of Abraham" appears synonymous with "the promise of the Spirit." This suggests seeing "in Christ Jesus" and "through trust" as being functionally equivalent. "Trusting" involves being "in Christ," which implies that the "trust," pistis, Paul has in mind is far from being, say, a detached assent to intellectual propositions. Such pistis is an attitude and/or action that involves joining to Christ. This is bound to involve belief in claims made about Christ, but it must also include a change of life. Socially it must have involved joining a Christian group. There must have been other changes in life too—we will watch for them later in the letter. Since this *pistis* involves incorporation into Christ, who was crucified, then, as Michael Gorman (2009) in particular has explored, this *pistis* must involve a life that is shaped by that specific identification: what he calls a "cruciform" lifestyle.

Theological Issues

Who Are "Those . . . of Trust" (Gal. 3:7)? A Crux in Galatians Scholarship

The statement "those who are of trust [*hoi ek pisteōs*], these are sons of Abraham" is very strange, not in itself but in the setting of Galatians. In itself, it probably works by fairly simple analogy: people who are characterized by trust are like Abraham, who trusted; being like Abraham, they can be thought of as his children. We would expect this category to encompass many people. Since Abraham's trust was in God (3:6), we might narrow "those who are of trust" down to cover religious believers or, even more specifically, believers in the God of Israel. This would yield a crowd of people, beginning maybe from those who called on the name of the Lord in Gen. 4:26, or perhaps from Isaac onward.

But in Galatians this does not work. In Galatians, "trust" is something that "arrives" in the world, doing so at a time related somehow to the life, death, and resurrection of Christ (3:24–25). Prior to this was the period "before trust arrived" (3:23). The ancient Israelites lived in a world where "trust," in the sense of Gal. 3, was absent.

This sounds strange and offensive to us: Jews show trust, and this has been the case since antiquity. In the NT it sits particularly awkwardly with the list of heroes of faith in Heb. 11. Even in Galatians, there is an odd juxtaposition with 5:22, where *pistis* ("trust" or, more likely, "fidelity") is one of a broad list of virtues. No doubt Paul would have seen many people prior to Christ as having exhibited such virtues.

A further strange assertion comes in 3:12: "The law is not *ek pisteōs*." This comes with an explanation drawn from Lev. 18:5, "Instead, 'the one who does these things will live by means of them.'" Whereas we (and people such as the biblical prophets) would see God's law, and the following of it, as being the main expression of Israelite "trust" in God, Paul here sees the fact of dependence on actions as excluding law from being *ek pisteōs*.

In all of Galatians except 5:22, Paul clearly uses *pistis* in some very specific sense that certainly does not carry the general idea of religious faith. For Paul, the Israelites of the Bible did not have the opportunity to exercise trust in the sense that Paul had in mind. In Gal. 3:6, Abraham is not trusting God in a general sense but is trusting promises by God that, for Paul, are promises of the coming of Christ and the gentile Christian mission (3:8, 14, 16). For everyone other than Abraham, the opportunity to trust in these things essentially comes with the arrival of Christ. For Paul, Gen. 15:6 shows a mode of reckoning righteousness that depends on trust in God's action fulfilled in Christ. "Those who are of trust" in 3:7 are specifically those who trust in Christ. The presence of Christ and the possibility of trusting in him provide access to a mode of obtaining righteousness, a mode that contrasts with the law-based method of obtaining righteousness through deeds.

Although this softens the potential offensiveness of what Paul wrote—he is not excluding non-Christians from having what we would call "religious faith"—it does not remove the central point that would offend many people. Paul sees the decisive issue in the world, from his time onward (which he expected not to be long), as being trust in Christ. This offends some because it is a universalizing claim: Paul calls all to trust in Christ, whether they are currently worshiping the gods of the first-century Roman Empire or those in any subsequent context. It offends others because it appears to be an arbitrary basis for a crucial classification of people, being based on human response to a particular message (which many would even seem unlikely to get to hear). Many scholars have produced often brilliant pieces of scholarship that soften the potential offensiveness of Paul's message. I encourage readers of this commentary to look into the work of these constructive scholars. However, my own conclusion from research so far is that, however wonderful Paul's message may be in many ways, he ultimately takes a line that will remain divisive, except in any world that unanimously accepts the Christ-based path that he has marked out.

Theologizing the Curse-Bearing Criminal

Galatians 3:13 should astonish us. It should probably tend to disturb us somewhat too. What is God doing, getting involved with a morally dubious social phenomenon, a practice that societies use to come to terms with problems by piling the responsibility entirely on the criminal? An answer is that all soteriology is morally dubious. Piling the curse upon a willing, crucified human (2:20) is probably morally less dubious than piling sins onto an unwilling, sacrificed animal, as was done in the Jerusalem temple, and as appropriated in some NT explanations of the cross.

We need to distinguish between reality and explanatory metaphor. The reality is that an innocent man was unjustly put to death by the authorities. The gospel message is that this unjustly killed, innocent man is God's Son; this unjustly killed, innocent man has been appointed universal ruler; this unjust death of God's Son, the universal ruler, is not going to be the basis of mass destruction by God: instead, God makes it the basis of liberation. The reality of the cross was among the worst possible expressions of human practice: public, humiliating death by torture. God has made the very worst the basis of the very best, reversing the outcome of an evil social practice. The metaphors used in explaining this reversal also take morally dubious human actions—killing an animal, focusing more-than-reasonable blame on a criminal—and reverse their normal outcome to produce good.

Galatians 3:15–29

Argument 2: For Unity in Christ

Introductory Matters

Having produced a chain of reasoning linking the Spirit, trust, Abraham, righteousness, blessing, and life and having connected these to gentiles via being "in Christ," who was crucified, Paul again uses Abraham to elaborate on what being "in Christ" means. In particular Paul uses the promise to Abraham of "a seed" to make an argument about Christ and the oneness of life in him. Paul also responds to issues raised by the negative side of his rhetoric in 3:2–14, in which he linked law with curse and separated it from trust and life. He positions law in relation to the Abrahamic promise and considers the function of the law in the period running up to the arrival of Christ.

The structure of 3:15–29 features an inclusio but is not chiastic at a level deeper than that. The key terms in the inclusio are "Abraham," "seed," "one," "promise," and "heir/inheritance." These are in 3:15–18 and recur in 3:28–29.

Tracing the Train of Thought

From the Nature of Covenants and the Wording of This One (3:15–18)

3:15–16. Brothers and sisters, I will explain this in human terms. In the same way as no one can set aside or add to a covenant enacted by a person, the promises were spoken to Abraham and to his seed—it does not say "and to the seeds," as if to many, but as to one: "and to your seed," who is Christ. Paul uses a human analogy to explain God's actions. In particular, he discusses the characteristic of human covenants, probably mainly thinking of wills, as being fixed documents. In 3:16 he notes that specific wording cannot be ignored. In 3:17 he uses the idea that a later provision, in this case the introduction of the law, cannot set aside the earlier provision.

As so often, Paul's syntax is rather irregular here. He begins a comparison, "in the same way as . . ." We expect him to say something like "As a human covenant cannot be set aside, . . . so the covenant with Abraham could not be set aside by the later law." He does effectively do this, but there is so much text between the setup and the payoff that the sentence structure grinds to a halt, and he needs to restart it in 3:17 with "I am saying this."

Galatians 3:16 picks up the word "promise" from 3:14. In 3:14 it was the promise of the Spirit. Now 3:16 effectively links that to the promises to Abraham, as Paul had indirectly done already in 3:6–9, 14 via the language of blessing. The words from Genesis that Paul cites in 3:16 are from Gen. 13:15, restated by God in 17:8 and by Abraham in 24:7. The promise involved there is that of the land. Paul generalizes by pluralizing "promise" to "promises." "The promises" lose the specificity that they had in Genesis and become a term that relates to the benefits brought by the gospel.

> ## Galatians 3:15–29 in the Rhetorical Flow
>
> **Letter opening (1:1–10)**
> **Letter body (1:11–6:10)**
>   **Narrative 1: Of a gospel revealed by God, not people (1:11–24)**
>   **Narrative 2: Of a gospel affirmed by unity at Jerusalem (2:1–10)**
>   **Narrative 3: Of a gospel betrayed by division at Antioch (2:11–21)**
>   **Argument 1: For blessing in Christ through trust (3:1–14)**
>   ▶**Argument 2: For unity in Christ (3:15–29)**
>   From the nature of covenants and the wording of this one (3:15–18)
>   From the nature of the law (3:19–25)
>   From the nature of being in Christ (3:26–29)

Matthew V. Novenson (2012, 140–42) builds on an argument by Richard B. Hays (2000, 264) that Gal. 3:16 also evokes the promise of a ruling descendant for David (2 Sam. 7:12), making the use of *Christos* in Gal. 3:16 specifically messianic. This is an interesting possible echo. More problematically, but with closer ties to issues central to 3:16, Novenson tries to extend A. J. M. Wedderburn's (1985) linking of 3:8 with 3:14 (see on 3:8, above) to include 3:16. Novenson does this by seeing Paul as here citing Gen. 22:18, in which the nations are to be blessed *en tō spermati sou*, "in your seed" (2012, 124–26, 140n11). The problem is the absence from Gen. 22:18 of the *kai* ("and") that Paul includes in his careful quote in Gal. 3:16. This means that Paul must be citing one of the other three Genesis texts noted above. However, 3:28–29 corresponds to 3:16, resolving its implicit conundrum: How can the many gentiles end up as heirs of the Abrahamic promises if there is only one "seed"? The answer of 3:28–29 is effectively that the gentiles are blessed "in" this one "seed" of Abraham, as Gen. 22:18 stated. Although Paul is not actually quoting Gen. 22:18

in Gal. 3:16, the idea of that Genesis passage does appear to be implicit. On the other hand, that does not help Novenson, because he follows Wedderburn in resisting reading 3:14 (and now 3:16) in terms of participation in Christ.

The argument of 3:16 really surprises us. We know, and Paul knew, that contextually the referent of "seed" in its many occurrences in the Genesis Abraham narrative is to his descendants who, in fact, were promised as being innumerable (e.g., Gen. 13:16). One explanation of Paul's exegesis is that he sees the fine detail of the scriptural text as pointing in the same direction as his overall reading of the scriptural narrative, a narrative heading toward the Messiah and the bringing about of a people who are in the Messiah (cf. F. Watson 2004, esp. 515–17). A second explanation is that an argument of the type seen in 3:15–16, based on a detail of wording of Scripture, occurs many times in ancient Jewish exegesis. Various scholars (e.g. Bruce 1982, 172–73; R. Longenecker 1990, 131–32) discuss instances in which rabbinic exegesis focuses on use of singular or plural forms of words such as "seed" and "blood."

Paul's argument in Gal. 3:16 is probably heading directly for the central issue in Galatians: unity between Jewish and gentile Christians. The promises of God, such as the Spirit (3:14), could only come to the descendants of Abraham (3:7), who were to include the gentiles (3:8), when there was one seed. The one seed was Christ (3:16). The blessing of Abraham had now come to the gentiles in Christ (3:14), that is, in the one seed. The people, Jew and gentile, who are in the one seed are necessarily one community. This will be spelled out in 3:28–29, but it is already present in 3:14–16. For Paul, the promises to Abraham "and to his seed" are being fulfilled in the diverse community united by their union in Christ. In practical terms, the promises to Abraham and his single seed exclude any behavior that splits apart the single community, as the Antioch incident has done. The community in Christ, even though it can be as many as the grains of sand on the shore, is one body.

3:17. I am saying this: a covenant enacted beforehand by God cannot be rendered invalid by the law, which came 430 years later, so as to nullify the promise. This picks up an issue that concerned many Jewish authors: the anomaly of the scriptural narrative including a long period prior to the giving of the law on Sinai. A major response to this concern can be seen in texts such as *Jubilees*. That book recounts incidents from Genesis but does so in a way that makes the characters directly fulfill the law (and the provisions of a particular calendrical system). Paul takes the opposite tack, stressing the length of time before the arrival of the law. His main point in doing this is to show that the provisions of the Abrahamic covenant (such as the promises about the gentiles) must stand, irrespective of anything that the Mosaic, law-based covenant might say. In particular, the law cannot be used to separate Jewish and gentile Christians, who have been brought together by the Abrahamic promises.

3:18. For if the inheritance came by law, it would no longer be by promise, but God has granted it to Abraham through promise. If inheritance were now by law (e.g., by the circumcision that some Galatians were inclining toward), then it would no longer be by promise: but that cannot be so, because God's mode of communication with Abraham was "through promise," not through law. The second clause of 3:18 may have a subtle lexical link to Paul's gospel via the word "granted" (*kecharistai*), a form of the verb related to *charis*, "grace" (1:3, 6, 15; 2:9, 21; esp. 5:4; 6:18). This word is a key expression of Paul's gospel in Galatians.

From the Nature of the Law (3:19–25)

3:19a–c. Why then the law? It was added on account of transgressions, until the seed came, to whom the promise was made. Hans Dieter Betz and Richard N. Longenecker take opposite positions on the place of 3:19–25 in the letter's argument. For Betz, this discussion is a *digressio*. Such a digression does offer indirect support for the main argument, but it is a stepping aside from the main line (1979, 163). In contrast, R. Longenecker sees this as the central response to Paul's opponents: the crunch issue is the nature of the law, and here is a discussion of it (1990, 135–36). Structurally, 3:19–25 forms the different middle section sandwiched between the halves of the discussion of oneness in Christ as Abraham's seed, in 3:15–18 and 3:26–29. Being in the middle can either highlight a passage as the central point or bracket it as a digression. However, in 3:15–29 there is another, insistently signaled structural factor: time. Although, thematically, 3:15–18, 19–25, 26–29 are somewhat in a pattern A-B-A′, there also is a clear A-B-C temporal flow between 3:15–16, 17–24, and 25–29: the time of Abraham, the time between Moses and Christ, and the time since the arrival of Christ. Even though (as elsewhere, e.g., Rom. 3:1, 9; 6:1, 15) Paul appears to digress by posing a rhetorical question that sounds as though it could be raised by an objector, he is actually moving his argument steadily forward. Here he shows the Galatians how a proper understanding of the narrative flow about God's dealings with people will lead them to reject the advice of Paul's opponents.

The semantics of 3:19a–b are tricky. *Ti oun ho nomos;*—"Why then the law?"—could, maybe just as plausibly, be read as "What then (is) the law?" *Ti* can have either meaning. Notably, $\mathfrak{P}^{46}$ makes it more specific, adding "Why then the law of deeds [*tōn praxeōn*]?" to replace the whole of the next clause. But even though $\mathfrak{P}^{46}$ is the earliest extant text, this reading is unlikely to be original. It would require extraordinary action by a scribe to remove *praxeōn* and insert *parabaseōn charin prosetethē*. In contrast, if the latter is original, it is quite easy to imagine a scribe, after reading *ho nomos tōn* ("the law of"; no question marks are in early manuscripts), then to expect the next word to specify a type of law.

121

The more substantive semantic problem is to understand the sense of the clause, "It was added on account of transgressions" (*tōn parabaseōn charin prosetethē*). The expression "it was added" reinforces 3:17–18, emphasizing that the law was not God's first means of interacting with people, or even his first means of interacting with Israel, as represented by Abraham. This relativizes the law. It is not the be-all-and-end-all that Paul's opponents are making it out to be. As to the reason why it was added, there are various possibilities. The easiest to understand would be that the law was added to limit or control sin or its effects (Betz 1979, 164–66; Vouga 1998, 82–83). This fits well with the image of the law as *paidagōgos* (3:24), the slave who protected, disciplined, and sometimes gave basic instruction to the children of wealthy Greeks and Romans (see on 3:24, below). Betz and François Vouga support their view by appealing to Greek philosophers. This looks reasonable, but there are complexities. F. Gerald Downing criticizes Betz as blurring Stoic and Cynic ideas. He argues that the latter were much more negative about the law (1998, 61). A second possibility is that the law was added in order to register, count, or give awareness of sins (Matera 2007, 132). The idea of the law giving awareness of sins is seen in Rom. 7:7–14: "I would not have known sin if not through law." Interestingly, in that passage the way the law makes sin known is by producing death (7:10–11, 13). This is an interesting counterpoint to Paul's argument in Gal. 3:21 relating to the law not producing life. A third and more radical possibility is that the law was added in order to multiply sins (Schreiner 2010, 240). This fits most easily with the syntax of 3:19 itself, in which there is no phrase denoting that the law was added to control or count transgressions. The verse just says, "It was added on account of [or "for the sake of," *charin*] transgressions." This third possibility sounds rather like the end of Rom. 5: "The law slipped in [*pareisēlthen*: what the "false brothers" did in Gal. 2:4] to increase the trespass" (5:20). That text continues, "But where sin increased, grace abounded, so that, just as sin reigned in death, so also grace would reign through righteousness for eternal life through Jesus Christ our Lord" (5:20–21). The relationship to themes in Gal. 3 is striking.

Which possibility best fits Paul's argument in Gal. 3? We need to bear in mind the overall characterization of the functions of the law in 3:1–4:7. The law puts those "of works of law" under a curse (3:10). "Scripture [here synonymous with the law] imprisons all things under sin" (3:22). People "were guarded under law, imprisoned" (3:23). "The law was our *paidagōgos*" (3:24). The Son of God set free "those under law," with the law implicitly tied in, somehow, with the action of the "elements of the world," which acted like "guardians" and "stewards" in enslaving "us" while "we" were "children" (4:1–5; yet on 4:1–2 notice differing overtones of the functionaries' titles, compared with the *paidagōgos*). This is language of control. More specifically, it is language of temporary control, designed to bring the controlled people safely to a state

Luther on the Law Added Because of Transgressions

"In other words, that transgressions might be recognized as such and thus increased. When sin, death, and the wrath of God are revealed to a person by the Law, he grows impatient, complains against God and rebels. Before that he was a very holy man; he worshipped and praised God; he bowed his knees before God and gave thanks, like the Pharisee. But now that sin and death are revealed to him by the Law he wishes there were no God. The law inspires hatred of God. Thus sin is not only revealed by the Law; sin is actually increased and magnified by the Law.

"... The Law is a mirror to show a person what he is like, a sinner who is guilty of death, and worthy of everlasting punishment. What is this bruising and beating by the hand of the Law to accomplish? This, that we may find the way to grace. The Law is an usher to lead the way to grace."

Luther 1949/1535, on Gal. 3:19, trans. T. Graebner

that is variously characterized as receipt of promise (3:22), "trust" (*pistis*, 3:23, 25), being considered righteous (3:24), adoption by God, and inheritance (4:1, 5–7). Taken together, these descriptions show the law as a power designed to control the situation, given the presence of the dangerous element sin and that the people being controlled had not yet reached the stage of being able to deal with the danger without the law's help. The law was a necessary, temporary protection during a period of growth and learning in a dangerous world.

3:19c. Until the seed came, to whom the promise was made. Not only does the law arrive late; it also leaves again when the promise is fulfilled. The idea that Jewish writers saw the status of the law as changing, on the arrival of the Messiah, is debated (see, e.g., Tait 2009). If there was such an idea, Paul's vision of the Messiah on the Damascus road would make it explosive. If the Messiah, as Paul believed, had arrived partway through the story of Israel and the present world, key assumptions underlying any Jewish idea of change of role for the law would be undermined. In some Jewish eschatology the arrival of the Messiah ushers in the new world after the resurrection of the dead (e.g., 2 *Bar.* 30). In Paul's belief, only the Messiah had so far been resurrected. Aspects of "the age to come" had arrived, notably the widespread presence of the Spirit (Joel 2:28; cf. Acts 2:17), but many aspects of the previous mode of existence continued, even for Christians, yet also for everyone else. In any case, probably for most Jews, there was no thought of the law coming to an end, even with the arrival of the Messiah: the law was imperishable (e.g., Wis. 18:4). For Paul to claim that the law operated until a certain point in time, a time that was now in the past, was something with which surely no non-Christian Jew of his day would have agreed. To judge by the Antioch incident and texts such as the Letter of James, many Christian Jews would not have expressed the matter in that way either.

3:19d–20. It was commanded through angels, by the hand of a mediator. The mediator is not of "one," but God is "one." This surprising addition to the description of the law appears designed to further reinforce its provisionality, its limited role. Unlike Paul's gospel, which came as a result of revelation directly from God (1:15–16), the law came through two stages of intermediaries. Paul takes Jewish established traditions about Sinai but draws conclusions opposite to the normal ones. Several texts placed angels at Sinai, and many saw Moses, who must be implied here, as a mediator (for angels: Deut. 33:2 LXX; *Jub.* 1.27–29; for Moses as mediator: *As. Mos.* 1.14; cf. Exod. 24, etc.; R. Longenecker 1990, 140–41). Josephus spoke of laws coming "through angels [*di' angelōn*] instructed by God" (*Ant.* 15.136, trans. de Boer 2011, 228). All these texts are far from wanting to use this idea to relativize the law. The presence of angels glorified Sinai. Moses was honored as mediator. Some texts did place value on direct communication from God, but did so by excluding an intermediary role for angels (e.g., *'Abot R. Nat.* B 2; R. Longenecker 1990, 142). Paul tapped into the type of rhetoric that valued direct communication but drew the angel traditions in as negative argument. He also problematized the role of Moses.

The oneness of God is also brought in to relativize a mediated law. The mediator not being "of one" presumably refers to the mediator acting in relation to at least two parties. Maybe the argument is that if Moses somehow represented the interests of both God and people, he could not properly represent the interests of the one God. In Gal. 3 more widely, there is strategic use of oneness language (3:16, 28). It feels as though the questioning of Moses's representing "one" would exclude Moses from being a voice that can promote the unity that Galatians is looking for. It is also noticeable that, in Romans, the oneness of God is invoked on behalf of soteriological unity between Jew and gentile (Rom. 3:29–30). Yet it is hard to see how the use of "one" in Gal. 3:20 can be fully brought together with its appearances in 3:16, 28.

3:21. So, is the law against the promises of God? Not at all! For if a law was given that was able to make alive, righteousness would actually have come by law. Paul argues that the law is not against God's promises, despite the way in which Paul seems to have set them against each other in 3:17–18. His argument in 3:21 is probably that the law does not trespass on the operating fields of the promises, which are implied to cover "making alive" and being the source of righteousness.

What does "to make alive" (*zōopoiēsai*) mean here? How do the issues in the verse fit together? One possibility is that it could be a term for conversion. It is used in this way in *Jos. Asen.* 8.10. Joseph, not wishing to kiss a nonbeliever but having pity on the gentile Aseneth, who is getting very upset about his reluctance, calls on God to "make alive [*zōopoiēson*] and bless this virgin," that is, to bring her to belief in God. Paul's argument then works neatly. The law cannot convert gentiles. If it could, it would already have brought them to righteousness. It has not done this. Instead, the Abrahamic promise to be the source of blessing for the nations (3:8), now fulfilled in Christ (3:14), has succeeded in this. It was never the law's role, so there is no conflict.

An alternative approach would be to look at *zōopoiēsai* in relation to its uses elsewhere in Paul. These are too few (six) to disprove the possibility of it implying conversion here, as above, but he is fairly consistent in using the term in relation to resurrection and related ideas (Rom. 4:17; 8:11; 1 Cor. 15:22, 36, 45). One text (2 Cor. 3:6) is more ambiguous: "The letter kills; the Spirit makes alive." This text links the Spirit to giving of life. The description of Christ in 1 Cor. 15:45 is as "a life-giving spirit." As Andrew Boakye explores, the relationship between spirit, life, and resurrection has strong roots in Jewish tradition, most notably in the "dry bones" scene of Ezek. 37. Life and its contrast with death also form a fairly pervasive motif in Galatians (1:1; 2:19–20; 3:11–12, 21; 5:24; 6:8, 14–15; Boakye 2014). If we go back to 3:11–12, we see the law having a problematic relationship to enabling people to live. We can probably deepen that because the curse of 3:10 would have overtones of death (which is the punishment for most of the misdeeds in the verses of Deuteronomy immediately preceding 27:26, quoted at Gal. 3:10). In contrast, the way of *pistis* ("trust") brings life to the righteous (3:11) and brings reckoning of righteousness (3:6–8). It also brings the blessing of Abraham and the promise of the Spirit, in Christ (3:14). In Galatians, the law does not operate in the sphere of promise, with blessing, Spirit, life, righteousness.

3:22–25. Instead, Scripture imprisoned all things under sin, so that the promise would be given on the basis of trust in Jesus Christ to those who trust. Before trust came, we were guarded under law, imprisoned until the coming trust would be revealed. So the law was our *paidagōgos* until Christ, so that we would be considered righteous on the basis of trust. With trust having come, we are no longer under a *paidagōgos*. A subtle point in 3:22 is that Paul has switched back to the promise being given to a group, "those who trust," whereas the promise was to "the seed" in 3:19. We can see how this works out once we reach 3:27–29, but how can Paul switch to the plural in 3:22? A way for it to work would be if living *ek pisteōs Iēsou Christou* ("on the basis of trust in Jesus Christ") already carries a connotation of being united as a single entity in union with Christ, that is, if *ek pisteōs Christou* is language of participation in Christ. That this is indeed how Paul is thinking is shown by 3:14. The gentiles receive the blessing of Abraham *en Christō Iēsou* ("in Christ Jesus") and the promise (of the Spirit) *dia tēs pisteōs* ("through trust"). *Pistis* and being in Christ are already tied firmly together in relation to gentiles receiving the promise. By 3:22, Paul is again heading rapidly toward this formulation: "You are all sons of God through trust, in Christ Jesus" (*dia tēs pisteōs en Christō Iēsou*, 3:26; see below). Being *ek pisteōs Christou* connotes being *en Christō*; hence the group in 3:22, "those who trust," are able to receive the promise made to the singular Christ.

   If this is right, why would Paul not simply put *en Iēsou Christō* ("in Jesus Christ") in 3:22 in place of *ek pisteōs Iēsou Christou*? The answer is that *pistis* is the central counterpoint to the law in 3:22–25. In these four verses, *pistis* or the verb *pisteuō* ("I trust") appear six times. Four times Paul writes that *pistis* is what the law is leading to. The law governs the time until *pistis* arrives. As 3:24 implies, the time when *pistis* arrives is the time when Christ arrives. *Pistis* is, in Galatians, a new mode of human existence that comes about when Christ arrives. With the arrival of Christ, *pistis* is revealed as the route to righteousness (3:23–24). Crucially for the argument of Galatians, as Paul has already spelled out, *pistis* is a route to righteousness that both Jews (2:16) and gentiles (3:6–14) can walk down. Trust in Christ is, in Paul's vision, the route to uniting Jews and gentiles in righteousness. The law could not do this. It had an honorable and vital role in controlling the situation prior to Christ, but it was a temporary and limited role.

   Supporters of the subjective genitive reading of *pistis Christou* (as "faith of Christ") may agree with much of this but no doubt would argue that a related case could be presented more straightforwardly if the *pistis* were that of Christ, toward which Paul was turning the Galatians' attention. They would also point out that this would eliminate the stylistic redundancy of 3:22. These are strong arguments. However, the factors discussed above (on 2:16, etc.) push forcefully in the other direction.

   Verses 23–25 elaborate on the logic of 3:22. There is language of constraint: "Scripture imprisoned"; "we were guarded under law, imprisoned"; "the law was our *paidagōgos*"; "under a *paidagōgos*." Then there is language of salvation: "so that the promise would be given"; "trust came"; "until the coming trust would be revealed"; "until Christ, so that we would be considered righteous on the basis of trust"; "with trust having come." The law constrained until a time when salvation arrived in Christ.

   Martinus de Boer challenges this flow from 3:22 to 3:23–25 by arguing that here "Scripture" is not synonymous with "law." Instead, "'the Scripture' that is so important for the new preachers has in fact shut up 'all things' (*ta panta*)—and this must then include (the works of) the law—under Sin's power," by which Paul probably means that Scripture attests the powerlessness of the law to make alive (2011, 235). It is clear how this could fit Paul's logic. However, it looks unlikely. As de Boer observes, Paul can use *nomos* ("law") to refer to parts of Scripture other than the Pentateuch (2011, 234n347; citing Rom. 3:19; 1 Cor. 14:21). That Paul is doing the converse here, using *graphē* ("Scripture") to refer to the law, is hard to deny, especially given that each of these "imprisons" (*synkleiō*) in successive verses (3:22, 23).

   De Boer's reading here is part of his wider argument that the law's role in 3:23–25 is negative, not constructive. It was not "protective or pedagogical, but only restrictive and oppressive" (2011, 241). Is he correct? How purposeful and benign, or otherwise, is the law's custody of sinful humanity prior to Christ in Gal. 3:23–25? As we saw above (on 3:19), Luther sees the law as actively leading the world to Christ. In favor of a purposeful role for the law (although not necessarily for Luther's specific view) are, paradoxically, statements such as "I, through law, died to law, so I might live for God" (2:19). This gives the law an instrumental role in what happened to Paul. There is also the choice of *paidagōgos* as analogy for the law's role (2:24). Although this was a slave who took children to school, rather than being a schoolteacher, that is at least some link to education. Also, as well as protecting and controlling children, there is some evidence of the *paidagōgos* supervising some basic educational tasks (see Lull 1986, 489–98).

In line with this view, Ernest deWitt Burton translates *paidagōgos . . . eis Christon* in 3:24 as "a pedagogue to bring us to Christ" (1921, 198, 200). However, the supposed near-parallels that he cites for this reading (Rom. 8:18, 21; Matt. 20:1; 1 Pet. 1:12) are unconvincing. It is much more likely that *eis Christon* is simply temporal, "until Christ." However, this translational decision does not determine the question of whether in 3:23–25 the law has a positive purpose. In the context of the argument of Galatians, Paul's choice of the term *paidagōgos* is probably quite carefully calibrated. The law was *paidagōgos*, not *didaskalos*: Paul is not arguing that the law was the "teacher." However, the law was *paidagōgos*, not *desmophylax*, "jailer." The law exercised constraint but not constraint for the sake of punishment. The law's constraint was the way of managing the circumstances up to the arrival of Christ, up to a time that Paul is about to identify in terms of reaching maturity (4:1–4). The law had an important role.

In 3:19–25, the focus is on a specific period, from Sinai to the arrival of Christ in the world. It is hard to be sure how sharp Paul envisaged the cutting-off of the law's role to be. Did the world stop needing a *paidagōgos* the day Christ was born? If not, then at what point? Paul may well not have had a very specific answer. However, he clearly thought that once the gospel of Christ was being preached, people were able to live in response to that, so they no longer needed the law as such (although we must keep reminding ourselves that the Scriptures themselves remain authoritative for Paul, albeit now interpreted in a Christian manner). It seems extremely unlikely that Paul envisages a long-term continuing role for the law, something like the classic Lutheran view of the law showing people their need for grace. Even simply from practical considerations, this would be very difficult to envisage in a mission to gentiles, most of whom would have known little about Jewish law.

From the Nature of Being in Christ (3:26–29)

3:26–29. **For you are all sons of God through trust, in Christ Jesus. For as many as were baptized into Christ, you have put on Christ. There is no Jew**

nor Greek. There is no slave nor free. There is no male and female. For you are all "one" in Christ Jesus. If you are of Christ, then you are Abraham's seed, heirs according to the promise. Here the argument flowing from Paul's decision to treat the threat of gentile circumcision as a threat to unity between Christian Jews and Christian gentiles reaches its climax (cf. Betz 1979, 181). Being in Christ means oneness. In the situation of the letter, this oneness is especially between Jews and gentiles (here called "Greeks"). However, Paul then points out that the same is true for whatever other social polarities there may be: "supply any category," as Douglas Campbell writes (2005, 108). Paul could even be progressively escalating the categories: "There is unity between Jew and Greek. But that's nothing! In Christ there is even unity across the most fundamental social divide in Greco-Roman life, that between slave and free. And beyond that: in Christ there is unity even across the first social distinction, instituted at creation: there is no male and female!"

Notice, though, that the aim of Paul's rhetoric is to preserve social diversity rather than to eliminate it. It is Paul's opponents who are seeking to eliminate diversity. They want gentiles to adopt circumcision, to Judaize, to become Jews, losing their distinction in identity. Paul wants unity between gentiles as gentiles and Jews as Jews, all together in Christ. (How far the historic churches ran from this vision!) Brigitte Kahl (2010, 281) sees Gal. 3–4 as "a grand restatement of Genesis that revolves around the theme of oneness—the one God who reconciles humanity as one (Jew) and other (Gentiles) into a new oneness as children of God and of Abraham and Sarah, as siblings of Christ." If gentiles are not to become Jews, what does it mean to say, "There is no Jew nor Greek"? The Antioch incident and the ethics of Gal. 5–6 probably show us. Eliminating social distinction, without eliminating diversity, means practices such as eating together, showing love and forbearance to one another, bearing one another's burdens, and not engaging in division, envy, or devouring one another (2:11–14; 5:13, 22, 20–21, 15). Some might see these as too trivial for such high-flown theological language as Gal. 3:28, but just as Paul can invoke epic Christology in service of encouraging mutual support among the Philippians (Phil. 2:1–11), here he can announce the disappearance of all the world's social polarities in service of loving daily existence within and between the house churches.

A common reading of Gal. 3:28 is to see it as announcing soteriological equality between the pairs of sets of people (e.g., Burton 1921, 206): Greeks, slaves, and women have access to salvation equal to that of Jews, free people, and men. This reading does address the most apparent issue in the letter: without adopting circumcision, Greeks have access to salvation equal to that of Jews. However, in two ways it is weaker than the reading above. First, it does not tie in as well to the section's argument about oneness. Most immediately, 3:28 does not read, "There is no Jew nor Greek. There is no . . . for you are all *saved* [or considered righteous, etc.] in Christ Jesus." It reads, "There is no Jew nor Greek. There is no . . . for you are all *one* in Christ Jesus." The point of the paradoxical assertion of the nonexistence of evidently continuing social polarities is that being in Christ brings oneness, unity, across these polarities. The second disadvantage of the purely soteriological reading of 3:28 is that it accounts less well for the inclusion of the slave/free and male/female polarities. Although, as many scholars note, there were some Jewish texts that are effectively disparaging about slaves or women (e.g., Bruce 1982, 187; citing *t. Ber.* 7.18), there was no prevalent Jewish thought that women or slaves were not part of God's people. For women in particular, the thought would undermine the very idea of Jewishness. Moreover, there is absolutely no sign that there was such thought among the first-century house churches. That women and slaves could be saved was not a point distinctive to Christians, and it was not a point that Paul would have had any reason to bother making in Galatians. In contrast, if the issue is practical unity across social polarities, this would always have been a pressing issue for the house churches. It would be generally pertinent for house-church life that Paul, having found a theological argument about oneness in Christ that dealt powerfully with the issue of Jew/Greek divisions, would then go on to say that the same argument applied to other social polarities in house-church life.

We must not get carried away with our perception of Paul as promoter of unity in diversity. Kahl (2010, 284), for instance, argues that Paul's "whole theology and practice are an uncompromising embrace of the other." We have already seen (on 1:6) that there are considerable limits to Paul's acceptance of "the other" in terms of what people preach. Joseph Marchal (2012, 223) astutely draws attention to the effect of 4:12 on the rhetoric of 3:28. Paul's call to imitate him places limits on his suitability as an apostle of diversity in an unconditional sense.

Turning to the details of the passage, the first point to notice is the introduction of the idea of all Christians being sons of God (3:26). The "all" here and in 3:28 fit together (along with "as many as" in 3:27) to reinforce the point that Paul's aim is to be inclusive here: gentiles as well as Jews are sons of God. In fact, 3:26 is where to find the soteriological inclusivity that some see as the point of 3:28. There would have been added inclusivity if Paul had chosen to speak of "sons and daughters" or "children." However, his argument still gets involved with inheritance, with its lack of gender-neutrality. He is also going to use an argument relating Christ's sonship to the Christian's sonship (4:6–7). There may even be a radical edge to his use of the masculine term, "sons," because, in the first-century house-church context, it could be significant that Paul describes the Christian identity of women and slaves among his expected hearers, in terms of the imagery of free male heirs. One further factor is that being sons of God was also an attribute of Israel (e.g., Hosea 11:1). Describing gentiles as having this identity undercuts Paul's opponents by asserting that gentile Christians already have the closest possible link to God, without needing circumcision.

The final expression of 3:26, *dia tēs pisteōs en Christō Iēsou*, could possibly be read all together as "through the faith in Christ Jesus" (the variant in $\mathfrak{P}^{46}$ reads *dia pisteōs Christou Iēsou*; Swanson 1999, 43). However, it looks more likely that the elaborate expression here should be read as a drawing together of the two phrases in 3:14, *en Christō Iēsou* and *dia tēs pisteōs*, in which case they act as two complementary descriptions of the means by which the Christian is son of God (see comments on 3:22).

Galatians 3:27 is then explicit about the practical process leading to union with Christ. The verse also offers an analogy for understanding the significance of the process. The practical process is baptism, to which this is the earliest Christian reference. The context here implies that baptism was an entry ritual (rather than, say, a periodic purification). Many have called it an initiation ritual (e.g., Meeks 1983, 150–57). Richard E. DeMaris prefers "boundary-crossing rite" because of the absence of any prolonged transitional ("liminal") state, usually a key characteristic of initiation rituals as analyzed by anthropologists (2008, 20). Although DeMaris is correct about the absence of an extended liminal state, especially in earliest Christianity, the nature of baptism as, to some extent, an ordeal does give it at least one key characteristic of initiation rituals. The term *baptizō*, "baptize," implies that the ritual involved dipping in water. This probably made it quite daring for many members of the house church. Although bathing in (single-sex) public baths was common in the Roman world, it would be rather radical for a group of various statuses and both genders to engage in a process that probably involved something such as the group going to a river and the new member being immersed in front of the group. Whether this took place naked or clothed, it is a ritual that imposed quite a high entry cost—although crucially, it was a cost that anyone could pay, unlike circumcision. The ritual involves, at least to an extent, an element of semipublic degradation. The ordeal of the member's degradation before the group and the physical discomfort of being covered in water makes this ritual a powerful marker of transfer of allegiance to the group.

There is a further aspect to this. Paul does not write *eis ekklēsian ebaptisthēte* ("you were baptized into the assembly") but *eis Christon* ("into Christ"). What would look to outsiders as initiation into the group is viewed by insiders as initiation into union with Christ. This gives a deeper dimension to the ordeal and degradation in the ritual. It is not an arbitrary, high barrier, guarding an exclusive group. It is a relatively easy, token degradation and suffering to demonstrate allegiance to a person viewed as having undergone the ultimate degradation and suffering on behalf of the new Christian. In Rom. 6:1–11, Paul expresses baptism in terms of dying with Christ and then sharing his risen life. In Galatians, Paul does not explain much about baptism, but the idea of it representing Christ's death and new life would clearly tie very well into the

Figure 8. Site known as Lydia's Baptistry, near Philippi.

letter's motif of sharing in Christ's crucifixion and new life (2:19–20; 5:24; 6:14–15, 17). What Paul does say in 3:27 is that baptism involves "putting on" Christ. The analogy is of clothing. Some scholars suggest a link to a practice of reclothing the baptized person (Dunn 1993, 204). Whether or not such practice happened in the Pauline house churches, the analogy is a powerful assertion of new identity. The person looking at the Christian should see Christ. The outer form that defined the identity was that of Christ. Conformity to the person of Christ is clearly an important strand in the letter (cf. esp. 4:19).

The NRSV translates 3:28 as "There is no longer Jew or Greek, there is no longer . . ." This follows the reading of $\mathfrak{P}^{46}$ which has *ouketi* ("no longer"; Swanson 1999, 44) in place of *ouk eni* (= *ouk enestin*, "there is no"; Betz 1979, 190). Since the NRSV does not even give its usual type of footnote, "Other ancient authorities read *There is no*," to acknowledge that $\mathfrak{P}^{46}$ is essentially alone in this, I imagine that this is just a straight translator's error. It is very easy to do, given the temporal context in Galatians, but despite $\mathfrak{P}^{46}$ being the earliest manuscript witness, this is almost certainly a scribal slip, misreading the less expected *ouk eni* as the expected *ouketi*.

Galatians 3:29 ties the final pieces of argument together. Since, in Christ, these people are "one" (3:28), they qualify as Abraham's singular seed (3:16, 19) and hence, plurally, can be "heirs according to the promise" (cf. 3:18). What would threaten being heirs is not uncircumcised gentile identity, as Paul's opponents would have it, but their demands, which effectively drive a wedge between Christian Jews and Christian gentiles, as happened in Antioch. This would threaten the diverse group being "one" and hence heirs.

Theological Issues

Church Entry Rituals

Baptism performed a very important social function in the early house churches. Meeting in houses generally meant all sorts of people potentially being present (e.g., 1 Cor. 14:23). Some will have been there out of commitment, presumably some would be there out of interest, and some by accident of ownership or family membership. Although the household baptism practice attested in Acts (10:47; 16:15, 33) should caution us against seeing the decision to be baptized as always being made by the individual, this moderately demanding and semipublic ritual provided a social process for expressing transfer into serious group membership.

Churches today have a range of practices and theologies in relation to baptism. In churches that baptize infants, the social significance of baptism probably has mainly to do with family allegiance to the church, either directly (for active church members) or less directly, where the church is seen as the proper body sanctioning something like the baby's entry into public life. In churches that baptize only more mature children or adults, the social significance of baptism is more about commitment to group membership. (There are, of course, theological matters too, for infants and the mature, but our reflection here is on social significance—which does, in itself, carry theological weight.)

The curious thing for Baptist (and similar) churches is that most of them today operate in a manner that minimizes distinctions between the unbaptized and the baptized. All are welcome, and there is a desire not to let any feel like second-class participants. The curious thing for churches that baptize infants is that most of them then operate almost without adult entry rituals at all. There are liturgies such as confirmation available, but essentially there is no general ritual differentiating the committed congregational member from the uncommitted.

In many churches, there has been a decline of entry rituals, of processes expressing specific commitment or, to turn it around the other way, of processes expressing God's commitment to a person at the point at which persons put themselves, in a way visible to others, into God's hands. This should be a cause for reflection. There clearly is virtue in everyone in a congregation feeling equally welcome. However, for the early house churches, baptism represented something theologically and socially vital, aspects of which many modern churches might be in danger of losing.

Galatians 4:1–11

Argument 3: Against Returning to Slavery

Introductory Matters

After reaching the climax of his argument about oneness and setting out a view of the role of the law, Paul now turns to deal with an aspect of the specifics of what at least some of the Galatians are now doing, contrary to his teaching. To reach this issue, he needs to introduce a new factor, "the elements of the world." He explains how "we" were once enslaved under these elements (4:1–3), but now God has sent his Son, who brings freedom and sonship (4:4–7). The Galatians had been under such slavery but now know God (4:8–9a). Paul is then incredulous that they have adopted calendrical observances of various kinds. He presents this as a return to slavery under the elements (4:9b–10).

Tracing the Train of Thought

From the Slave-Like Nature of Childhood and the Liberating Action of God (4:1–7)

4:1–2. I tell you, for as long as the heir is a child, he differs in no way from a slave, despite being lord of all, but he is under guardians and stewards until the point set by his father. Again Paul picks up the images of inheritance and of the child being constrained by keepers of one sort or another. The words used for the keepers are different from the one used for the law: *paidagōgos* (3:24–25). This may be because the *paidagōgos* had at least some specific

133

connection with the period of education. The law's function in 3:19–25 could perhaps be described as constraint, with educative overtones. The functionaries in 4:1–2 have roles centered on responsible control of people and management of assets (Goodrich 2010, 265–73). The constraint of 4:1–3 has different overtones from that of 3:19–25.

4:3. So too we, when we were children, were enslaved under the elements of the world. This needs to be interpreted with the beginning of the next verse: "But when the fullness of time came, God sent out his Son." As in 3:15–29, there is a scheme here of dividing history into periods. In 3:15–29 we had the time of Abraham (3:15–16), then that of Moses (3:17–18), then the period from Moses to the arrival of Christ (3:19–24), and finally the current situation since the arrival of Christ (3:25–29). In 4:1–7 we have the period prior to Christ's arrival (4:1–3), then the events of Christ's arrival and action (4:4–5), and finally the current situation (4:6–7). In neither scheme is time divided up on a personal, individual basis, contrasting time before and after conversion. The time periods relate to the world as a whole. Childhood is used as an analogy for the time before the arrival of Christ in the world.

This causes difficulties. Galatians 4:8 has the preconversion Galatians enslaved to "beings that by nature are not gods," a situation which, from 4:9, we discover to be equivalent to looking toward the "elements," which are the entities controlling life (4:3) before the arrival of Christ. Few of the Galatians can even have been born before the birth of Christ. Moreover, in 4:8, clearly Paul is effectively describing the Galatians' life as enslavement to "the elements of the world" right up to conversion, in the 40s or 50s of this era.

One proposed solution is to take the "we" of 4:3 to refer specifically to Jews. This would fit with the note that God's Son came to "redeem those under law" (4:5). Jews cannot be excluded from 4:1–5 (which implies that being under the law is somehow linked with being under the "elements"). However, the varying use of pronouns in 4:1–7 suggests that the Galatians are included in the whole scheme. Christ redeems those under law "so that *we* might receive adoption. Because *you* are sons, God sent out the Spirit of his Son into *our* hearts" (4:5–6). Paul must be using the pronouns in a rather loose and inclusive way.

There does also appear to be an element of looseness in the chronology of Paul's overall scheme, as indeed there is also a slight looseness in Paul's pulling together of the events of Christ's life, death, and resurrection as though they are effectively a single point in time. Paul thinks that the time of slavery essentially ended for both Jews and the rest of the world when Christ arrived. However, he also thinks that some people have remained in slavery even after the great freeing event has occurred. As well as the preconversion Galatians in 4:8, that can be seen for Jerusalem in 4:25. Perhaps the way to put it is that God has, in Christ, produced freedom, which has now been proclaimed, but some people have either not heard the proclamation or have refused to act on it. The era of freedom has arrived, but some people continue to choose slavery. Paul's bewildered fear (4:11) is that the Galatians, even after experiencing freedom, will choose to adopt what for them is a new form of slavery.

A surprise in this passage is the introduction of "the elements of the world" (4:3). Some have argued that "elements" here refers to basic teaching (e.g., Lightfoot 1890, 167). This would make 4:1–3 closely parallel to the situation of 3:19–25, with its links to the schoolroom. However, "the elements of the world" would be a strange way to refer to such teaching. The reference to the Galatians' preconversion experience also tells against it. The "weak and poor elements" are linked to the "beings that by nature are not gods" (4:8–9). The "elements of the world," *stoicheia tou kosmou*, also had a meaning well known in Greek-speaking society. They were the fundamental substances constitutive of the world (e.g., Wis. 7:17). The best-known set was earth, air, fire, and water. Often the idea of them was linked with a view of time in which the world went through repeated cycles, each of which ended in a great conflagration, with all things being reduced to fire (cf. 2 Pet. 3:12). Some Jewish sources directly linked the elements with Greco-Roman gods by observing that some gentiles worshiped the elements. Thus Wis. 13:2 describes worship of fire, wind, air, and also of the luminaries of heaven. In Greco-Roman sources are broader links between the divine and the elements. These could operate at an overall level, as in the Stoic view that identified the divine with the material substance of the cosmos (Cicero, *Nat. d.* 1.15, citing the Stoic Chrysippus). They could also operate through ties between various gods or spirits that were linked with aspects of the physical universe (e.g., Apollo and the sun). By the second century AD, we have evidence of Christian writers using the term "elements" in describing the heavenly bodies that govern the seasons (Justin, *2 Apol.* 5). Since Gal. 4:8–9 identifies "the elements" with the objects of the Galatians' former worship, and then 4:10 links this to the calendar, Paul must be thinking of "the elements" in 4:3 as something like heavenly bodies, with some presumed link to deities (in gentile minds, if not his own). Paul's tendency to see gentile worship in such terms was encouraged by texts such as Deut. 4:19.

**Deuteronomy Bans Worship
of Celestial Bodies**

"And when you look up to the heavens and see the sun, the moon, and the stars, all the host of heaven, do not be led astray and bow down to them and serve them, things that the LORD your God has allotted to all the peoples everywhere under heaven." (Deut. 4:19 NRSV)

The greater puzzle is how Paul ties the law into this cosmic chronological scheme, especially given that the law specifically banned the worship of created features of the cosmos. In terms of the letter's rhetoric, Martinus de Boer probably has the correct answer for this. The aim of 4:1–10 is to challenge an aspect of the Galatians' behavior, the practice of calendrical observance, "observing days and months and seasons and years" (4:10). Some Galatians (as Paul presents it) are now doing this, presumably in that they are observing some Jewish festivals and other special days such as Sabbaths, at the instigation of Paul's opponents. Such observances are specifically linked to the movements of the sun or moon, that is, celestial phenomena associated with the elements of the world. The preconversion Galatians also practiced calendrical observances, with the dates in question being linked to Greco-Roman cults. As de Boer writes, "In this sense both Gentile and Jewish believers in Christ were once 'enslaved [together] under *ta stoicheia tou kosmou*'" (2011, 257).

In 4:1–3, an effect of Paul broadening his canvas from constraint under the law (3:19–25) to constraint under the elements of the world (which includes constraint under the law) is to bring all the world into his chronological scheme, rather than just Jews. The whole world faced a slavery and did not realize that this was in fact a temporary constraint imposed by God while the people of the world were in "childhood." God then produced freedom from this constraint through the actions of Christ. Paul presents this picture to the Galatians, living after the arrival of Christ and after accepting the proclamation of Christ. It is probably unwise to press the text here too hard to try to learn details about Paul's view of the world before the coming of Christ. Paul presents his view as a backdrop against which the Galatians are to consider their present situation and choices.

4:4–5. But when the fullness of time came, God sent out his Son, born of a woman, born under law, so that he might redeem those under law, so that we might receive adoption. The language of constraint takes a particular turn here. Paul has spoken of people being imprisoned (3:22, 23), guarded (3:23), enslaved (4:3). He has also used the preposition *hypo* ("under") in relation to this. In 3:10, people were under a curse; in 3:22 under sin; in 3:23 guarded under law; in 3:25 under a *paidagōgos*; in 4:2 under guardians and stewards; in 4:3 under the elements. Now God's Son is born "under law" (4:4) and redeems those under law (4:5). Later, Paul characterizes some Galatians as wanting to be under law (4:21) and comments that those led by the Spirit are not under law (5:18).

The consistent pattern is that being "under" means living under constraint. It fits in with the other expressions of constraint. This point is reinforced by the term *exagorasē* ("redeem") in 4:5. This means to free someone (or regain something for its owner) by payment. In the context of first-century life, the most prominent situation of the term's use was in freeing slaves.

There are two unexpected points in this. The first is that a Jewish writer, Paul, would view people under the law as being thereby enslaved, so needing freeing and indeed needing adoption. However, Paul's untypical Jewish view to this effect has already been seen in Gal. 3, for instance in his presenting being a son of God as based on being in Christ rather than on being Israelite. The second is that Christ's redeeming those under law leads directly to a group that includes the Galatian gentiles receiving adoption (3:5–6). This startling move relates to one seen in 3:13–14: "Christ redeemed us from the curse of the law, . . . so that the blessing of Abraham would come to the gentiles in Christ Jesus." The curse of the law was, rather surprisingly, a barrier to gentiles receiving the blessing of Abraham. The cross removed that barrier. We might, instead, have expected the curse of the law to apply only to those "of works of law," meaning Jews or law-observant gentiles. However, as we noted in discussing that passage, Deut. 27:26, quoted in Gal. 3:10, would mean that gentiles are cursed, being lawbreakers, so Christ would indeed need to remove the curse in order for gentiles to be blessed.

In acting to free Jews from the curse of the law, Christ also frees gentiles. In Gal. 4:4–5 we see the pattern put in more general terms: Christ frees Jews from slavery under the law, which has the effect of freeing gentiles too, bringing them into God's family. Another way of looking at this may be that Paul develops the rhetoric of 3:19–4:5 by tracing the law's enslaving function, then generalizing from that to the enslaving function of the elements. The Jewish law's rule becomes a representative of all cosmic constraint prior to Christ. Redeeming of those under law could then be representative of redeeming all under cosmic constraint.

Why does Paul mention that Christ was "born of a woman"? It is hard to discern a gender-related point that Paul makes here. It seems more that Paul is emphasizing the idea of the Son of God being a real human. The ascription of the title, Son, to Jesus represents quite a high Christology. It links Christ to God by Jesus being Son of God in some unique sense. Throughout Israel's history, many people had been called sons of God (e.g., Ps. 2:7), but their lives did not represent "the fullness of time." Christ was, in Paul's view, Son of God in such an absolute sense that his birth changed the world. However, it is probably overreading the passage to see it as demonstrating Christ's preexistence. In the Bible, God "sends out" (*exapostellei*) various people, such as Paul (Acts 22:21) and even "the rich," whom God "sent out empty" (Luke 1:53)!

Adoption, the goal in 4:5, was a very far-reaching social institution in the first-century world. It gave the fullest possible sense of incorporation into the adoptive family. This is seen most graphically among the Roman emperors, who gained prestige by their descent from their imperial predecessors, even though the connection was usually of adoption rather than birth. Octavian (later Augustus), for instance, issued coins claiming to be *divi filius* ("son of the deified one") on the basis of his posthumous (!) adoption by Julius Caesar. For house-church members, the idea of being adopted into God's own family represented a meteoric jump in their concept of their status.

4:6–7. Because you are sons, God sent out the Spirit of his Son into our hearts, crying out, "Abba, Father!" So you are no longer a slave but a son: if a son, also an heir through God. Paul brings the argument of 4:1–7 to a close at the same place as 3:29, with the conclusion that the Galatians are heirs. However, this time he reaches this conclusion by a more predictable route. Whereas in 3:15–29 he got there via a surprising argument about oneness, this time he goes via sonship. Adoption, *huiothesia* (4:5), leads to being sons, *huioi* (4:6). Now we go back to the topic of the Spirit, the focus of the Galatians' experience in 3:2–5 and of the promise in 3:14. This time the Spirit is designated as being the Spirit of God's Son (4:6). In some sense, the Christian's sonship is the same kind of attribute as Christ's sonship, making it appropriate that his Spirit inhabits each Christian, leading Christians to verbal expression of their own sonship. The way sonship is expressed is in a form that, in itself, unites Jewish and gentile Christians in the doubled Aramaic and Greek expression, *Abba ho patēr* (4:6).

The Christology here is striking. The Spirit sent out from God, known from its many excursions in Scripture, from the predawn of creation (Gen. 1:2) to the anointing of kings and prophets (e.g., 1 Sam. 16:13; Isa. 61:1), is now sent out as the Spirit of God's Son. God's key means of intervention in the human heart is now mediated through the identity of Christ. Being in Christ implies being inhabited by the Spirit of God's Son, a Spirit that affirms the Christian's identity as child of God. For the house-church members, this is astonishing. Octavian might claim to be son of a god. For a craftworker's slave girl to claim this turns the status hierarchy upside down. And how does she feel when Paul switches to the singular and writes, "You are no longer a slave but a son, . . . also an heir" (4:7)? The vision is dazzling, even though the everyday reality must have been much more prosaic (Oakes 2009, 149).

From the Absurdity of the Galatians Returning to Former Slavery (4:8–10)

4:8–10. But then, not knowing God, you were enslaved to beings that by nature are not gods. How is it that now, knowing God—or rather being known by God—you are turning back again to the weak and poor elements, to which you are wanting to enslave yourselves again? You are observing days and months and seasons and years. The Greek construction in 4:8–9 uses the words *men . . . de*, which act as grammatical signals. These are hard to translate directly into English. However, their function here is to compare two situations: "given that then . . . , how is it that now . . . ?" (*tote men . . . , nyn de . . . pōs . . .*).

In 4:10, Paul attacks actions that at least some Galatian Christians appear to have taken already, in contravention of his teaching. These are described in calendrical terms. Given the argument of Galatians as a whole, they are presumably calendrical observances relating to Jewish law, even though the terminology here does not explicitly relate to Jewish festivals (de Boer 2011, 276). In 4:8–9, Paul depicts the Galatians' move as a return to enslavement to "the elements," relating these to beings that they formerly worshiped.

On the face of it, this is a very negative evaluation of the adoption of Jewish practice. For some scholars, the tension that this produces between 4:8–9 and general Pauline evaluations of the law is too much. Peter Pilhofer expresses this strongly: "There is no sharper criticism of the law, of Judaism, anywhere in our letter—not to speak of other texts by Paul, . . . an evaluation of Judaism that does not have its equal in the NT, even in Hebrews" (2010, 293, AT).[1] For Pilhofer, the difficulty of fitting this passage into the argument of the letter drives him toward Thomas Witulski's radical theory about this passage.

Witulski solves the problem of the oddness of the rhetoric of 4:8–10 by taking it at face value: the Galatians have been converted from Greco-Roman religious practice to Christian religious practice, but now they are reverting to what they used to do. In particular, Witulski links this to the development of prominent imperial cult facilities in Pisidian Antioch at about this time. He sees the chronological observances as especially being those of the imperial cult (2000, 158–68, 183–214). This neatly solves the problems of the rhetoric of 4:8–10. However, it complicates Galatians by introducing a second and quite different strand to the situation that Paul is addressing there. Witulski's answer is to split Galatians into two documents, written for different situations, with 4:8–20 probably a later document, added to the rest of Galatians to tackle the imperial cult issue that had just come about through the development of the cult at Antioch (2000, 71–81).

Bruce W. Winter argues that the imperial cult is indeed in view in 4:8–10, but he links this with 6:12, where Paul describes his opponents as seeking "to make a good showing in the flesh." Winter produces a scenario for the whole letter in which Paul's (Galatian Jewish-Christian) opponents were persuading the Galatian gentiles to adopt full Jewish practice because Jews were permitted not to perform imperial cult rituals. The opponents were doing this to avoid suffering persecution for associating with gentile Christians who have ceased imperial cult practice (Winter 1994, 123–44). Justin Hardin agrees that the imperial cult is in view in 4:8–10 but disagrees that Jews were exempt.

---

1. The German original reads, "Eine schärfere Kritik am Gesetz, am Judentum findet sich an keiner Stelle in unserm Brief—von andern Texten des Paulus ganz zu schweigen, . . . einer Einschätzung des Judentums, die im Neuen Testament selbst im Hebräerbrief nicht ihresgleichen hat."

© Burak Karaman 2012

Figure 9. Temple of the imperial cult at Ankara. The *Res Gestae* inscription is along the lower section of the visible outer wall.

Instead, they practiced the cult by making offerings to God for the emperor's well-being. Gentile Galatian Christians were being urged by Paul's opponents to follow this route too, as part of the general desire to normalize their social identity by adopting circumcision (Hardin 2008, 103–14). Hardin also points out that Witulski's dating of the imperial cult at Pisidian Antioch has now been overthrown by a rereading of a crucial inscription, redating it from AD 50 to 2 BC. In any case, it would not necessarily imply the date of first establishment of the cult (Hardin 2008, 71–78, 131). This undermines Witulski's theory of 4:8–20 as a late addition to cope with the new cult. Hardin also reasonably accuses Witulski of unlikely exegetical gymnastics as he seeks to overcome the (for him) problematic repeated use of "elements" (4:3, 9) by arguing that "elements" was edited into 4:3 in order to assimilate it to 4:8–20 when that was added to Galatians (Hardin 2008, 129–30; Witulski 2000, 75–77).

If we maintain the idea that 4:10 criticizes Galatian law-observant behavior, are we left in the difficult position depicted by Pilhofer (Paul's sharp criticism of the law)? Also, what about evidence that Witulski and Hardin offer showing that the calendrical terms in 4:10 are likely to fit the imperial cult rather better than Jewish traditions? Martinus de Boer's argument shows a way through (see on 4:3, above). That the calendrical terminology may fit the imperial cult (or other Greco-Roman cults) somewhat better than Jewish law

Partition Theories

Members of English-speaking churches may go through their whole lives without encountering partition theories about NT texts. However, they have been common in continental European scholarship for over a century. Such theories view various NT texts as being edited together from shorter sections. Among Paul's Letters, 2 Corinthians is most frequently handled this way. Many scholars also split Philippians, and there are various proposals relating to the end of Romans. These theories seek to account for several features, such as awkward transitions between passages, changes of tone, and (most powerfully) changes of apparent situation—as Witulski sees here in Galatians.

English-speaking scholarship has tended to resist partition theories (although they would still be common for 2 Corinthians). This resistance has particularly taken the form of appeal to rhetorical motives for such features as sudden changes of tone, where partition theorists would see evidence of documents (clumsily) edited together. Scholars have also built cases against partition theories by seeking to demonstrate lexical, thematic, or (most powerfully) argumentative links between the allegedly separate texts.

is not a problem for de Boer's reading. Paul's point is to compare the two. The gentile Galatians had given up calendrical observances when they became Christians; now they are taking them up again, albeit for different reasons from before. For Paul, either means slavery to the elements governing time. He is not regarding Jewish law-keeping per se as a form of paganism. Paul is probably not even viewing gentile adoption of the law's ethnic boundary markers as embracing again a form of paganism, as N. T. Wright (2000, 217) more subtly argues. However, Paul is seeing Jewish law-keeping and Greco-Roman cultic observances as both being forms of slavery. He has been saying this at least since 3:22. The point is not special to 4:8–10. Christ has brought the Galatians freedom from their former gentile cultic slavery. They should not replace it with Jewish cultic slavery (a slavery that no longer has a relevant function). Paul is still being harsh about the law, but not unprecedentedly so, in the way Pilhofer fears.

Paul's Fear about the Galatians (4:11)

4:11. I fear about you, in case somehow it is in vain that I have labored for you. Just as the argument section of the letter (3:1–4:11) began with an expression of bewilderment about the Galatians, so it ends with an expression of Paul's fear about what they are doing, or considering doing. In saying this, he also introduces the topic of his ministry among them. This will be the topic of the next section, in which he turns to begin giving the Galatians direct instructions.

In 4:12–20 Paul will make a personal appeal to the Galatians' sympathetic loyalty to Paul. This actually begins here. He reminds them that he has "labored" on their behalf. He is on their side. The bringing of the gospel to Galatia was a demanding undertaking. Geographically, it was a large area, whether it was the south of the province or included the north too. According to Acts, Paul's mission also involved flight, rejection, and stoning (Acts 13:50; 14:2–6, 19). Paul reminds them of his struggle and suggests that their current behavior, in calendrical observances, may render that struggle worthless. He seeks to elicit their sympathy and, from this, to bring them back to the way of life that he taught them.

Theological Issues

Slavery to Calendrical Observance

Ironically, gentile Galatians' observance of Greco-Roman ritual calendars, prior to accepting Christ, probably did not feel like slavery. The house-church members lived in a society built around these calendars. A free theatrical show on the emperor's birthday would certainly feel like no imposition—even less so if there was some kind of handout linked to it. In a romanized household, any slaves would no doubt enjoy the holiday element of Saturnalia. Everyone might be worried by festivals relating to the dead, such as Lemuria, but even these probably felt like the natural turning of the year, in which a regular time for appeasement of the restless dead was perceived as something that needed to happen sometime. (On Roman religious festivals, see Beard, North, and Price 1998; on specifically Anatolian cultic practice, see S. Elliott 2003, 58–232.)

It is more burdensome to follow a calendar at odds with that of the prevailing culture. Diaspora Jews were mocked for practices such as Sabbath keeping (Seneca, *Ep.* 95.47). However, at least they had a vigorous, long-established subculture, so they would have grown up with the complexities of negotiating the interactions between Jewish festival times and the cycle of the Greco-Roman year. For gentile Christians, to take on Jewish patterns of time must have been very trying. Some gentiles may have had prior links with synagogues, and hence some knowledge of how to make things work. However, adoption of Christian practice was, in itself, likely to have separated these people from the synagogue links that they had. The difficulties of trying to follow a Jewish calendar would have been particularly acute for gentile Christians who were part of households with a non-Christian head.

Although Jewish calendrical observance was likely to be a burden for gentiles, we should notice that Paul does not directly say they are slaves to calendrical observance. He says that calendrical observance makes them slaves to the elements, the celestial elements that govern the calendar. Although his argument probably would draw some force from burdensome experience in relation to the calendar, his real point is irrespective of whether calendrical observance feels slave-like. His point is that it places the Christian under other powers, in this case the motion of celestial bodies, which in Paul's day were generally thought of as powerful beings, or as closely linked to such beings. This compromises the Christian's freedom, won for them by Christ.

Galatians 4:12–20

Instructions with Argument 1: "Be like Me"

Introductory Matters

After long sections of narrative and argument, we finally reach the first really direct instruction to the Galatians. It is not the instruction we were expecting. "Be like me!" (4:12). We might have expected an instruction to reject Paul's opponents, or not to get circumcised. If imitation is needed, would it not surely be of Christ? In fact, that does come up in 4:19, but Paul's first call is to imitate Paul. He then switches into personal appeal based on previous interactions between the Galatians and himself. "What has now changed?" he asks. The opponents' aims in relation to the Galatians are then contrasted with his own. He ends the section with longing for a good meeting with them, because he is in despair.

Tracing the Train of Thought

"Be like Me, as I Am like You" (4:12a)

4:12a. The long wait for the first substantial instructional imperative in the letter (the only previous imperatives are "Let them (him) be accursed" [1:8, 9] and "Know" [3:7]) gives the instruction considerable weight. This weight is further increased because 4:12 follows 4:11 without use of any grammatical linking word. This type of Greek construction, called anacolouthon, is fairly rare and adds emphasis. However, this emphatic instruction is unexpected:

Be like me, as I am like you, brothers and sisters, I implore you (4:12a). Why a call to imitate him?

The call should not be as unexpected as it tends to seem to us. Paul has already been writing about himself in a paradigmatic fashion and will do so again at the end of the letter. Such writing is most evident in 2:19–21, where much of what he has done or experienced is surely presented as a pattern for Christian life. He lives for God (2:19). Paul has been crucified with Christ; he no longer lives but Christ lives in him, and he lives by trust in God's Son (2:19–20). Paul does not set aside God's grace (2:21). The rhetoric clearly implies that these are what Christians should seek: especially Christian Jews, such as Peter, and the Galatians in their particular situation.

The paradigmatic nature of Paul's "crucifixion" with Christ in 2:19 suggests a similar function for Paul's being "crucified to the world" and the world to him, in 6:14. As a paradigm, this could lead in one (or conceivably both) of two directions. Especially if Paul's bearing

Galatians 4:12–20 in the Rhetorical Flow
Letter opening (1:1–10)
Letter body (1:11–6:10)
Narrative 1: Of a gospel revealed by God, not people (1:11–24)
Narrative 2: Of a gospel affirmed by unity at Jerusalem (2:1–10)
Narrative 3: Of a gospel betrayed by division at Antioch (2:11–21)
Argument 1: For blessing in Christ through trust (3:1–14)
Argument 2: For unity in Christ (3:15–29)
Argument 3: Against returning to slavery (4:1–11)
►Instructions with argument 1: "Be like me" (4:12–20)
"Be like me, as I am like you" (4:12a)
Contrast between the Galatians' previous and current attitudes toward Paul (4:12b–16)
Contrast between the aims of Paul's opponents and his own (4:17–20)

"the marks of Jesus" (6:17) is also paradigmatic (although it could also be true without that), Paul could be a paradigm of suffering for Christ. As Ernst Baasland (1984), A. J. Goddard and S. A. Cummins (1993), Susan Eastman (2007), and Justin K. Hardin (2008, 101–2) argue, suffering and persecution are more prominent themes in Galatians than many suppose. Persecution and its avoidance are topics in 5:11 and 6:12. The next verses in 4:12–20 are also about to describe Paul's sufferings. An element of the "cruciform" Christian life in Galatians is preparedness to suffer for Christ (cf. Gorman 2008, 149–50). Willingness to go down a road that might lead to suffering could be an aspect of Paul's call to imitate him.

Another possible paradigmatic direction is flagged most clearly in 5:24: "Those who are of Christ Jesus have crucified the flesh, with its passions and desires." This is more specific than simply meaning conversion. As we will discuss below, it sees identification with the crucified Christ as involving a freeing from certain morally limiting forces, enabling a free and effective ethics. It also implies that identification with Christ involves a type of disconnection from certain aspects of the world (though not avoiding concern for situations in the world). For the world being crucified to Paul, and him to the world (6:14), he is probably modeling this. That would then fit with points in Paul's narrative about himself, in which he emphatically links not to the world but to the divine realm. We see this in relation to his apostleship (1:1), whom he seeks to please (1:10), and the origin of his gospel (1:11–12, 15–24). Paul is a paradigm of dependence on God and Christ, rather than on the flesh. This works well as an element of his rhetoric directed at the Galatians choosing God, Christ, and the Spirit, rather than the flesh and circumcision.

However, a particular clue to the likely direction of Paul's call to imitate him lies in the way he relates it to his assertion "as I am like you." What does he mean by this? Goddard and Cummins (1993, 99) argue that Paul is referring to his and the Galatians' common experience of conflict and persecution. This is not unreasonable. It would certainly work well with Eastman's reading of 4:12–20 (2007; see below). However, given that this is the first main imperative of the letter, it looks more likely to relate to the letter's central issue, especially since that also relates it to 4:9–10, which it closely follows. In Paul's speech to Peter, he comments on the possibility of discovering "that we too" are "sinners" (2:17). Given that he has just used "sinners" as a characterization of gentiles (2:15) and has described even Peter's life as being "in a gentile manner" (2:14), Paul is implying that, in some senses, Christian Jews are effectively acting as if they are gentiles. In 4:12, Paul could therefore be suggesting that he has become effectively a gentile like the Galatians. For instance, since Paul has "died to law" (2:19), his plea to Galatians who have begun to take up Jewish practices, such as the calendrical observances of 4:10, could be, "You too should die to the law (that you have begun to observe)" (cf. de Boer 2011, 278). It looks most likely that Paul calls the Galatians to imitate him by maintaining the law-free lifestyle that he has adopted as part of being like the gentiles to whom he ministers. However, Paul's law-free example is part of his overall example of turning his back on the flesh and adhering to God, a process most strongly represented by the idea of Paul being crucified with Christ, a process that Paul expects Christians everywhere to share in.

Contrast between the Galatians' Previous and Current Attitudes toward Paul (4:12b–16)

4:12b–15. You did me no harm. You know that it was through a weakness of the flesh that I proclaimed the gospel to you initially, and you did not despise what tested you in my flesh, nor did you spit. Instead, you received me as if I were an angel of God, as if I were Christ Jesus. So where is your happiness? For I can testify that, if it were possible, you would have torn out your eyes and given them to me. Beginning with 4:11, a note of personal appeal has come into Paul's rhetoric. The way the call to imitate Paul was phrased as an urgent request made it an emotional appeal. Now Paul builds the emotion by evoking their concern and generosity toward him in the past.

In particular, he describes their behavior on his arrival among them. (Incidentally, this sounds like a relatively local incident or set of incidents. It certainly sounds as though all the groups to which the addressees belonged heard the gospel during the same period. This has implications for ideas about how Paul spread the gospel in Galatia.) Something was physically wrong with him. "Flesh" in 4:13 sounds like a reference simply to the physical body, without the moral overtones elsewhere in the letter (esp. 5:19). Paul's physical problem was probably some disfigurement. That would offer an explanation of it being a *peirasmon*, a "trial," something that "tested" the Galatians. It would also account for their possible inclination to "despise" or to "spit" (4:14): "They were not put off by his physical condition, . . . nor did they 'spit' . . . in his presence—two reactions to be expected of persons fearing strangers and physically disabled persons as potential possessors and casters of the evil eye" (J. Elliott 2011). John Elliott's suggestion is supported by the reference to eyes in 4:15. Paul's assertion that the Galatians would have given him their eyes suggests that his physical problem probably involved his eyes. A disfigurement relating to one or both eyes would incline a Mediterranean audience to view the sufferer as possessing an evil eye (J. Elliott 2011; see on 4:17, below).

There is a long tradition of discussing the medical possibilities. One popular idea has been to relate it to the itinerary of Acts 13, combined with some geographical knowledge about the area, to suggest that Paul picked up a disease while traveling in the supposedly swampy region of Pamphylia (Acts 13:13; Ramsay 1920, 94–97). This mainly shows the strange willingness of NT scholars to construct theories about text A from minor snippets of information from text B. Even if the mission in question is that described in Acts 13–14, the probability that the note in Acts 13:13 about arriving at Perga in Pamphylia explains the discussion of physical problems in Gal. 4:13–15 is remote. In fact, if we were looking for a theory based on the events in those chapters of Acts, a more obvious one would be that Gal. 4:13–15 refers to injuries suffered in the stoning of Acts 14:19, which left Paul apparently at the point of death (Goddard and Cummins 1993, 120). However, this would require Paul or Luke to be a bit loose in expressing the sequence of events (Gal. 4:13). Susan Eastman (2007, 104) supports the emphasis on persecution by appeal to Paul's emphasis on his scars in contrasting himself to his opponents at the end of the letter (6:11–18).

Whatever the medical details, Paul's point is that the Galatians went far beyond normal cultural bounds in receiving him and providing him with care. In fact, they received him *hōs angelon theou, . . . hōs Christon Iēsoun* (4:14). We could read this "as an angel of God, . . . as Christ Jesus" or, given the ambiguity of the word *angelos*, "as a messenger of God, . . . as Christ Jesus." This would mean receiving Paul so much as a representative of God and Christ that they viewed him as some sort of representation of Christ. The wording could have a specific angle. Since Paul was physically afflicted, he could somehow have been viewed as offering, to some extent, a visual representation of the crucifixion. He says in Galatians that he bears "the marks of Jesus on [his] body" (6:17). This could act as a reminder of the time when the wounded Paul provided, in himself, a presentation "before [their] very eyes" of "Jesus Christ . . . crucified" (3:1; Eastman 2007, 103–4).

However, to see Paul as a representation of Christ in 4:14 in particular could well be an overreading of the evidence. It may be better simply to read 4:14 as complimentary hyperbole: "You received me as warmly as if I was an angel or Christ" (R. Longenecker 1990, 192). Even so, there is undoubtedly some significance in using angel/messenger and Christ as the points of comparison. Paul is not simply praising the Galatians' hospitality but also points out that they gave that hospitality because they perceived Paul and his message (if not Paul's body itself) as coming from God, as representing Christ.

4:15–16. So, where is your happiness? For I can testify that, if it were possible, you would have torn out your eyes and given them to me. So have I become your enemy by telling you the truth? The expected answer to the second question is "No, of course not." The main point of reminding the Galatians about their previous generous behavior toward Paul is to point out how sharply their attitude has changed, without there being any new action by Paul that could have given proper reason to change it. This verse raises a slight mystery about the sequence of events. When did this "telling . . . the truth" take place? Martinus de Boer regards this just as a reference back to 4:8–11 (2011, 282). However, the force of 4:15–16 (and indeed, the occasion of the letter) springs from Paul having already heard that their attitude to him has changed. The implication of 4:16 is that the letter is not Paul's first word on the Galatians' inclination toward his opponents' teaching. In fact, 1:9 has already suggested this: "As we have said before and I now say again . . ." The reference could be to an earlier letter, with a hostile reply from the Galatian Christians. However, we might then have expected Galatians to contain clear traces of the existence of the hostile letter (cf. 1 Cor. 7:1). An alternative would be an unpersuasive visit by Paul. However, again we might expect clearer traces of that. The use of the first-person plural in 1:9 suggests that there may, instead, have been a visit by some people from Paul's entourage, sent to try to head off problems in Galatia. They would have carried a message from Paul encouraging the Galatians to return to his teaching. If so, they were evidently unsuccessful. We might expect Paul to refer to such a scenario only obliquely, as is the case in Galatians.

In describing the change in the Galatians' attitude, Paul is effectively appealing to the cultural value of honorably consistent behavior. To waver in behavior without good cause was a characteristic of the "flatterer" (see on 2:11–14), the false friend. The supposed reason that Paul ascribes to their change, that he told the truth to them, strengthens this picture, because telling the truth to someone was a key characteristic of a friend (see, e.g., Cicero, *Amic.* 44: "Dare to give advice with all frankness"; trans. in Betz 1979, 232). The Galatians should be ashamed of their inconsistency. Paul also seeks to reawaken their friendly feelings toward him by reminding them of their past friendship.

Contrast between the Aims of Paul's Opponents and His Own (4:17–20)

4:17–18. They are zealous for you, not in a good way. Instead, they want to exclude you, so that you will be zealous for them. It is good for someone to be zealous for you on behalf of what is good, always, and not just when I am with you. *Zēloō* is difficult to translate. It has a range from the negative "be jealous," "envy" (e.g., Acts 7:9, the patriarchs envying Joseph; and 1 Cor. 13:4, love *ou zēloi*, "does not envy"), through to positive, "be concerned about," "be keen" (e.g., 1 Cor. 14:1, *zēloute . . . ta pneumatika*, "be eager for spiritual gifts"). Martinus de Boer reads it here as "to zealously court" (2011, 282). Even trickier is *zēlousthai*, which is probably to be read as a Greek passive (rather than a middle voice), with the Galatians as an implied object of the verb. This means reading the first clause in 3:18 as something like "It is good to be zealously courted." Turning it around by introducing an unnamed subject gives "It is good for someone to be zealous for you." Paul's key point, though, is that this should be *en kalō*, "in good," "on behalf of what is good." Hans Dieter Betz offers, "Good is always to be courted in a good way" (1979, 231). This is conceivable, although we might have expected a definite article with *kalon* (the first "good" in Betz's expression). Paul has probably been deliberate in switching from *kalos*, "in a good way" (4:17), to *en kalō* (4:18), meaning roughly "in something good." Thus Paul is asserting that his mission, his zeal for the Galatians, is on behalf of something good, and that his zeal always continues, even in his absence.

For John H. Elliott, Paul's characterizing of his opponents as those who *zēlousin*, "envy," brands them as possessors of the evil eye, especially as they do this *ou kalos*, "not in a good way" (2011). Although this would fit well with 3:1 (see above), Paul's positive use of *zēloō* in 4:18 raises questions over the idea. *Zēloō* in 4:17–18 as a whole looks more like a term about eager activity, with the question being whether the aims or methods of the activity are good or bad.

The opponents are eager on behalf of the Galatians, but not to direct them to anything good. Instead, "they want to exclude" the Galatians. "Exclude" is a surprising word here. Martinus de Boer (2011, 283) argues that Paul's opponents teach the Galatians that they are excluded from God's people unless they accept circumcision and law observance. This is possible, although it looks a rather unusual way for Paul to express it. However, de Boer adds the suggestion that "the pressure of the new preachers may have taken the form of literally excluding the Galatians from their table fellowship." This certainly makes Paul's sentence work smoothly. It would also link neatly with the Antioch incident. However it is rather speculative. More mundane but fairly straightforward is the view of F. F. Bruce and Richard Longenecker that the opponents are excluding the Galatians "from Paul's leadership and fellowship," which, in Paul's view, is tantamount to exclusion from Christ (R. Longenecker 1990, 194; Bruce 1982, 211). This is maybe the most likely reading, although it still assumes an unstated "from us" after "exclude you."

In 4:18, Paul says that he is happy about eagerness but is concerned about its direction. He again implicitly reminds them of his time with them, evoking the eagerness for the gospel that they showed then.

4:19–20. My children, for whom I am again in pains of childbirth until Christ is formed in you, I wish that I could be with you now and change my tone, for I am in despair about you. Paul's mention, in 4:18, of being with the Galatians triggers an exclamation that Paul would love to be with the Galatians. The very fact of expressing this was, like truth-telling, a standard characteristic of friendship: friends desire to be together (Betz 1979, 232). In fact, it could be that a long absence of Paul from Galatia is actually a key underlying issue in the letter. The Galatians may well have felt that Paul was neglecting them, in favor of big crowds in cities such as Ephesus. In such circumstances it is rather natural to listen attentively to the next religious teachers who actually come and spend time with the house churches. If the scenario suggested above is correct, of a prior delegation from Paul having gone to Galatia to try to argue the Christians out of giving allegiance to these other teachers, who perhaps were still present, we can easily imagine the Galatians being further annoyed that, despite this crisis in their allegiance to Paul, he still did not come to talk to them himself.

Paul is still not coming to them. Instead he sends this letter. However, he does express his desire to be with them and his overwhelming concern on their behalf. It is unclear how far we should take the childbirth imagery here. As Conrad Gempf argues, Paul's general emphasis in using childbirth imagery is on the pain involved (1994). This is true here too. Paul's pain is intensified by the "again." Paul has given birth to them once. He should not need to go through these same pains again. Susan Eastman (2007, 97) argues that pains were, specifically, the effects of persecution suffered during his preaching in Galatia. This may be correct. However, Paul uses various metaphors of struggle in many texts (e.g., Gal. 4:11). This should make us cautious about tying the use of pain in Paul's metaphor in 4:19 to experience of actual pain. Less likely than Eastman's idea is Beverly Roberts Gaventa's argument that the labor pains in 4:19 are, in terms of what is most significant about them, "not the birth pangs of an individual apostle, but the birth pangs of the cosmos itself" (2007, 37). Gaventa is right that birth pangs are used in some texts about God's intervention in the world (e.g., Isa. 13:6–8). However, the metaphor is used in other contexts too. For instance, in Mic. 4:10 (Gaventa 2007, 33) the birth pangs in the oracle relate to the fall of Jerusalem to the Babylonians. God's redemption of Jerusalem is a later event, referred to at the very end of Mic. 4:10. Rather than evoking apocalyptic ideas, Paul appears much more likely to be using the metaphor of labor pains because of its inherent structure, of acute pain involved with bringing new life.

In contrast to the "not good" aims of his opponents, Paul's aim is clearly to the benefit of the Galatians, namely, that Christ would be "formed in" them (4:19). Paul's program is clearly what the Galatians should opt for. Furthermore, not only is it clearly beneficial; in itself it also addresses the matters at issue in Galatians. The key to the new existence is being in Christ, and Christ being in the Christian. In 4:19 this is not a static condition but a form of development: Christ is being progressively formed in the Christian. The internal dynamic (Hooker 1990, 7), rather than just an external pattern to imitate, brings about the lived content of the new existence. It is the same as the operation of the Spirit (of Christ, 4:6) in the Christian, the effects of which will be spelled out in 5:22–23. This process, not the law observance called for by the opponents, is the way to the life that is "good."

Paul not only wishes to be with the Galatians. He also desires to be with them and able to speak in a different tone from the often-stern rebuke of this letter. The apostle wants to be there, reconciled with them. Paul may not be present, but he is cut to the heart, in despair.

Theological Issues

Imitation and Uniformity

"Anyone is welcome to join, as long as they then become like us." We noted above (see on 3:28) Joseph Marchal's (2012, 222–23) juxtaposition of 4:12 with 3:28 to point out that Paul's call to imitate him puts a limit on the extent to which he can be seen as sustaining diversity. How uniform a life is implied by imitating Paul?

Paul somewhat deconstructs his call to imitate him by saying that he is like the Galatians. As discussed above, that suggests focusing on Paul's gentile-like behavior. The Galatians should imitate his stance toward Jewish law. However, Phil. 3:17, "Be imitators together of me," shows that Paul can see himself as a model in quite a broad way. Philip Esler puts this in terms of social psychology. Writing on Romans, Esler argues, "Paul needed to demonstrate that he was representative of the shared social identity and consensual position of the group; in short that he was an ingroup exemplar, . . . an actual person who embodies the identity of a group" (2003, 223). In Romans, Paul does not call directly for imitation of him but, as Esler argues, he does present himself as exemplifying key values of the group. In Galatians, he has done this extensively before reaching the call of 4:12. Galatians is a polemical letter. The nature of the values of the group is being contested. In much of 1:1–4:11, Paul reminds the Galatians of his role as exemplar for a group with particular values. By calling for imitation of himself in 4:12, Paul is effectively calling them back to share in those values. That reminder is then reinforced by retelling the story of their initial encounter with him.

In the context of the polemic of Galatians, the content of imitating Paul will be the readoption or maintenance of the values of which Paul is exemplar. Paradoxically, this does include providing a welcome to socially different people, without requiring them, in overall terms, to become the same as the rest of the people in the group.

Galatians 4:21–5:13a

Instructions with Argument 2:
"Do Not Be Subject Again to . . . Slavery"

Introductory Matters

In 4:21, Paul returns to the theme of 4:1–11, calling the Galatians to stay clear of bondage. He emphasizes the Galatians' inheritance of freedom in an extended passage that treats the story of Hagar and Sarah as an allegory of current circumstances (4:21–31). Among the surprising elements of this is an application of the story to persecution (4:29–30). Paul issues a clear call to stand firm in freedom (5:1). He then applies this specifically to the way of circumcision that some Galatians appear to be considering. Paul contrasts this way with Christian life and hope (5:2–6), and contrasts himself with his opponents, whom he condemns vituperatively because the Galatians were called to freedom, not to the bondage that the opponents would bring about (5:7–13a).

Readers will notice that we are taking 5:13a with 5:12, rather than using it to begin the next section, as is conventional. Richard N. Longenecker argues that in Gal. 5, verse 13a, "For you were called to freedom, brothers and sisters," is "reintroducing the theme of freedom that was declared in v 1a and is now being refocused after the digressional remarks of vv 7–12" (1990, 239). This is quite possible. However, 5:13a actually looks more like a bridging text. As well as setting up the topic for the contrasting tack that is taken in 5:13b, it works very well as an explanation for the depth of Paul's anger expressed in 5:12 (see below). Hence 5:13a can be seen as forming an inclusio with 5:1. In this view, *adelphoi* ("brothers and sisters") in 5:13a concludes this section of the letter (cf. 5:31), and *monon* ("only") in 5:13b introduces the next section (cf. *monon* in Phil. 1:27), albeit with a tight link to the preceding clause, which acts as a bridge, as noted above. Dividing the sections after 5:13a provides the best topical coherence and makes the most natural sense of the *gar* ("for") in 5:13a, which suggests a logical link backward from the verse.

Tracing the Train of Thought

Allegory of Freedom and Call to Stand Firm in It (4:21–5:1)

4:21. Tell me, you who want to be under law, do you not listen to the law? Paul explicitly uses the rhetorical technique that he has persistently turned to since 2:16, using the law, meaning the text of Scripture, against arguments calling for gentile allegiance to the law, meaning the commands of Scripture. As in 4:5, the use of "under" with law probably carries, in itself, a connotation of subjection to a form of slavery.

4:22–31. For it is written that Abraham had two sons, one by the slave girl and one by the free woman. But the one by the slave girl was born according to flesh, whereas the one by the free woman was born through promise. These things are being said allegorically, for the two women are two covenants. One is from Mount Sinai, born for slavery. This is Hagar. Hagar is Mount Sinai in Arabia. She represents the present Jerusalem, for she is in slavery, together with her children. But the Jerusalem above is free. She is our mother, for it is written,

> Rejoice, barren woman who has
>   not given birth!
> Break forth and shout, you who
>   have not had birth pains!
> For many are the children of the
>   deserted woman,
> more than those of the woman
>   who has a husband.

You, brothers and sisters, like Isaac are children of a promise, but just as then, the one born according to flesh used to persecute the one born according to Spirit, so

---

Galatians 4:21–5:13a in the Rhetorical Flow

Letter opening (1:1–10)

Letter body (1:11–6:10)

Narrative 1: Of a gospel revealed by God, not people (1:11–24)

Narrative 2: Of a gospel affirmed by unity at Jerusalem (2:1–10)

Narrative 3: Of a gospel betrayed by division at Antioch (2:11–21)

Argument 1: For blessing in Christ through trust (3:1–14)

Argument 2: For unity in Christ (3:15–29)

Argument 3: Against returning to slavery (4:1–11)

Instructions with argument 1: "Be like me" (4:12–20)

▶ Instructions with argument 2: "Do not be subject again to . . . slavery" (4:21–5:13a)

  Allegory of freedom and call to stand firm in it (4:21–5:1)

  Law and the danger of falling from grace (5:2–6)

  "The one harassing you will bear the judgment" (5:7–13a)

also now. But what does the Scripture say? "Cast out the slave girl and her son, for the son of the slave girl shall certainly not inherit with the son of the free woman." Therefore, brothers and sisters, we are not children of the slave girl but of the free woman.

Let us try to follow the twists and turns of Paul's surprising argument here. Galatians 4:22 is straightforward. Paul narrows down the scriptural list of sons of Abraham (see Gen. 25:1–6) to the two to whom the Genesis account gives its major attention. Isaac is mentioned in 4:28, but Ishmael is never named. Evoking Ishmael's Arabic descendants would clearly complicate Paul's linking of him with Jerusalem. Yet Paul does not avoid the topic entirely. In 4:25, Hagar can represent Mount Sinai because Sinai is described as being in Arabia. The two mothers in 4:22 are described as *paidiskē* and *eleuthera*. *Eleuthera* is the feminine noun form of *eleutheros*, "free": hence the translation "free woman." *Paidiskē* is the feminine of *pais* ("boy" or "slave boy"), hence "slave girl." However, there is no deliberate contrast between Hagar as immature and Sarah as mature. Indeed Sarah, like Ishmael, is not named. None of her actions or qualities are discussed except that she was free. The basic contrast maintained throughout Paul's argument is between the slave and free status of the two mothers (4:22, 23, 24, 25, 26, 30, 31).

In 4:23 a second element is added to the contrast. The slave girl's child is born *kata sarka*, "according to flesh." The free woman's child is *di' epangelias*, "through promise." So far in the letter, *sarx* ("flesh") has generally been a fairly neutral term, denoting humans and their mortal bodies (1:16; 2:16, 20; 4:13, 14). The only clearly loaded use has been 3:3, where Paul asks, "Are you so foolish that, having begun in the Spirit, you are now ending in the flesh?" The two modes of birth are presented as giving the children characteristics of those modes. The children of one mode are in the "flesh" category, the category into which 3:3 sees the Galatians' recent actions leading them. The others are "children of a promise," as Paul points out in 4:28. That puts these children into the categories already linked with "promise" in Galatians, as recipients of the Spirit (3:14) and heirs through participation in Christ as the one seed of Abraham (3:16, 17, 18, 22, 29).

Martinus de Boer (2011, 294) is probably correct in translating the Greek *estin allēgoroumena* (4:24) as present continuous action, "are being said allegorically." J. B. Lightfoot cites Josephus (*Ant.* proem 4) for this usage. However, as Lightfoot (1890, 180n24) shows, the verb could also be read as "are being interpreted allegorically" (citing Philo, *Contempl.* 3.11 [see 3.28–29; 10.78]). In fact, de Boer is in substance using the second sense of the verb because he sees Paul as the one "saying": "These things are [now] being said [i.e., interpreted] allegorically [by me]" (2011, 295). However, J. Louis Martyn is probably stronger in thinking that Paul sees this allegorical sense as inherent in the Genesis text: "For Paul, as for Philo, the two women in the Genesis story point beyond themselves" (1997a, 436; citing Philo, *Post.* 130, etc., on the two as representing differing human qualities). The logic of Paul's argument, from the point in 4:21 where he calls the Galatians to listen to the text, requires him to see Genesis as saying these things allegorically. He is not claiming a specific divine revelation for an idiosyncratic reading of the text. Paul expects that the Galatians, reading Genesis with Christian eyes, will see it this way too.

The women "are two covenants" (4:24). Paul argues that, in reading about Hagar, Sarah, and their offspring, Christians should be hearing the text as a narrative about the Sinai covenant (4:24) and the . . . —well, his sentence gets rather carried away, and we never get a second covenant explicitly described, although he does say quite a lot relating to it. To think about Sinai, the Galatians should think about Hagar. They should think of this as a covenant "born for slavery." Paul backs this point up with the geographical point mentioned above: Sinai is "in Arabia." To feel the force of this argument, the hearers need some unstated knowledge, namely, that Hagar was the ancestor of the peoples of Arabia (Gen. 25:12–18). Even without that knowledge, the hearers would realize that Paul is setting up a counterintuitive link based on the fact that Sinai is not in Israel. Israel received its law in a place that was outside the holy territory.

Having reached Sinai, we might have expected Paul to repeat the moves of 3:19–24, saying that the law came from Sinai so, like Hagar, it represents slavery. Instead, Jerusalem appears: in fact, two Jerusalems appear! The "present Jerusalem . . . is in slavery, together with her children" (4:25). In contrast, "the Jerusalem above is free" (4:26). Why Jerusalem? Jerusalem has appeared several times already. Curiously, he earlier uses a different Greek word, *Hierosolyma* (1:17, 18; 2:1) rather than *Ierousalēm* (4:25, 26). *Ierousalēm* is the form used in Scripture. *Hierosolyma* is frequent in Greek authors but in the LXX appears only in texts from the Apocrypha. Apart from Gal. 1:17–2:1, Paul always uses the biblical form (Rom. 15:19, 25, 31; 1 Cor. 16:3), and it is natural that he uses that form in the context of 4:25–26. The narrative in Gal. 1–2—about Paul not going to Jerusalem, then going, and what happens there—has been viewed by many scholars as indicating that his opponents had links with Jerusalem and could be promoting forms of Christian practice in line with those of the Jerusalem Christians (Elmer 2009). Paul certainly sees the "false brothers" at Jerusalem as representing the same teaching as his opponents. If the opponents' link with Jerusalem is indeed the reason for the appearance of Jerusalem in 4:25, that has a very strange effect on the rhetoric of these verses: it means that Jerusalem is discussed here because it is the center of a particular type of Christian practice, rather than because it is the Judean capital and the location of the temple.

However, it does not seem possible that Paul would use the term "the present Jerusalem" actually to denote the Christian community in the city (contra de Boer 2011, 300). "The present Jerusalem" must refer to the city itself, probably with particular reference to its identity as the Jewish center for festivals and other temple rituals. If there is an implication about the place of Jerusalem in the Jesus movement, it must be derivative from this main sense. Paul asserts that Jerusalem "is in slavery" (4:25). That could be taken politically, with Jerusalem being under Roman control. Such terminology could be used in rhetoric about Roman rule of provinces (e.g., Galgacus's speech, according to Tacitus, *Agr.* 30). It could also be seen as particularly fitting for rhetoric by a Jewish writer because Jewish texts asserted the authority of God and Israel (e.g., the rhetoric of the Sicarii, according to Josephus, *J.W.* 3.8.1). Justin K. Hardin sees 4:3 as referring to being slaves to pagan powers and gods, in fulfillment of the curse of Deut. 28:58–68 (2008, 137). This could also work for 4:25. An alternative referent for the "slavery" of 4:25 could, of course, be the slavery that Paul has been discussing as being involved in law observance (Dunn 1993, 253). If so, Paul's introduction of Jerusalem into the argument would not seem very far-reaching. It could have some secondary connotation of questioning the geographical focus that his opponents probably had. Even Jerusalem was in slavery. God had given revelations in or near Damascus (Gal. 1:16–17; cf. Acts 9:3; 22:6)—and indeed in Arabia (Gal. 1:17). How could Paul's opponents maintain the fixation that everything had to be subject to Jerusalem and the authorities there, whether Christian or non-Christian? "The present Jerusalem" could also appear here mainly because Paul wishes to bring in his contrasting entity, "the Jerusalem above."

This idea is reminiscent of the cosmology of Phil. 3:20, "our *politeuma* [community? commonwealth?] is in the heavens." The struggling Philippians (1:27–30) are directed toward their belonging to an entity whose location gives a status and power above (lit.) those of communities on earth. Membership can only depend on trust (*pistis*), for the place is currently unseen. So too for "the Jerusalem above," although what is distinctive about this expression is its appropriating the idea of the Jewish central place (cf. the temple in the Letter to the Hebrews). In the context of Galatians, a key effect of this appropriation is that, once again, it encourages the hearers to ignore the calls for circumcision, viewed as a means of joining the ethnic community focused on Jerusalem. For Paul, that movement would be in a mistaken direction, to an earthly entity that is enslaved. The Galatian Christians already belong to the free Jerusalem, which is not in Judea but in heaven.

Then Paul bursts out in a scriptural song, of the triumph of the barren woman (Gal. 4:27), cited at length from Isa. 54:1. The extent of the space given to this makes it reasonable that scholars such as Susan Eastman and Matthew Harmon (see below) have argued that this is climactic in the letter. The passage is very surprising. In the Isaianic context, it follows the song of the Suffering Servant (52:13–53:12) and is the start of a passage about the redemption of Israel, with the text often focusing on Jerusalem. Israel in exile or the consequently empty Jerusalem is portrayed as a woman who has been abandoned but will now have a large family. This gives many possible links to

Galatians, but it is not clear that Paul uses the text in this way. In the context of Gal. 4:21–31, the text looks like a triumph song for the barren Sarah, outmatching the fertile Hagar. More immediately it appears to be a triumph song for the heavenly Jerusalem, outmatching the earthly one. It is hard to know how far to press the imagery. In general terms it could fit Paul's argument if it is asserting that the Jerusalem above, despite having none of the institutions and power of the earthly Jerusalem, is producing new members and even heading toward outnumbering those focused on the earthly Jerusalem. The song of 4:27 probably also introduces a fresh nuance into the use of "promise" in describing Isaac's birth in 4:28. Barren Sarah could not produce children by natural means. She needed a dramatic divine intervention. This intervention is encapsulated in God's promises to Abraham and Sarah for the birth of Isaac, against all natural expectation (cf. Rom. 4:13–25).

Susan Eastman builds on Richard B. Hays's (2000, 304) work by exploring Gal. 4:27 in relationship to the context of Isa. 54:1 as a key text about Israel's redemption. She argues that the implicit link to Sarah adds to the idea of the gentile Galatians as a sign of fulfillment of God's promise to Abraham and Sarah. Eastman also proposes that the abundance despite barrenness differentiates Paul's apocalyptic gospel (following Martyn [see introduction]) from one "according to flesh," and that Paul's link between Isa. 54:1 and the heavenly Jerusalem conveys a glorious picture of the Christians' future (Eastman 2007, 127–55). Matthew Harmon (2010, 123–203) sees Gal. 4:27 as one end of an Isaianic argument running from Gal. 3:1 to 5:1, drawing on a sequence of passages from Isa. 51:2 ("Look to Abraham your father") to 54:1. The ends of Harmon's Isaiah range work well in relation to Galatians. Whether Isa. 53 has a significant place in the soteriology of Gal. 3 (esp. 3:13; Harmon 2010, 145–46) is more open to question.

In Gal. 4:29 the allegory enters a dark phase: "Just as then, the one born according to flesh used to persecute the one who was according to Spirit, so also now." Paul has undergone what he sees as persecution from non-Christian Jews (esp. 2 Cor. 11:24). Acts and John portray this as a wider experience of first-generation Christians (e.g., Acts 6–7; John 9). If 1 Thess. 2:14–16 is by Paul, he too sees Christians in Judea as undergoing such persecution. However, that text is also interesting because it mentions the gentile Thessalonian Christians as having undergone persecution from fellow gentiles ("their own fellow-tribespeople," 1 Thess. 2:14) rather than from Jews. What from Paul's perspective looked like persecution of Christian Jews by non-Christian Jews would presumably have looked from the other side like the exercise of community discipline, as is most obvious in Paul's statement in 2 Cor. 11:24 about having received what was an exact-count formal synagogue punishment.

To what does the persecution idea refer? The puzzle is deepened by the next scriptural quotation. This quotes Sarah's words in calling for the expulsion of Hagar: "Cast out the slave girl and her son, for the son of the slave girl shall certainly not inherit with the son of the free woman" (Gal. 4:30). This is Gen. 21:10 LXX, amended by changing a final "my son" to "the son of the free woman," which has the effect of taking it out of Sarah's voice and making it sound more like a divine proclamation.

For Susan Elliott, the references in 4:21–31 to a mountain, mothers, and slavery, together with various details of the text and its relationship to the issue of circumcision, lead her to read it in relation to the Anatolian Mountain Mother cult. Then Gal. 4:30 becomes the climax, in which "Paul enjoins the audience to rid themselves . . . of the Mother of the Gods and her 'son' Attis and his imitators, whether as *galli* or as advocates of circumcision" (2003, 288). Strengths of her suggestion are in accounting for various unexpected features of 4:21–31, and doing so in relation to local context. Weaknesses are in introducing local cults as a factor not directly signaled by Paul, and in reading the circumcision issue indirectly via the castrated cult attendants, the *galli*. Other scholars, such as Martinus de Boer, also take 4:30 as a call for the Galatians to throw out Paul's opponents but do so without drawing on the Anatolian context (2011, 307).

In fact, we ought to consider 4:30 with the following verse, to see how Paul applies some or all of the preceding text. "Therefore, brothers and sisters, we are not children of the slave girl but of the free woman" (4:31). What is noticeable here is that Paul does not give an application of the "cast out" instruction in the text (Eastman 2007, 132). Instead, what Paul does in 4:31 is to restate the conclusion about Christian identity that has been implied in 4:26, 28. Christians are not of the slave girl but of the free woman. They are of the Jerusalem above, not the present Jerusalem. They are not of the Sinai covenant. How does the persecution point of 4:29–30 come into this? It looks as though Paul is using it as evidence of who are heirs and who are not heirs: the fact that non-Christian Jews have persecuted Christian Jews such as Paul (as the Galatians well know) puts them into the category of the son of Hagar, who taunted Isaac and was excluded from the inheritance. It is therefore foolish for the Galatians to put themselves under Jewish law (4:21), because not only is that putting themselves into the family of slavery, but it also excludes them from the inheritance of Abraham that they have been promised in Christ (3:29).

5:1. For freedom Christ has set us free. Stand firm then and do not be subject again to a yoke of slavery. The same grammatical move happens here as at 4:12. Paul uses anacolouthon, the unusual absence of a linking word, to bring an imperative in with something of a punch. This is the climax of the slavery/freedom theme that has been running vigorously since 3:22 (following its introduction in 2:4–5 and its link to the cross in the redemption language of 3:13). Christ did not set people free in order for them to look around, feel the air to be a bit chilly, and retreat back into slavery. Freedom is difficult, full of the uncertainty brought about by having choices. It is easy to want to hand over responsibility to other people, to law codes, to religious authorities. But Christ has freed people for freedom. To retreat is to throw his work back at him.

Law and the Danger of Falling from Grace (5:2–6)

5:2–4. Look, I Paul say to you that, if you get circumcised, Christ will be of no use to you. I testify again to every man who gets circumcised that he is under obligation to do the whole law. You were alienated from Christ, those of you who are being considered righteous by means of law. You fell away from grace. Again, Paul uses a very emphatic construction, this time to be absolutely clear about what the Galatians should not do: get circumcised. Circumcision does not, in itself, make one Jewish. Many people were and are circumcised for many reasons. However, in this case it is clear that the issue is about gentile men undergoing this operation because it is part of Jewish law. What is not clear is how much of the rest of Jewish law these Galatians have been planning to observe. The fact that Paul's rhetoric so far in the letter has covered Jewish law in general rather than circumcision in particular would make us think that obedience to the law as a whole was in view among the Galatians. However, now Paul rather surprisingly points out that this would be required (5:3), as though these Galatians had been planning only to be circumcised. It would be helpful if Paul had explained in 5:3 what he had in mind that was beyond circumcision (and calendrical observance). Many points spring to mind that would be very difficult for gentiles (or most Diaspora Jews) to observe: for instance the requirement of regular attendance at Jerusalem festivals (Exod. 23:14–19a). Other points, such as Jubilee laws (Lev. 25), would be impossible in a gentile context. The force of Paul's rhetoric in 5:3 could be to say, "You don't understand how much you are taking on here, or the incredible difficulty of going down the road you have started on."

Paul warns the Galatians in the strongest terms of the consequences of circumcision: "Christ will be of no use to you" (5:2); "You were alienated from Christ"; "You fell away from grace" (5:4). Incidentally, there is a curious mixture of verb tenses here: future in 5:2, with aorist in 5:4. Current linguistic scholarship makes clear that we cannot push the Greek aorist tense in directions that many scholars (and preachers) have done in the past. We cannot infer from the aorists in 5:4 that this group of people underwent an event at a specific point in the past (relative to the date of the letter) in which they were suddenly alienated from Christ and fell from grace. The aorist is the default tense in Greek and does not in itself carry emphatic information of the kind above. However, the present tense in 5:4 ("are being considered righteous by means of law") is combined with the aorists there; this pair is set in contrast with the combination of conditional clause in 5:2 ("if you get circumcised") with the future tense ("Christ will be of no use"). Thus the rhetoric probably does give us a good clue about Paul's view of where some Galatians have arrived in terms of acting on his opponents' teaching. Probably few or none of the Galatian men have actually undergone circumcision, but some of the Galatians (men or women) have begun some actions that reflect the idea of Jewish law being a source of righteousness. This last point fits with our reading of 4:10 as relating to Jewish calendrical observances that some Galatians were currently undertaking.

Coming back to Paul's threats themselves, to say that "Christ will be of no use to you" (5:2) could principally relate to 5:1. Christ has freed the Galatians. Circumcision means giving up that freedom, taking on a new "yoke of slavery." However, the implications of what Paul warns would be more far-reaching than just about slavery. As he implies in 5:4, without Christ the Galatians give up on their "hope of righteousness" (5:5). The fact that this is described as "eagerly awaited" implies that it includes concepts of eschatological reward (although see "Theological Issues"), of eschatological salvation (cf. 6:8). Contrary to the impression given by some Christian theological systems, Paul clearly thinks that the Galatians are in danger of losing a salvation that they have been given.

The seriousness of this is reinforced by the language of 5:4. Those "being considered righteous by means of law" (a rather woodenly literal rendering: it is probably reasonable to follow de Boer in reading you who "are being" as, in effect, you who "are seeking to be"; 2011, 314) *katērgēthēte apo Christou*, "were alienated from Christ." The phrase *katargeomai apo* occurs three times in the NT. The other two are Rom. 7:2, 6. A wife is "released from" the law about husbands if her husband dies. This is then used as an analogy for the Christian being released from the law. However, the idea of the phrase is not about liberation but about the breaking of a link. It can therefore be used in the negative sense of Gal. 5:4, which describes separation from Christ. This is the opposite process from the participation in Christ, the union with Christ that is central to salvation in Galatians. Similarly, falling "away from grace" (5:4) reverses the process of salvation. In Galatians, grace has been associated with God's calling the gentile Galatians (1:6). In turning to the law for righteousness, the Galatians abandon the terms on which they were called (see also on 2:21).

5:5–6. For we, by the Spirit, by trust, eagerly await the hope of righteousness. For in Christ Jesus neither circumcision matters nor uncircumcision, but trust, working through love. The role of trust in 5:5 is reminiscent of Heb. 11:1: "the assurance of things hoped for, the conviction of things not seen" (NRSV). In Gal. 5:5–6, "trust" involves acting today, being convinced of hope of righteousness coming tomorrow. Such a life is enabled by the Spirit. This focus on the future is rather a surprise, given the way righteousness and trust have been discussed earlier in the letter. The impression has been that, when Christ arrived, people who had trust in him were now considered righteous, which involved them becoming one in Christ, becoming children of Abraham, and receiving the Spirit. However, the reality always was that these things are matters of trust. Being "in Christ" or "a son of Abraham" or "being considered righteous" are not directly visible. The visible things are "miracles" worked among the Galatians (3:5) and, as 5:6 emphasizes, the life of love that trust creates. Even these would be open to question and interpretation, especially as to whether they are really manifestations of God's Spirit. In fact, "being considered righteous" as such is never described as a past event in Galatians (contrast Rom. 5:1). It is a present-tense process (2:16a, 17; 3:8, 11; cf. 5:4) or a purpose (2:16b; 3:24) or something in the future (2:16c). However, Paul does see it as having effects already, in being "in Christ," "a son of Abraham," and experiencing "the Spirit."

Galatians never explicitly shows us what is righteous, in an ethical sense, about Paul's use of righteousness language. He does not, for instance, give a point of reference for this terminology by using it to describe Christ's actions (contrast Rom. 5:18) or God's character (contrast Rom. 3:5). Neither is this language linked to the ethical section at the end of Galatians, nor to the last judgment (contrast Rom. 2:13–16). The only event that Paul links to this language is that of Gen. 15:6, in which Abraham trusts God's promise that he will have children. We do not even see a reference to the sacrifice of Isaac: contrast the interpretation of Gen. 15:6 in James 2:21–24. Abraham trusts. God "reckons" this as righteousness. In the same way, in Galatians, Christ arrives; Jews such as Peter and Paul trust in Christ (2:16); gentiles such as the Galatians trust in Christ (3:2–9, 14, 22–29); God reckons these people as righteous on the basis of their trust (3:8). Paul has divided the world into two groups, "the righteous" and the rest. He sees membership among "the righteous" as belonging to "those who are of trust" (3:7, 9), "those who trust" (3:22). Final, definitive, public knowledge of who has this "righteousness" remains in the future (5:5). In somewhat circular fashion, Paul sees current awareness of this righteous status as being a matter of trust: trust in Christ brings righteousness; trust in the future confirmation of that righteousness enables the Christian to live as having that status in the present.

"Righteousness" is not a term tightly defined in Galatians. Its specific sense is hard to be clear about. By contrast, being "in Christ" is very well defined in terms of its ethical implications. Here in 5:6 we see that definition again, essentially in the same terms as 3:28–29: being in Christ removes the division between Jew and gentile. "Neither circumcision matters, nor uncircumcision." Being in Christ means unity across that division. So Peter's actions at Antioch were wrong, actions tantamount to requiring gentiles to "Judaize" (2:14): the very thing that Paul's opponents are calling for in Galatia.

The positive assertion at the end of 5:6 backs this up. Not only is the Jew-gentile division done away with, but what comes in instead is love. In the same way that 1 Cor. 13, on love, reinforces the call to unity in 1 Cor. 12, in Galatians too the ethics of love reinforce the ending of division. *Pistis* is absolutely not to be the new shibboleth, the list of beliefs guaranteeing the distinctiveness of our group over against others. *Pistis* is the trust in Christ that works itself out in active love.

On the subject of ways in which many churches have historically lost sight of Paul here, the most dreadful of all is the church's gross historical neglect of the second half of Paul's "neither . . . nor" pair: "nor uncircumcision." The church has constantly forgotten that Paul's vision is of gentiles as gentiles and Jews as Jews, united in allegiance to Christ. Churches have repeatedly demanded that Jews cease Jewish practice if they are to be seen as acknowledging Christ: the church's aim usually is to eliminate distinctively Jewish identity. Ironically, the church has typically acted in a way similar to Paul's opponents, seeking to erase difference by merging one community into the other. All that differs is the direction in which the church has sought to do it.

"The One Harassing You Will Bear the Judgment" (5:7–13a)

5:7–13a. You were running well. Who cut in on you to stop you from obeying the truth? This persuasion does not come from the one who called you. "A little yeast leavens the whole lump." I am persuaded about you, in the Lord, that you will not think otherwise at all. The one harassing you will bear the judgment, whoever he may be. But I, brothers and sisters, if I am still preaching circumcision, why am I still persecuted? In that case the offense of the cross would be done away with. They ought to castrate themselves, those who are stirring you up, for you were called to freedom, brothers and sisters. Paul's rather heroic athletic imagery elsewhere in his letters (e.g., Phil. 3:12–14) is better known than this depiction of more dubious athletic goings-on. Yesterday (I am writing this section during the 2012 Olympics) a cyclist in the head-to-head sprint competition in the velodrome got her front wheel slightly ahead of her opponent, then cut into the sprinting lane, where her opponent was riding but was now blocked. The balked rider raised her hand in protest (surprisingly, the front rider was not disqualified). So too for the Galatians. According to Paul, this incursion had particularly blocked them from "paying attention to" or "obeying [*peithesthai*] the truth" (5:7). As Paul recently mentioned, he told them truth that made them regard him as an enemy (4:16). "The truth of the gospel" is what was at stake over Titus and circumcision (a truth remaining "for you," 2:5) and was what Peter betrayed at Antioch (2:14). In referring to "the truth," Paul ties the effect of the Galatians being blocked to the central issues of the letter.

It is self-evident that "persuasion" preventing people from obeying the truth must be bad, hence not from a good source, certainly not from the source of their original calling (5:8; cf. 1:6). Since it would not seem rhetorically very worthwhile for Paul to be talking about himself here as "the one who called you," the reference is probably to God. Again, the appeal is effectively to the value that the Galatians must inevitably put on the message that first brought them to trust in Christ. Anything contradicting that message would clearly be problematic for them, once they realized that that was what had happened.

"A little yeast leavens the whole lump" (5:9). Since Paul elsewhere likens the house churches to communities celebrating Passover (1 Cor. 5:7–8), it is conceivable that he could be thinking in those terms here too, with the opponents as the problematic leaven in the house that should be free of it. However, the text sounds more like a general warning that the opponents' teaching could affect every element of the house churches. Incidentally, this could also suggest that the opponents' current influence is far less than is implied by the letter's repeated address as if to people who have already all abandoned Paul. In fact, Paul now expresses his confidence, rooted in Christ as Lord, that the Galatians will actually stick with the truth of the gospel (5:10).

Paul's references to his opponents in this passage suggest that he does not know a great deal about them: probably not who, specifically, they are. Although we might allow for the "Who?" in 5:7 to be a rhetorical device to belittle an opponent whose name he well knew, and although we could say the same about "whoever he may be" (5:10), the two expressions together, alongside the indefiniteness of all the other references to the opponents, suggest that he really does not know them. In fact, the references in 5:7, 10 give the impression that there is only one of them. However, the description of the figure in 5:10 as *tarassōn hymas* ("harassing you") is the same as in the plural in 1:7. Paul also switches without comment to a plural expression: "Those who are stirring you up" (*hoi anastatountes hymas*) in 5:12. The singular terms in 5:7, 10 are probably just indefinite expressions covering any of the opponents.

In 5:10, the opponent "will bear the judgment." This appears somewhat out of the blue. However, the verse as a whole expresses Paul's confidence that the Galatians will stick with his views but that this happy outcome still does not excuse whoever has been stirring up discontent. God will deal with such people. "Whoever he may be" appears to have a connotation that, if Paul does know something about the opponents, it could be that one or more of them makes high claims about his status or connections in the Jesus movement. If so, these would presumably be connections to the Jerusalem church.

In between comments about his opponents, Paul makes a rather mystifying comment about himself. "But I, brothers and sisters, if I am still preaching circumcision, why am I still persecuted? In that case the offense of the cross would be done away with" (5:11). This appears to be a response to an accusation that Paul is preaching circumcision. It is unclear what this refers to. One possible explanation is linked to the accusation apparently behind 1:10, that Paul sought to please people. If he was "all things to all people" (1 Cor. 9:22), maybe he could be commending circumcision when preaching to Jews, seeking to please his audience, to try to win them over (for this and other possibilities, see R. Longenecker 1990, 232). A second possibility is that Paul's opponents did not see themselves (or present themselves) as opponents of Paul at all but said that what they were teaching was what Paul taught generally, as the next step for maturing Christians to take (see introduction). The second of these would be more relevant than the first, since "preaching circumcision" in this context presumably means preaching that gentiles should be circumcised. However, we would expect such a far-reaching scenario to have left more definite traces in Galatians.

Paul's response, on the other hand, is fairly clear, although surprising. We might have expected him to respond by pointing out that, with all he had already written in Galatians, it was obvious that he would not preach (gentile) circumcision. Instead, as he did in 4:29–31, he brings in the topic of persecution in order to use the fact of persecution as evidence in support of an assertion. The Galatians knew that Paul was persecuted: they should infer that he cannot be preaching a message acceptable to Jewish authorities. Preaching of gentile circumcision would remove the offensive element from the cross. Again, this is not what we would regard as the element of the cross most obviously offensive to Jews. We might think instead of the idea of the Messiah being crucified. However, Paul sees the key offense of the cross as being that it leads to preaching to gentiles without preaching circumcision. We can see how this indeed could be offensive to Jews if the preaching promised the gentiles blessing that would be thought specific to Israel, but did not require them to become part of the Jewish community.

Having promised (divine) judgment in 5:10, Paul descends to vituperation in 5:12. He takes their concern for circumcision and argues that in their case the cut should be taken further. This is rather reminiscent of his renaming possibly similar opponents as "the mutilation" in Phil. 3:2. Paul explains his anger by pointing out what a precious thing his opponents are undermining: "For you were called to freedom, brothers and sisters" (Gal. 5:13a). As J. B. Lightfoot writes, "This is the justification of the indignant scorn poured on their offense: 'They are defeating the very purpose of your calling: ye were called not for bondage, but for liberty'" (1890, 208).

Theological Issues

Living in Hope of Righteousness

What do you hope for? In many expressions of Christian theology, Paul's righteousness language becomes something of a metonym for eschatological reward: the emphasis is on the benefits that we would receive as a result of God considering us righteous. Texts relating to Israelite lawcourts do indeed demonstrate how righteousness language can be used to signal the giving of benefits to people through a favorable verdict (e.g., Ps. 82:3 [81:3 LXX]). However, it looks semantically very risky to promote exclusively the sense of reward over any ethical meaning in interpreting Paul's language of righteousness. This point is maybe most pressing here in Gal. 5:5: "We . . . eagerly await the hope of righteousness."

It is particularly risky because a hope for ethical righteousness is widely attested in the Greco-Roman world. Thus for Plato, virtue was a key aim (e.g., *Euthyd*. 278D.2–3). As in Christian belief, it was indeed tied in with hope for happiness, since he thought, as did others, that the good life was the happy life. However, virtue was pursued as a good thing in itself (Annas 1996, 1191). In the Sermon on the Mount, Jesus teaches the way of righteousness (Matt. 5:6, etc.). This is not just because being righteous gains reward (although there is reward, e.g., 5:6). Righteousness is clearly valued for its own sake. It brings glory to God (5:16) and represents a person's likeness to God (5:9, 45, 48). Paul would no doubt agree. We live in a hedonistic age (without the moral aspect that Epicurean hedonism had). *Pistis Christou* involves a reorientation of life that does not just mean trusting Christ to give us good things. It involves allegiance to Christ so that his aims become ours. Christ aims for righteousness among his followers. This should not plunge Christians into a mire of guilt and desperate moral effort. However, it should affect our ambition. Christians should have an eager hope for righteousness, including moral righteousness.

Galatians 5:13b–6:10

Instructions with Argument 3:
"Through Love Be Slaves to One Another"

Introductory Matters

Galatians 5:13–6:10 is often thought of as "the ethical section" of Galatians. It is indeed a piece of ethics. In it, Paul makes points that in effect, albeit unsystematically, communicate a theory of how to behave well. Among the key elements of the theory are that love fulfills the whole Jewish law (5:14); the person is a site of struggle between "spirit" and "flesh" (5:16–17); the person led by "spirit" is not subject to law (5:18); good qualities are produced by "the Spirit" and bad qualities are "works of the flesh" (5:19–23); Christians have put to death "the flesh," along with its "passions" and "desires" (5:24); life "by spirit" still requires a decision to "walk by spirit" (5:25). The mix between references to "spirit" as a component of the person and possible references to the divine Spirit make decisions on capitalization of the word significantly difficult.

The passage also includes what is popularly called ethics, instructions for behavior (5:13, 15, 16, 25–26; 6:1–6, 9–10). They are also implicit in the vice and virtue lists of 5:19–23. We will argue, below, that by far the strongest emphasis of these instructions is toward unity. This makes the behavioral instructions a significant part of the letter's overall drive toward unity. Alongside the ethics, the passage also includes a certain amount of argument, further strengthening the letter's earlier case that the Galatians already have a Spirit-led Christian life, which means that they should not accept the opponents' calls to make themselves subject to Jewish law. Arguments are advanced on

Galatians 5:13b–6:10 in the Rhetorical Flow

Letter opening (1:1–10)

Letter body (1:11–6:10)

  Narrative 1: Of a gospel revealed by God, not people (1:11–24)

  Narrative 2: Of a gospel affirmed by unity at Jerusalem (2:1–10)

  Narrative 3: Of a gospel betrayed by division at Antioch (2:11–21)

  Argument 1: For blessing in Christ through trust (3:1–14)

  Argument 2: For unity in Christ (3:15–29)

  Argument 3: Against returning to slavery (4:1–11)

  Instructions with argument 1: "Be like me" (4:12–20)

  Instructions with argument 2: "Do not be subject again to . . . slavery" (4:21–5:13a)

▶ Instructions with argument 3: "Through love be slaves to one another" (5:13b–6:10)

  Call to make freedom an opportunity not for the flesh but to love, which fulfills the law (5:13b–15)

  The effects of Spirit and flesh (5:16–26)

  Doing good (6:1–10)

love as fulfilling the law (5:14), on the struggle between spirit and flesh (5:16–17), and on Christians crucifying the flesh (5:24). Galatians 5:18–23 also mounts an argument that life by the Spirit does not require subjection to law. The ethics of 5:13–6:10 have their strongest focus on behavior conducive to unity, and the arguments of 5:13–6:10 support Spirit-led life without the need for law; these features offer a way of integrating 5:13–6:10 into the letter as a whole.

One popular alternative theory about 5:13–6:10 is that Paul is tackling a different issue from the rest of the letter. This is sometimes seen as "libertinism," espousing a morally anarchic life. It is an idea that might be imagined as behind problems tackled in 1 Corinthians. It could stem from people who have accepted Paul's message of freedom but taken it to extremes (e.g., Betz 1979, 273). One variant of this theory is that of Robert Jewett, who sees the Galatians as Spirit-inspired libertines yet at the same time drawn toward aspects of Jewish ceremonial law (2002, 345–47). A second theory is that of John M. G. Barclay, according to which Paul is not fighting libertinism but is helping tackle the Galatians' moral uncertainty, to which his opponents have offered an attractive solution in advocating a turn to the law. He also seeks to do so in a way that shows the sufficiency of his moral strategy (1988, 70–74, 217).

The textual point that these two theories fit better than does the one in this commentary is in 5:13b, where Paul specifies freedom as being the thing that should not become an "opportunity for the flesh." This makes it sound as though Paul's aim is to head off a conceivably problematic consequence of his own gospel. However, if we look at the overall intended effect of the rhetoric of 5:13–6:10, we can see that it drives the hearer further toward unity and life by the Spirit, and away from the need for dependence on Jewish law. That is, the rhetoric of 5:13–6:10 pushes in the same direction as the rhetoric of the rest of the letter. The argument of the whole letter works toward maintenance of freedom from law and toward unity. Galatians 5:13–6:10 does this along with the other parts of the letter. Moreover, the starting point for all of Paul's argument is effectively that the Galatians are currently free (although tending to slip from it), so it is consistent with the rest of the letter for Paul to use the Galatians' freedom as the starting point for the letter's ethics.

Two points in particular do distinguish 5:13–6:10 from the rest of the letter. This is the only place where Paul gives detailed positive instructions to the Galatians. Elsewhere, apart from the call to imitate Paul, the explicit or implicit instruction has been negative: do not follow the way that the opponents are calling you to! Now he tells them what they should actually do, with a particular focus on love, the key quality promoting unity. However, while doing this, he takes every opportunity to continue showing them why they should not submit themselves to the law. The second point is that there appears to be a problem in the Galatian house churches that only comes to shape in this passage: some sort of disunity and rivalry within or between house churches (5:15, 20–21, 26). Given that unity is a central rhetorical concern of the whole letter, this problem may be implicit throughout. It could have influenced Paul's decision to focus the circumcision issue onto the topic of unity. Divisions would also be an inevitable effect of a situation in which some Galatian house-church members began accepting the teaching of Paul's opponents. Apart from anything else, there must have been factions, divided by whether or not they accepted it. As we shall see, Paul also in effect argues that the move of some toward law observance is a move toward "the flesh," which is a move with a range of deleterious effects, especially in producing vices characteristic of disunity.

Tracing the Train of Thought

Call to Make Freedom an Opportunity Not for the Flesh but to Love, Which Fulfills the Law (5:13b–15)

5:13b. Only, do not make freedom an opportunity for the flesh, but through love be slaves to one another. On "flesh," see on 5:16 (below). Paul's language now takes a paradoxical twist that we also see from him repeatedly elsewhere. Having consumed a large amount of papyrus in defending the Christians' freedom, he now turns around and tells them to be slaves (cf., e.g., Rom. 6:15–23; 7:6; 12:11; 14:18). He writes, *douleuete allēlois*, "Be slaves to one another."

The first point to make is that, throughout the letter, Paul has a very demanding view of Christian discipleship. He exemplifies it in himself. His general pattern is of connection to the divine realm rather than "the flesh" (while still being in "the flesh"). This is seen, from Gal. 1:1 to 6:17, as a pattern of radical commitment and self-sacrifice. When he writes that "the world was crucified to me, and I to the world" (6:14), this is not a cheap, imaginary link to the death of Christ. It bears the weight of what the translator of Dietrich Bonhoeffer's *Nachfolge* calls "the cost of discipleship" (Bonhoeffer 1948 [German, 1937], trans. R. H. Fuller). For the house-church members too, participation in grace was a costly matter. These first-generation Christians were all, in one way or another, converts: people who had gone through a profound social change, continuing to live among people who would disapprove of that change. Some of us may read of Paul's gospel of freedom and unity, and imagine that this is ethically very easy. Paul has no such idea. The life of freedom in Christ is a life of obedience and self-sacrifice. Christ has indeed made the sacrifice that renders all sacrificial systems unnecessary. But in identifying with Christ's cross and resurrection, the Christian dies and rises to a life that is reoriented toward God. Galatians 5:13–14 shows that this also means a reorientation toward other people.

A second way into the issue of Paul's paradoxical writing is to consider it in practice in the house churches. All, whatever their place in the social hierarchy, are to act, through love, as slaves to one another. On the face of it, this is extreme social radicalism. The owner is to be slave to the slave. The husband is to be slave to the wife. The parent is to be slave to the child (more radical then than now!). But this is not slavery in the same sense that submission to the law would be. It is a social reorientation, effectively again breaking down the polarity between slave and free, as proclaimed in 3:28. Again as in 3:28, its essential effect is unity between the two groups. In 5:13 it is clear that the unity in question is essentially that of practical matters, such as cooperation and mutual support. It is mutual slavery through love. (On the complexities of what this might or might not mean in practice, see Oakes 2009, 98–126.)

A third point is that slavery to God, or to the good, had a long tradition in scriptural and philosophical writings, without it being seen as compromising the free, good life. Biblical examples abound, culminating in the Servant Songs of Isa. 40–55. Among philosophers, although Epictetus (and other Stoics) had been "set free by God" (*Disc.* 4.7.17, trans. Oldfather 1925), he submitted his will to God (4.7.20). Indeed Epictetus, like all the parts of the divine cosmos, is a servant of the whole (frg. 3 [in Stobaeus, *Flor.* 4.44, 66]). However, although Epictetus's idea fits Paul's general willingness to use slavery language, it does not parallel his talk of mutual slavery among Christians in Gal. 5:13. Stoics, drawing on their Cynic roots, would not approve of this language since submission to another person compromised the very independence of action that enabled one to serve God. This helps us clarify a key issue. Galatians is eloquent testimony to Paul's unwillingness to submit to other people in terms of their opinions or their actions if that could threaten the gospel. However, in the Thessalonian and Corinthian correspondence, we see his willingness to do manual labor in order to serve the people there, rather than seeking financial gain from them (1 Thess. 2:9; 1 Cor. 9:3–18). That kind of slavery was compatible with Paul's idea of freedom (1 Cor. 9:19) and is presumably a pointer toward the type of idea in Gal. 6:13. However, at some level we always need to remain aware that this language of slavery is metaphorical. Paul deploys it in deliberately paradoxical ways. "Slavery" to one another is not actual slavery. It shows us something of the shape of the life for which Christian freedom is intended, but it does not remove the freedom itself.

5:14. For all the law is fulfilled in one saying, in "You shall love your neighbor as yourself." Here is another paradox: Paul commends fulfillment of the law. However, only in an apparent sense is this at odds with Paul's teaching in the rest of the letter. The key issue probably is not Paul's specific lexical choices here: "fulfill" rather than "do"; "all the law" rather than "the whole law" (for discussion of the issues, see de Boer 2011, 343–50). This is fulfillment that is a justification of practical nonfulfillment. Love does duty instead of many of the specific commands, which the Galatians need not keep. The gentile Christians should love and need not circumcise, nor observe calendrical festivals, and so on. It is theologically necessary to Paul that the law is fulfilled by life in Christ. As is evident from Paul's widespread appeal to Scripture in the argument of the letter, this remains for him the inspired Word of God. For Paul, all aspects of Scripture are fulfilled in Christ and in the life of the community in Christ (cf. 1 Cor. 10:11). This includes the commands of the law.

Paul can express the law as being encapsulated in a couple of key commands. In terms of commands for interaction between people, such as those against adultery, murder, theft, and coveting, Paul explains in Rom. 13:9 that they are summed up in Lev. 19:18, cited both there and here in Gal. 5:14. Crucially, he sees the love that is the product of the Spirit-led life (5:22) as fulfilling this and hence, he believes, the law as a whole (cf. Rom. 8:4). The Galatian Christians do not need to adopt Jewish law: their Spirit-led life of love already fulfills it (cf. end of 5:23).

Martinus de Boer follows this line of thought (as above) and argues that we should take the citation of Lev. 19:18 in Gal. 5:14 as a promise: "You will love your neighbor." That is, the law (i.e., the Scripture, understood as promise rather than law) is fulfilled in Christ (2011, 350–51; see on 6:2, below). This would fit well with the rhetoric of Galatians. However, we need to be cautious, because the use of the second-person singular "you shall" to represent an imperative in the expression of Jewish law was so deeply established that Paul would seem likely to need a more elaborate explanation to communicate to his hearers that this was to be understood as a future indicative rather than an imperative.

5:15. But if you bite and devour one another, watch out in case you are destroyed by one another. This verse is a great surprise and tends to have little impact on scholars' overall readings of Galatians. However, it is not alone. The next section ends in a similar vein: "Let us not be full of empty glory, provoking one another, envying one another" (5:26). In between these texts, eight of the "works of the flesh" relate closely to divisions within communities.

How much can we mirror read here? Does this warning imply that Paul actually knows of disunity among the Galatian house churches? We know that Paul has heard some things about what is happening among the churches. News of some sort has clearly triggered the letter's impassioned rhetoric. Galatians 5:26 might just be about general teaching for life in community. However, 5:15 has such unusual and pointed rhetoric that it looks most likely to be responding to a situation that Paul believes to be happening. This conclusion is reinforced by the volume of contextual material that would be relevant to the problem. It could provide one reason for Paul extending the assertions of 3:28 beyond the Jew-gentile polarity to other key social polarities in the house churches. It could even provide an extra reason for the relevance of the Antioch incident, as an example of the wrong of breaking fellowship.

The content of the warning in 5:15 is very stark. The implied problem appears to be something such as rather violent intragroup or intergroup quarreling. The threat is that this will lead to destruction of the community, brought about from within. Civil war was and is one of the ultimately terrifying catastrophes. The Romans were appalled when it broke out among themselves. Everyone would have agreed with the saying of Jesus that a house divided against itself is bound to fall (Mark 3:25).

The Effects of Spirit and Flesh (5:16–26)

5:16–17. I tell you, walk by Spirit, and you will certainly not fulfill the desire of the flesh. For the flesh desires contrary to the Spirit, and the Spirit contrary to the flesh, for these oppose each other, so that you do not do the things that you want to do. The previous few verses have called the Galatians to moral action, to moral effort. Galatians 5:16 brings in another factor: spirit/Spirit. Paul instructs Christians to walk *pneumati*, "in spirit" or "by spirit," in which case they will not fulfill the *epithymia* ("desire") of *sarx* ("flesh"). As we will shortly see, the things that the "flesh" desires, which are presumably equivalent to "the works of the flesh" (5:19), are a catalog of morally disastrous qualities, including many that would fuel the "biting" and "devouring" that Paul warned about as a community danger in 5:14: one of the "works," *phthonoi* ("envies," 5:21), is also the final communal issue warned about at the end of this section of the letter (5:26).

In this context, "the desire of the flesh" is unequivocally a bad thing. Paul's way to overcome it is not directly through moral effort. It is through walking in (Schlier 1989, 247–48) or by (R. Longenecker 1990, 244) spirit. But what does this mean? Syntactically, *pneumati* is modifying *peripateite*, "walk," so it is acting adverbially. This is typical for Paul. He always uses *peripateō* metaphorically (rather than of literal walking) and always modifies it with one of four types of accompanying term. The types are: (1) with a straightforward adverb (e.g., *euschēmonōs,* "decently," Rom. 13:13), (2) with *kata* ("according to," Rom. 14:15; 2 Cor. 10:2) or *dia* ("through," 2 Cor. 5:7), (3) with a specifying Greek accusative (*tous echthrous tou staurou,* "as enemies of the cross," Phil. 3:18), or (4) with a dative (with *en,* Rom. 6:4; 2 Cor. 4:2; 10:3; without *en,* here; Rom. 13:13; 2 Cor. 12:18).

Generally, *peripateō* with a modifier is used by Paul to describe a manner of life. There is usually no distinction between the dative modifiers and others. In particular, the datives do not tend to be instrumental ("by means of"). For instance, in 2 Corinthians, *peripatountes en panourgia* (4:2) means "behaving deceitfully," and *ou tō autō pneumati periepatēsamen* (12:18) means "Did we not behave in the same spirit?" However, the dative with *en* can also be used to describe a life situation rather than a chosen manner of life, as in 2 Cor. 10:3, where some think Paul's group are *kata sarka peripatountas* ("walking according to flesh"); but he responds that although we are *en sarki . . . peripatountes* ("walking in flesh," living as humans), we do not *kata sarka strateuometha* ("wage war according to flesh"; 12:3). The dative modifier without *en* in 2 Cor. 12:18 describes manner of life (see above). The same is true of Rom. 13:13, *peripatēsōmen mē kōmois . . .* ("let us walk . . . not in debaucheries"; the list that follows this overlaps with Gal. 5:19–21). Elsewhere in the NT, Acts 21:21 has *tois ethesin peripatein* ("to walk according to the customs"), and John 11:54 has *ho . . . Iēsous ouketi parrēsiā periepatei en tois Ioudaiois* ("Jesus was no longer openly walking among the Judeans"). Our brief lexical study of this syntactical form suggests taking *pneumati* in Gal. 5:16 as describing a manner of life. It is probably synonymous with *kata pneuma* in Rom. 8:4, where Paul speaks of those who "walk not according to flesh but according to spirit."

Peripateite is probably an imperative ("walk") rather than an indicative ("you walk"). The verse reads more naturally as an instruction rather than a statement. But what does the instruction mean in practice? *Pneuma* has occurred often enough already in Galatians to give us some help. *Pneuma* is introduced in 3:2, where it has a definite article, "the Spirit," and is something that has been received by the house churches (also in 3:5). *Pneuma* is not here an aspect of human makeup (as, say, body, soul, and spirit). In 3:3 and 5:5 *pneumati* is a manner of life. The Galatians have begun "in spirit," and Christians eagerly await "in spirit." In 3:14, "the promise of the Spirit" is the key result of "the blessing of Abraham" received by the gentiles in Christ. In 4:6, God sends the Spirit of his Son into the hearts of God's new sons. In 4:29, the identity of Isaac and Christians is *kata pneuma,* "according to spirit." The main effect of all this in Galatians is that the Spirit is a key element of the Galatians' Christian life, received from God and under threat from their inclination to follow Paul's opponents. This suggests giving *pneumati peritateite* in 5:16 somewhat the same sense as *stēkete* ("stand firm [in the freedom of the gospel]") in 5:1. The main thrust of 5:16 is probably that the Galatians should continue to live in the manner of Christian life that they began in, having accepted the gospel from Paul, and that, if they do so, the dire effects of "the flesh" will be avoided. This conclusion is reinforced by noting that *pneuma* is here being contrasted with *sarx* ("flesh") and by considering how the previous two such contrasts have worked. Galatians 3:3 contrasts the early Christian life of the Galatians with what is happening now that they are turning toward Paul's opponents. Likewise 4:29 contrasts Sinai-based identity with Christian identity.

Up to this point in Galatians, the Spirit-flesh contrast has operated as a contrast between a gift of God, resulting from acceptance of Paul's gospel, and law-observant life, resulting (for the Galatians) from acceptance of the opponents' message. Now Paul begins a progression toward giving this contrast moral content. He begins by setting up two irreconcilable sets of desires, "the flesh desires contrary to the Spirit, and the Spirit contrary to the flesh, for these oppose each other" (5:17). (Note that *epithymia* ["desire"] is not in itself bad; what matters is having the right set of desires.) One function of this may be to stress to the Galatians that there is no halfway house between his message and that of his opponents. There is no possibility of a pick-and-mix approach to the two theologies. However, Paul also appears to be drawing on the overtones of anthropological (ideas about the nature of a human) senses of "spirit" and "flesh" as components of a person. The ambiguity of the terms allows him to slide to this from Spirit as an external gift from God. His readers would presumably begin hearing in the spirit-flesh distinction a contrast between constituents of a person. As George H. van Kooten (2008, 384) writes on Rom. 8:4 (with a reference to Gal. 5:16):

> The use of the term "spirit" here is ambiguous and, I would argue, deliberately so. Anthropologically speaking . . . the distinction here is between, on the one hand, those who walk according to the lowest possible level of their anthropological constitution . . . and, on the other, those who walk according to their highest possible level.

This rhetorical coup has been latent in the letter ever since 3:3, where Paul attached his message and that of his opponents to "spirit/Spirit" and "flesh" respectively.

Paul ends his point with the observation developed at length in Rom. 7, that the presence of "the flesh" in a person prevents actions that the person would aim to do out of wishing (philosophically self-evidently) to act in line with the impulses of "the Spirit." As with Rom. 7, commentators tend to put much energy into trying to decide whether the downbeat tone of "You do not do the things that you want to do" could be part of Christian life (e.g., Bruce 1982, 244). In Galatians, the letter as a whole gives a strong steer on what is going on here. Paul sees "the flesh" as a perennial danger, one that the Galatians have been falling into through infatuation with the opponents' teaching. The result has been tension, as in 5:17. The solution is to "walk by spirit" (5:16), "be led by spirit" (5:18), that is, stay faithful to Paul's gospel of unity.

5:18. If you are led by Spirit, you are not under law. Paul has almost certainly switched back here to the Spirit as the external gift from God. The counterpoint in this verse is between two benefits from God: the Spirit and the law. A person is not exempt from God's law because of being philosophically adept, hence led by the "spirit" part of one's being. It is because another gift from God has provided what God requires. The first phrase here is equivalent to Rom. 8:14, *hosoi . . . pneumati theou agontai* ("as many as are led by the Spirit of God"). In Gal. 5:18 too, it is the Spirit of God, the force that came on prophets and kings and which, the early Christians believed, was now residing among the churches (Acts 2, etc.). There is therefore justification for capitalizing the "S," although there seems little value in seeking to be entirely consistent since Paul also uses other senses of "spirit." The construction *pneumati agesthe* probably means "you are led by the Spirit." The NT evidence is only slight, but the relationship between Luke 4:1 and Mark 1:12 suggests taking it this way. Mark's "the Spirit drove him out into the desert," becomes Luke's *ēgeto en tō pneumati en tē erēmō* ("He was led by the Spirit into the desert"). Those texts, and even Gal. 5:18, which lacks a desert, have an exodus feeling to them (cf. Wright 2000, on Galatians more generally). Here, as elsewhere in Paul (e.g., Phil. 2:14–15), there is a sense of seeing the Jesus movement as a new people being led through the wilderness, with the Spirit as the pillar of cloud going ahead of them.

5:19–21. The works of the flesh are obvious: they are sexual immorality, impurity, indecency, idolatry, sorcery, enmities, strife, jealousy, angers, selfish ambitions, divisions, sects, envies, drunkennesses, debaucheries, and the things like those, about which I warn you now, as I warned you before, that people who do such things will not inherit the kingdom of God. Galatians 3:2–3 taunts the Galatian Christians for going after works of law (*erga nomou*) and ending up with *sarx* ("flesh"). In 5:19, *erga* ("works") are ascribed to "the flesh" itself. The Galatians are chasing *erga nomou*, but they end up only in *sarx*, which in fact produces its own *erga* of a type that all people of that time would agree to be wrong (and which surely are contrary to God's law). The content of the list of works overlaps somewhat with many Jewish and non-Jewish vice lists (see esp. R. Longenecker 1990, 249–52). As noted above, a particularly striking overlap is with Rom. 13. In 13:8–14 we have a call to love one another, "love your neighbor," as summation of the law (13:8–10), and a vice list of six "works of darkness" (Rom. 13:12–13), five of which are in Gal. 5:19–21, with the other also being a close synonym of *porneia*, at the head of the Galatians list. The person doing the "works of darkness" of Rom. 13 is effectively described as carrying out the "desires" of "the flesh" (13:14). This shows that some components of the Galatians list were probably part of a general vice list that Paul carried around as part of his mental furniture.

However, there is an interesting shape to the list of "works of the flesh." Martinus de Boer (2011, 358–59) follows J. B. Lightfoot (1890, 210) and others in dividing them into four groups: sexual misconduct, religious misconduct, sources of communal discord, and excessive drinking and its consequences. Remarkably, eight of the fifteen works are in the "communal discord" group. This includes several excessively close synonyms. Paul piles up the pressure on vices that go against unity. The list of "works of the flesh" contributes to the letter's rhetoric on unity. Moreover, the list ends with a dire warning against those who do these things. If, as looks likely, there is actual divisiveness among the Galatians as a result of the arrival of Paul's opponents, his warning is effectively seeking to pull the Galatians out of this situation, back into united acceptance of his gospel and, with it, the life of Spirit, which generates very different produce.

5:22–23. But the fruit of the Spirit is love, joy, peace, patience, kindness, goodness, fidelity, humility, and self-control. Against such things there is no law. Again, there would be fairly wide agreement for Paul's list of "fruit of the Spirit" to be virtues (R. Longenecker 1990, 258–60). Hans Dieter Betz (1979, 286) distinguishes 5:22–23 from virtue lists by arguing that the concepts in 5:22–23 "are not virtues in the Greek sense of the term. They do not represent qualities of personal behavior which man can elect, cultivate, and appropriate as part of his character." In literal terms, this is not true. At least some of the items in the list are, in themselves, virtues. A person could indeed cultivate them. Yet in Gal. 5:22–23, Paul is not prescribing rules for self-improvement. His point is like the one in 5:16: it is the Spirit that is the source of these virtues. Curiously, Betz goes on to argue that the "context of ethical exhortation" in Gal. 5 implies that "fruit" was not simply given to the Galatians but that "by receiving the Spirit they were enabled and motivated to bear that fruit themselves" (1979, 286–87). This appears to take him back to more or less seeing the fruit as a list of virtues to cultivate. In the context of Paul's rhetoric about Spirit, flesh, and law, it looks more likely that Paul is implicitly arguing that, since the Spirit produces these virtues among the Galatians, the best path is that of faithfulness to his gospel, rather than turning to the law as a source of virtue: that only ends up in "works of the flesh."

Many of the virtues in the list are conducive to unity. In communal terms, for "peace" to be a virtue makes it rather synonymous with maintenance of unity. Certainly Pax (Latin for "peace") was the deified virtue representing lack of strife in the empire. For instance, coins celebrating "PAX" were issued at the end of Roman civil wars. Moreover, "love" heads the list, as it heads the whole of this section of the letter and is threaded through its moral instructions. Love is the virtue that seeks the kind of practical unity expressed in mutual concern and support in and among the house churches. One virtue that fits naturally in such a list but looks a bit surprising in the context of Galatians is *pistis*. As a virtue partway down a list, it cannot be the *pistis Christou* to which Paul has given a vital role in the letter's soteriology. The *pistis* of 5:22 is among Christians, or between Christians and non-Christians. It is a virtue of the person who is trustworthy or loyal. As such it is clearly another virtue central to group cohesion.

The final virtue on the list is *enkrateia.* Calling this "self-control" is slightly confusing because in this context it clearly does not imply a self-sufficiency that rejects the leading of the Spirit of God. However, this virtue, prominent among Greek philosophers writing on ethics (Stowers 2003), forms an appropriate end point to Paul's list because it is central to the thesis of 5:18. It is because the Spirit produces in Christians the ability to control their decisions and actions that the Spirit-led person does not need to be subject to law. As Paul concludes, against the virtues of 5:22–23 "there is no law" (5:23). The law ceases to have anything to control when these virtues are in existence in the community. Again, the message is that the Galatians should follow Paul's gospel of the Spirit and of uniting love, not the opponents' message of law and of the creation of distinctions and divisions between people.

Figure 10. Pax coin, Ephesus (?) 28 BC. Obverse: Octavian; reverse: Pax standing on a sword and holding a *caduceus* (symbolizing world communication), a *cista mystica* (symbolizing Asia), and a laurel wreath. Drawing by the author, of Mattingly (1923, Augustus 691).

5:24. Those who are of Christ Jesus have crucified the flesh, with its passions and desires. Philosophically, this may be the sharpest point in the letter. Paul takes a common philosophical goal, control of both normal and extreme emotions and volitions, and offers a solution that is a philosophical tour de force. This *enkrateia* ("self-control"), which is essentially where we are again, is achieved not through years of philosophical study but through identification with a Jewish craftworker at the point of his shameful execution. Instead of moving upward to virtue via education, the Christian moves downward to virtue through identification with the dying Christ in the shameful ritual of baptism (see on 3:27) and in the social dislocation of abandoning a former life and social connections in favor of the humble life of the house church. This conversion and subsequent life "crucifie[s] the flesh" in ways that Paul exemplifies in the letter (see on 2:19; 4:12). This crucifixion brings the life of the Spirit, which offers the virtues that philosophy seeks.

Looking back at 5:16–24 as a whole, we do see ethics, yet probably also, to some degree, another argument based on the Galatians' experience. As he does in 3:2–5, Paul can point to the history of the community's life as an argument for the validity of his gospel. Conversion to Christian life, as a result of Paul's gospel, brings changes in behavior. House-church members

177

recognize vices that they engaged in before conversion but now do not. They recognize virtues that have been developed. They recognize degrees of control over "passions" of the flesh that they did not have before coming to identify themselves with the crucified Christ. Did this come about through the recent arrival of Paul's opponents? No! It came about through Paul's gospel. To a greater or lesser extent, the Galatians have actually experienced the life of the Spirit that Paul describes here. The implicit and, at times, explicit message is that they should stick with it.

5:25–26. If we live by Spirit, let us also walk by Spirit. Let us not be full of empty glory, provoking one another, envying one another. Given all the above, it is a surprise that Paul now moves into moral exhortation. Surely the life of the Spirit made that redundant? Evidently not. Again Paul draws on language of pedestrian locomotion. This time the verb is *stoicheiō*, the verb related to the noun for the elements (4:3), although it is hard to see any link to that topic (de Boer [2011, 372] suggests a possible allusion implying a contrast with their former life). The instruction appears to be the same as that of 5:16, in which case they could form an inclusio, neatly drawing together 5:16–25 as a unit. However, the move from 5:25 to 5:26 and beyond makes 5:25 look more like a transition into the series of instructions beyond. The first clause of 5:25 draws the hearer into the world of Paul's gospel, identifying the group as being safely back in allegiance to the Spirit-led life to which he had introduced them: "If we live by Spirit [which we do], . . ." The second clause then calls for a life of practical steps in accordance with that situation. Although paradoxical, it is what Paul does all the time in his theology and ethics.

In 5:26 Paul returns to issues of communal dysfunction, less sharply expressed here than in 5:15, but presumably relating to similar issues. The syntax of 5:26 suggests that people's excessively high estimates of their worth (they have *kenodoxia* [lit., "empty glory"], a vice also criticized in Phil. 2:3) are leading to provocation and envy. Paul does not directly link this with his opponents (although 6:12–13 probably shows that he would view them as *kenodoxoi*). What 5:26 reinforces is Paul's concerns for communal unity.

Doing Good (6:1–10)

In most of Paul's Letters, it is hard to resist resorting to a title such as "Miscellaneous Instructions" for the snippets of guidance that Paul tends to offer at some point in the letter (e.g., Phil. 4:4–9). The title "Doing Good," although drawn from 6:10, is not much sharper. The issue of communal unity, seen in 5:26, is to some extent continued through 6:1–10, especially in 6:2. Galatians 6:4–5 is closely related to the matter of "empty glory" (5:26). The humility called for in 6:1 would also lessen potential provocation (again, 5:26). It is probably reasonable to see 6:1–10 as, broadly speaking, continuing the agenda of love and unity from Gal. 5. However, the continuity is not strongly marked. The overall pattern of 6:1–10 is unclear.

6:1. **Brothers and sisters, if actually a person is caught in some sin, you who are spiritual should set such a person right, doing so with a humble spirit, watching yourself in case you too are tempted.** It would be neat if the sin (*paraptōma*, "trespass") in view was that of following Paul's opponents. However, Paul does not signal that. A more likely link is that 6:1 continues the community theme by discussing rebuilding of group relationships.

The affirmation of the Galatians as "spiritual" fits with the rhetorical shift in the later part of the letter, from projecting the idea of the Galatians as generally abandoning the gospel to projecting the idea of them as generally faithful to the gospel (e.g., 5:10; see on 5:18). The reference is probably to the group in general (rather than a subset), evoking their identity, seen from 3:2 onward, as people of the Spirit (Fee 2007, 230, leading him to prefer translating *hymeis hoi pneumatikoi* ["you who are spiritual"] as "you who live by the Spirit"). However, the next use of *pneuma* in the verse probably uses the word in a very general sense. "With a humble spirit" probably means just "in a humble manner" (contra Fee 2007, who appeals to consistency with 5:23 to read this phrase as "by the Spirit's gentleness").

Despite the confidence expressed in the Spirit producing good fruit (5:22–23), Paul still needs to give advice on responding to sin in the community. He even needs to warn the "spiritual" people correcting the sin, both of the need for humility, despite it being part of the Spirit's fruit in 5:23, and of the danger of temptation. The "spiritual" may not be under law, but they do not escape the need for being morally vigilant about themselves.

6:2. **Bear one another's burdens, and so you will fulfill the law of Christ.** This is the most surprising verse in the letter. It seems perverse for Paul, after all the rhetoric of Galatians, to ascribe to Christ a law. Theories to explain this abound. One sees "the law of Christ" as the teaching of Jesus, especially on love (Burton 1921, 329). This has the advantage of fitting well both with the specific instruction here and with the general focus of 5:13–6:10 on love. However, apart from the general methodological difficulties of using material from the Gospels to explain Paul, or of seeing Paul as giving a key role to teaching of Jesus that he does not describe elsewhere, there is also the problem that this really would tend toward being law, a set of commandments. That would seem in danger of having simply substituted one list of laws for another (as the church has indeed tended to do), which really would undercut the rhetoric of the letter.

A particularly prominent current explanation is that law here means torah, Jewish law, as it has done throughout the letter, and what we see here is torah (instruction) as it was always meant to be, brought into its proper nature through Christ. For James D. G. Dunn (1993, 323) and others, Christ enables a torah free from its divisive identity as the sponsor of "works of the law," such as rules about eating, which separated Jew from gentile. This is a very attractive theory. However, there are two key difficulties. One is the slenderness of the positive evidence for Paul believing in this renewed torah. Where Paul speaks positively about Jewish law (e.g., Rom. 7:14), he tends to be referring to Jewish law in its normal sense. In other positive expressions such as "law of the Spirit of life" (Rom. 8:2), "law" looks capable of being taken in a sense other than referring to torah. On the negative side, Paul's argument in Galatians about the specific and time-limited role of the law (3:19–25) makes it very difficult to see some sort of torah as having a continued place in Christian life. It remains authoritative Scripture, but not law as such.

Martinus de Boer makes the fascinating suggestion that "the law of Christ" refers to Scripture (cf. 4:21) "containing divine promises pertaining to Christ" rather than to any law as such (2011, 381). This fits with him taking the citation of Lev. 19:18 in Gal. 5:14 as a promise (see above). This is attractive, but likely Paul would need to signal more clearly such a use of "law" if his audience were to hear it in that sense here.

The best clue to understanding "the law of Christ" may lie in the specific injunction in this verse: "Bear one another's burdens" (*allēlōn ta barē bastazete*). Bearing other people's burdens is precisely what Christ did on the cross, in acting *hyper* ("on behalf of") people. In 3:13, Christ became "a curse on our behalf [*hyper hēmōn*]." He "gave himself on behalf of [*hyper*] our sins" (1:4). Paul says the Son of God "gave himself on behalf of me [*hyper emou*]" (2:20). Although Paul does not use the verb *bastazō* in describing Christ's action on the cross, the concept does appear to be present, and *bastazō* is a term highlighted by repetition in Gal. 6. As well as bearing one another's burdens, Christians should bear (*bastasei*) their own load (6:5); and Paul says, "I bear [*bastazō*] the marks of Jesus on my body" (6:17), which also gives an indirect lexical link between *bastazō* and the cross, albeit not in the way that we are particularly interested in. Looking further afield, Heb. 9:28 speaks of Christ bearing sins, although the verb is *anapherō*. The theme is, of course, prominent in Isa. 53, in which the Suffering Servant bears our infirmities, diseases, and punishment (Isa. 53:3–4). This way of reading "the law of Christ" has substantial advantages in terms of its fit with the rhetoric of the rest of the letter. If the phrase refers not to a spoken or written law but to the action of Christ on the cross, seen as normative for the life of those "in Christ," this avoids clashing with the rhetoric of the letter. The "law of Christ" is not law in the sense that is criticized elsewhere in the text (Hays 2000, 333). Instead, it is the action of Christ on the cross, to which Christians become conformed through their existence in Christ (cf. Gorman 2008, 145–66). This reading of "law of Christ" fits well with key aspects of the rhetoric elsewhere. It still looks quite strange to call this "law," but maybe here we do have an instance of Paul adopting terminology because it is the area of dispute with his opponents.

6:3–5. For if someone thinks they are something, being nothing, they deceive themselves. Let each test their own work, and then they can boast just in themselves, and not in someone else, for each person is to bear their own load.

Paul returns to the topic of being *kenodoxoi,* having "empty glory" (5:26), expanding on how something like that can be avoided. Just as Gal. 5:13–26 is in similar territory to Rom. 13:8–14, this text fits with ideas in Rom. 12:3: "You shouldn't think more highly of yourself than you ought. Instead, you should assess soberly, as God has distributed to each an amount of faith" (Oakes 2009, 100). Just as Gal. 6:1 warns "the spiritual" that they still need to watch themselves to avoid temptation, 6:4 requires people to be testing themselves, as Rom. 12:3 calls for assessment of oneself. This is not to say that Paul's vision of Christian life is dominated by introspection. In contrast to various Christian and other religious systems, Paul's calls to self-reflection are brief notes in the midst of community-focused ethical practice. However, it is clear that possession of God's Spirit is far from legitimating existential carelessness in the Christian life.

A paradox lurks here, which would become evident on a second reading of Gal. 6. By testing oneself, a person "can boast just in themselves" (6:4). Paul, whom the Galatians have been called to imitate (4:12), will soon deny boasting in anything other than the cross of Christ (6:13). How can the Christian boast in self? There is then a more immediate paradox. In 6:5, the verb *bastazō* ("I bear") is back very soon after 6:2, but in contrast to 6:2, Paul in 6:5 calls for each to bear their own "load" (*phortion*), which does not appear significantly different from *baros* ("burden") in 6:2.

The paradoxical teaching does make practical sense. Christians are called to bear one another's burdens but to be realistic about themselves. The sense of "boast" in 6:4 is presumably rather limited. Paul is not commending advertisement of one's good deeds. He is advocating realism in ascribing to oneself only one's own actions, not those of others. One direction Paul is certainly not advocating in 6:5 is cutting off support to people on the grounds that they should support themselves. That is not the topic here. It would also make the relationship between 6:5 and 6:2 go beyond paradox into antinomy.

6:6. Let the person who is being instructed in the word share with their instructor in all good things. Thus far Paul has shown no signs of interest in particular ministries in the Galatian house churches. However, here he is probably referring to local teachers (R. Longenecker 1990, 278) rather than making some reference to himself: such a reference would probably be made more obviously and be set within a more relevant context. In other Pauline texts we meet "teachers" (e.g., Rom. 12:7). "The instructor" (*ho katēchountos*) here presumably carries out the same function, rather than house churches (or groups of them) having people whose ministry is specifically instructing newcomers, to which the *katēch-* word group later came to refer. It would seem unlikely that Paul would address his remark just to the transitional group of people who are currently in the process of becoming full church members.

The substance of the instruction appears to be encouragement of material support for people who devote time to teaching. Presumably the implication is that such people give up time when they could be working in ways that earn money or produce food, and so forth. However, in the Greco-Roman economy, relatively few people had regular wage-earning employment. This means that the issue of financial support of teachers often involves other parties. If the teacher is, say, the adult daughter of a craft-working householder, her teaching time would reduce the amount of her economic contribution to the household. Financial support of her as a teacher would contribute to the household as a whole. The general effect of Paul's instruction would be to share the cost of teaching among all the households in the house church, rather than letting it devolve solely on the household to which the teacher belongs.

Thinking about the situation addressed in Galatians, it is interesting that Paul does take a step here that would strengthen the teaching structures of the house churches. There clearly are ways in which such a move could act as part of a strategy to rebuild the mechanisms by which his message was, presumably, previously well implemented in the Galatian house churches, but which had recently been disrupted in some way. However, Gal. 6:6 is too isolated a text to represent a serious strategy of this kind (contrast, e.g., the long discussion of ministry topics in 1 and 2 Corinthians). If the rhetoric of Galatians does include an attempt to restore Pauline leadership structures, it seems most likely to be found in the material about imitating Paul. However, even that seems essentially aimed at the church membership as a whole, rather than at leaders.

6:7–8. Do not be deceived: God is not mocked. For whatever a person sows, that is what they will also reap, because the one who sows to their flesh will, from the flesh, reap destruction. But the one who sows to the Spirit will, from the Spirit, reap eternal life. The penultimate element of the body of the letter is the application of what must be a fairly universal proverbial expression: you reap what you sow. Paul leads into this with an assertion about people being unable to act in a way that could bring mockery on God. The proverb indicates that people cannot escape the consequences of their actions. Paul's application of this relates to life as a basic choice between flesh and Spirit. He states their consequences as being eschatological: destruction or eternal life.

Thomas R. Schreiner reads 6:7–9 primarily in moral terms, although also with some reference to the general law-related argument of the letter. He sees the most prominent issue as being about giving: "Sowing to the flesh in this paragraph means that one uses one's worldly goods for one's own advantage and in accord with selfish desires" (2010, 369; partially following Hurtado 1979). However, he also applauds Hans Dieter Betz in recognizing sowing to the flesh as "placing one's hope for salvation upon circumcision and obedience to the Jewish Torah" (1979, 308). Betz is surely right here, especially given the emphatic reference to eschatological consequences. Reading the text as moral instruction appears to miss the main line of Paul's argument. The reference to flesh and Spirit returns the reader to the issues of 5:13–25 and potentially right back to 3:2–5. The return to issues of flesh and Spirit in 6:7–9 makes the body of the letter end with a heavy warning about choices in the matters central to the letter. The Galatians are in danger of moving from Spirit to flesh (3:3) as they wander off after the teaching of Paul's opponents. Paul sees the stakes for the Galatians as being the highest possible ones: destruction or eternal life.

6:9–10. Let us not become weary in doing good, for we shall reap at the proper time, if we do not give up. Therefore, as we have opportunity, let us do good to all, especially to the household members of the faith. The instructions attached to the final occurrence of "reap" do not immediately sound like the most obvious ones to use to bolster the main argument of the letter. "Doing" (6:9) was on the wrong side of the equation in 3:12. "Doing" the law was clearly not to be sought, according to 5:3. Now Paul makes "doing good" (*to . . . kalon poiountes*) the criterion for "reaping." Why? Again, in 6:10, Christians are instructed to do good (*ergazōmetha to agathon*). Here Paul's term for good is *to agathon*. In 6:9 he uses *to . . . kalon*. Are 6:9 and 6:10 talking about the same thing?

Let us take 6:9 first. Elsewhere in Galatians, *kalos* has been used to contrast what the Galatians used to do, and should be doing, with the behavior of Paul's opponents. The Galatians had been "running well [*kalōs*]" (5:7). The opponents are zealous *ou kalōs*, "not in a good way" (4:17). "It is good [*kalos*] for someone to be zealous for you on behalf of what is good [*en kalō*]" (4:18). *To kalos* ("the good"), in its (few) previous occurrences in Galatians, is a positive term used for faithfulness to the good life of the Pauline gospel. It is therefore natural for Paul to end his instructions by calling the Galatians not to give up on *to kalon*. "Doing" (*poiountes*) is not a problem either. In itself it is a neutral term. In 2:10, Paul is "keen to do [*poiēsai*]" what is needed for the poor. In 3:10 and 5:3 the problem relates to the law, not to "doing" as such. Even in 3:12, the problem for the law does not lie in "doing" inherently being a bad thing. The problem is that, according to Hab. 2:4, it is the one who lives on the basis of trust (rather than by means of doing) who is righteous (see on Gal. 3:11–12, above).

The usage in Galatians relating to *to agathon* is different from that for *to kalon*. *Agathosyne* ("goodness") is sandwiched between "kindness" and "fidelity" among the fruit of the Spirit (5:22), in a context rich in material relating to communal life. The instructee is to share with the instructor "in all good things" (*en pasin agathois*, 6:6). Two is too small a number of uses from which to draw safe inferences, especially given Paul's extensive use of *agathos* elsewhere as a general term for "good" (e.g., Rom. 2:7). However, the contextual proximity of the uses in Gal. 5:22 and 6:6 does suggest taking *agathos* in 6:10 as a virtue having to do with communal life (for B. Longenecker [2010, 214–16], it is particularly giving to the poor, making 6:10 the end point of a rhetorical arc running from 2:10. He also draws 6:9 into this, but not 6:7–8). This is further supported by the sentence itself: while being an interesting instance of encouraging Christians to help outsiders, it sees the main recipients of the good deeds as members of the Christian community. Moreover, the community is described in terms of the classic locus of communal life, the household ("of the faith"; cf. 1:23). Likely the main instructional sense of 6:9–10 is something like the following: "Do not give up on the life of the Pauline gospel [6:9]. Take every opportunity to be a supportive community member to all, especially to fellow Christians [6:10]." That makes the verses, together, an appropriate ending to the body of this letter, calling for faithfulness to Paul's gospel of communal unity.

Theological Issues

Limits to Acting as Slaves to One Another

All institutions, including churches, have people who are inclined to give, and people who are inclined to take. The work of the gospel among the latter will not do away with the category in any group in these already-and-not-yet times. In general, the main ethical issue in a group will be that people tend not to give as much as would be good (I am not here talking particularly about financial giving, although that would be relevant). However, there are situations where "takers" exploit "givers." The risk of some degree of exploitation is inherent in giving and cannot be eliminated. However, the exploitation is always wrong, and there are many types of situations in which it is abusive. Clearly, leadership or peer pressure in a well-functioning group ought to deal with these situations. However, it will clearly also often be right for the "giver" who recognizes exploitation to stop giving to that person. The "slavery" to one another in Paul's gospel is a mutual slavery of love. If it becomes problematically asymmetric, it is not the same thing. Of course, there are types of relational asymmetry that arise unavoidably, such as care for someone who is in a medical condition of high dependency. But this is not the same thing as the kind of exploitative relationship in which the dominated Christian may need to stand up for his or her freedom. Cruciformity is so radical that it knows no limits to what Christians could be called upon to give up for the gospel. However, that does not sanction Christian communities functioning in ways that permit the use of the rhetoric of service to sustain abusive exploitation.

Galatians 6:11–18

Letter Closing

Introductory Matters

The end of the letter body is not strongly marked. Galatians 6:10 is in the form of a conclusion, but not one that signals an end by using a substantial rhetorical flourish or theological marker such as a prayer or doxology (cf. Rom. 15:13). However, 6:11 almost certainly does signal a very specific transition, from the writing down of the main part of the letter by a scribe (cf. Rom. 16:22), to Paul himself taking up the pen for the ending. He uses the same phrase, *tē emē cheiri* ("in my own hand"), in 1 Cor. 16:21; Philem. 19; and if by Paul, 2 Thess. 3:17 and Col. 4:18. Except for Philem. 19, which has another specific function, the phrase only occurs when the letter is about to end. Although Gal. 6:11–18 is the letter ending, there is a fair amount of substance in it. We have the most specific discussion of the motives that Paul ascribes to his opponents (6:12–13). We have some key assertions relating to Paul's sense of identity (6:14, 17). Paul also gives an interesting variant on one of the letter's expressions of the end of Jew-gentile divisions (6:15). The blessing pronounced in 6:16 mystifyingly speaks of "the Israel of God." The letter ends with a grace wish and "amen." As in the letter opening, it is notable that many of the usual polite and friendly elements of his letter endings, such as personal greetings, are missing.

Tracing the Train of Thought

Paul's Handwriting (6:11)

6:11. See with what large letters I write to you in my own hand. A long-standing view links the comment on the size of Paul's handwriting with his assertion about the Galatians' willingness to tear out their eyes for him (4:15) and that consequently his "weakness of the flesh" (4:13) when he arrived there was an eye disorder. However, a more likely explanation for the comment in 6:11 (and much more widely accepted by scholars) is that the large letters signal emphasis or depth of emotion: he is passionately concerned about what is in the letter and, maybe, particularly the points that he is about to make (Lightfoot 1890, 221).

Contrast between the Opponents and Paul about Circumcision and the Cross (6:12–15)

6:12–15. Those who want to make a good showing in flesh, these are the ones who are compelling you to be circumcised, only so that they would not be persecuted for the cross of Christ. For not even those who are circumcised keep the law themselves, but they are wanting you to be circumcised so that they might boast in your flesh. As for me, may I never boast except in the cross of our Lord Jesus Christ, through which the world was crucified to me, and I to the world. For neither circumcision is anything, nor is uncircumcision, but new creation is. This text is in three parts: about the opponents (6:12–13), about Paul (6:14), and about what is significant (6:15). However, they are worth taking together to discuss the lexical and syntactical relationships between them. The key repeated terms are *peritomē* ("circumcision," with the related verb), *sarx* ("flesh"), *stauros* ("cross," with the related verb), and *kauchaomai* ("I boast," with a similar verb, *euprosōpeō*, "I make a good showing"). The basic syntactical relationships are that, first, the opponents' motives are characterized in a certain way (6:12), for which further explanatory reasons are then given (6:13); then this is contrasted with Paul's attitude (6:14), for which an explanatory reason is given (6:15).

The opponents are castigated as being self-interested, effectively disloyal to Christ (in avoiding persecution on his behalf), hypocritical, and deceptive. The outer parts of Paul's accusation form a chiastic structure:

A Those who want to make a good showing in flesh
  B   these are compelling you to be circumcised . . .
  B′ they are wanting you to be circumcised
A′ so that they might boast in your flesh

The basic message is clear: your circumcision would be for their reputation. The opponents no doubt present it as being for the Galatians' benefit, but Paul sees this as a deceptive cheat: the opponents are only thinking of themselves.

Bruce W. Winter sees "making a good showing" as a legal term: the opponents seek to gain a good legal standing for the gentile Christians by bringing them under the umbrella of the protected legal status enjoyed by Jews, the aim being to avoid persecution of the Christian community because of nonobservance of imperial cult rituals (1994, 137–39; see Hardin [2008, 102–10] for a more nuanced discussion of the legal issues). The theory's linking of the "good showing" (6:12a) with avoidance of persecution (6:12b) is clearly a strength for this view. However, it is far from clear that the persecution in view is by gentile authorities and is in relation to matters such as nonobservance of imperial cult rituals. In the letter thus far, all the references to persecution have been to persecution of Christian Jews by non-Christian Jews. The pre-Christian Paul persecuted the churches (1:13, 23). The Sinai-related child, who is "according to flesh," persecutes the child "according to Spirit" (4:29). The Christian Paul is persecuted (5:11), with persecution by non-Christian Jews probably in mind. The most likely reading of 6:12 is therefore that the opponents, who are Christian Jews, fear persecution from non-Christian Jews if the gentile Christians do not undergo circumcision (Dunn 1993, 336–37).

It is easy for Paul's heavily loaded rhetoric to carry us away into seeing the opponents' motives as being dreadful. However, if our reading is correct, even from Paul's description of them in 6:12, the opponents' motives would be quite understandable. If the opponents are synagogue members who have come to believe in Jesus as Messiah, their association with gentile members of the Jesus movement could easily be seen as problematic by the synagogue authorities and other members. The opponents' attempt to bring the gentile Christians into the ambit of Jewish life would seem positive in itself and as something that would ease the situation of Christian Jews. In fact, if the opponents succeeded and the Jesus movement

Galatians 6:11–18 in the Rhetorical Flow

Letter opening (1:1–10)

Letter body (1:11–6:10)

Narrative 1: Of a gospel revealed by God, not people (1:11–24)

Narrative 2: Of a gospel affirmed by unity at Jerusalem (2:1–10)

Narrative 3: Of a gospel betrayed by division at Antioch (2:11–21)

Argument 1: For blessing in Christ through trust (3:1–14)

Argument 2: For unity in Christ (3:15–29)

Argument 3: Against returning to slavery (4:1–11)

Instructions with argument 1: "Be like me" (4:12–20)

Instructions with argument 2: "Do not be subject again to … slavery" (4:21–5:13a)

Instructions with argument 3: "Through love be slaves to one another" (5:13b–6:10)

►Letter closing (6:11–18)

Paul's handwriting (6:11)

Contrast between the opponents and Paul about circumcision and the cross (6:12–15)

Final blessing, plea, and grace wish (6:16–18)

became a means of bringing more gentiles into the Jewish community, the Jesus movement could indeed become something that Christian Jews might be proud of in the synagogue (6:13), rather than allegiance to Jesus being a somewhat covert matter, seen by many other Jews as shameful.

Mark D. Nanos advocates a variant on this view. He sees Paul's opponents as indeed seeking to bring the Christian gentiles fully into synagogue life, but holds that the opponents are not necessarily Christians. Instead, they are synagogue officials responsible for regularizing the position of any gentiles who wish to become members. Paul's gospel has led Christian gentiles to expect synagogue membership. His opponents have explained on what terms that can happen. The fear of persecution, which Paul attributes to them in 6:12, is of criticism and possible loss of status and role if they fail properly to perform their office (Nanos 2002, 217–25). A major advantage of this reading is that it locates Paul's opponents firmly in synagogues, therefore making a fear of "persecution," albeit in a weakened sense, by other Jews a more likely possibility. However, we have seen above (in the introduction) evidence suggesting taking the opponents to be Christian Jews. Paul also implies that it is his opponents who have taken the initiative in drawing the Galatian gentiles toward Jewish life (e.g., 5:7), rather than that the Galatians were seeking synagogue life and his opponents responded to this.

Who are "those who are circumcised" who do not, according to Paul in 6:13, keep the law? Interpreting this verse would be straightforward if the reference were to some gentiles who had already undergone circumcision at the instigation of people like the opponents (cf. Burton 1921, 352–53). Paul could be asserting that, once the ritual had been carried out, so that the opponents could add another name to their list of proselytes, this was not followed through in serious law keeping (which, to be consistent, ought to happen: as Paul writes in 5:3).

However, "those who are circumcised" in 6:13a appear to be those "who are wanting you to be circumcised" (6:13b). In that case, "those who are circumcised" would probably be the opponents, as Christian Jews, and Paul's point would now be that they lived hypocritical lives because they did not keep the law. Luther thinks that they do not keep the law because they do not have the Holy Spirit (1949/1535, on 6:13). However, Paul does not give any indication of that here. Instead, he moves on to draw a contrast with the opponents' desire to boast in the Galatians' flesh. The logic of 6:13 would work particularly neatly if that action of boasting in the flesh were in itself a form of law breaking. In Nanos's view, Paul's assertion that his opponents really seek their own ends, not those of the Galatians, means a breach of the key command to love their neighbors (2002, 228). Again, we can imagine how a case could be made for that, but it is unclear that Paul makes it. Thomas R. Schreiner suggests that Paul has in mind a general characterization of Jews as not fully keeping the law, as seen in Rom. 2:17–24 (2010, 378). It is hard to be sure how Paul's assertions in 6:13 about nonobservance of the law and about boasting are to be taken. What is clear is that both charges are part of his general strategy of linking his opponents with hypocrisy.

6:14. Paul contrasts them with the absoluteness of his own commitment. **As for me, may I never boast, except in the cross of our Lord Jesus Christ, through which the world was crucified to me, and I to the world.** The opponents avoid persecution for the cross. Paul takes a contrasting stance: the cross is his very boast. He is done with boasting in fleshly things. In fact, he is so closely identified with the cross that he is done with the world altogether. Paul is a model for Christians, who have "crucified the flesh" (5:24). They have been called to be like Paul (4:12). Although Paul still lives in the world, indeed "in the flesh" (2:20), all the key drivers of his life lie beyond it. This is reminiscent of the ethics of Phil. 3:19–21, which Paul grounds by pointing Christians to their place of belonging, in heaven. Paul's death to the world probably also connotes a willingness to undergo persecution, even to the point of martyrdom, in contrast to his opponents. Of course, paradoxically, in asserting his refusal to boast in himself and his identification with the cross, Paul is presenting himself as more admirable than his opponents (cf. Puca 2011). The Galatians should follow him, not them.

6:15. **For neither circumcision is anything, nor is uncircumcision, but new creation is.** The opponents' insistence on circumcision is countered by a re-statement of the key motif of the letter, given previously in the form of 3:28, "There is no Jew nor Greek," and of 5:6, "neither circumcision matters, nor uncircumcision." Here the denial of the division is in terms almost as stark as 3:28. It is then reinforced by a fresh alternative, "new creation." The letter has previously spoken about "life" (2:19–20; 3:11–12, 21). The possibly closest of these to the vocabulary of creation is the comment in 3:21 about the law being unable "to make alive" (*zōopoiēsai*; see on 3:21). The description in 1 Cor. 15:22, 45 of Christ as "the last Adam," as a "life-giving spirit" (*pneuma zōopoioun*), suggests a link to the breath of God that gives life to Adam in Gen. 2:7 (LXX: *pnoē zōēs*). However, the Corinthian correspondence also offers the more direct point of comparison in 2 Cor. 5:17: "If anyone in Christ, new creation. The old things went: look! new things have come about" (keeping nearly to Greek word order). This shows that Paul can use "new creation" to indicate the new condition brought about through Christ. Scholars debate whether, here in Galatians, Paul is thinking of re-creation of Christians in particular or of the world in general (Hubbard 2002, 133–232). In Gal. 6:15, we do not have much helpful context. However, in some way Paul is seeing the events that have happened through the arrival of Christ as comparable to the events of Gen. 1–2. Christ has brought about some sort of new start, either for the world or for people who are "in Christ." Paul's key point is that this new start, not the old divisions of Jew and gentile, determines existence now. As in 3:28, the old social polarities have been put aside through Christ's arrival.

J. Louis Martyn on 6:11–18 as the Key to Galatians

"To take one's bearings from the subscript, then, is to see that fundamentally the letter is not about what should not be (the Teachers' inferior preaching). Nor is it even about what should be (Paul's superior preaching). It is about what does not exist and about what does exist. No longer having real existence is the cosmos of religion, and taking its place is God's new creation, that is to say, Christ and the church (the Israel of God), in which the Spirit is bearing the fruit of love." (1997a, 560)

If the Galatians follow Paul's opponents back into the world where these polarities are given decisive significance, that would mean that the Galatians do not understand Christ's new creation. For J. Louis Martyn, Martinus de Boer, and others, this is the key to understanding the entire letter (see sidebar).

For Martyn (1997a, 572), Paul announces "the horrifying crucifixion of the cosmos." In particular, this produced "the end of all religious differentiations, such as the differentiation of holy, circumcised people from profane and uncircumcised people" (1997a, 561). This is breathtaking scholarship (esp. Martyn's 1985 paper announcing these ideas). There are many theologically attractive points. However, it struggles in terms of detailed exegesis and of relation to the rest of the letter. Galatians 6:14 does not quite say what Martyn wants. This can be seen in his comment on the text:

> The cross—not the advent of the law—is the watershed event for the whole of the cosmos, affecting everything after it. . . . Putting the matter in terms of his personal witness, he speaks of this watershed event by saying that it was by the cross . . . that he himself suffered the loss of one cosmos, and saw the birth of another, God's new creation. (1997a, 564)

For Paul to suffer the loss of his own cosmos is not the same as saying that the cosmos itself died. There is more chance of something absolute in 6:15 with the unqualified reference to "new creation." However, even here it is not clear whether the term refers to the re-creation of a person or of the world. This is just one point in the letter, and its exegesis is open to question. It seems highly risky to make it the basis for reinterpreting the whole letter.

Martyn would respond that, in fact, the letter as a whole suggests his hypothesis. However, that is surely not the case (see, e.g., on 1:16, above). Even the most apocalyptic point of the whole letter, Christ's rescue of us from the present evil age (1:4), is an action directed toward people rather than toward changing the nature of the world. From there, the point can be made more broadly. It is the same as the broad argument against Richard B. Hays's reading of *pistis Christou* as "faithfulness of Christ" toward God. The implicit soteriological narrative about Christ in Galatians is overwhelmingly about Christ's salvific action on behalf of people (see on 2:16, above). It is between Christ and people. Not between Christ and God, as Hays argues. Neither is it between Christ and the cosmos, as Martyn argues.

Final Blessing, Plea, and Grace Wish (6:16–18)

6:16. And to as many as walk by this rule, peace be upon them, and mercy even upon the Israel of God. There is still a "rule" (*kanōn*). The rule is that what matters is new creation in Christ, not the old social polarities. This is not the kind of rule that constitutes a new, burdensome law—although it could be turned into the basis of one, given enough perverse ingenuity or, more likely, given the desire to impose this rule on others who do not wish to live by it. But for those who freely live by it, abandoning the divisions of the old world in favor of the new creation, Paul has already shown in Galatians that there is, inherently, blessing that can be described as including peace. The Galatians who stick with Paul's gospel inherit these anyway, but Paul now wishes it to them afresh.

Most commentators and translators add "mercy" to the above blessing, adding a comma after "mercy" to create a double blessing of peace and mercy on those who "walk by this rule" and also on "the Israel of God," who may be the same people or may be a different group. Recently, Susan Eastman (2010) and Martinus de Boer (2011, 404–408) have argued that Paul intends two separate blessings, each on a distinct group. Each of these types of interpretation, the double-blessing one and the separate-blessings one, raises various options for the meaning of the term, "Israel of God." We will take each type of interpretation in turn.

Richard Longenecker supports the double-blessing interpretation, arguing that, given Paul's concern throughout the letter "to treat as indifferent the distinctions that separate Jewish and Gentile Christians . . . , it is difficult to see him at the very end of that letter pronouncing a benediction (or benedictions) that would serve to separate groups" (1990, 298). However, even among scholars who see a double blessing here, there are some who see Paul making reference to more than one group. A key issue is the meaning of *kai epi* in the phrase, *kai epi ton Israēl tou theou*. The *kai epi* could mean "and upon," signaling that Paul is about to add a further set of people to be recipients of the blessing, or "even upon," signaling either a second way of describing the recipients of the blessing or the naming of a subset of those blessed. These three options roughly map onto three alternative ways of reading the phrase *ton Israēl tou theou* ("the Israel of God"). If *kai* means "and," so Paul is adding a group other than those who walk by the rule of new creation in Christ, "the Israel of God" could refer either to Jews in general, including non-Christian Jews (Bruce 1982, 274), or to Christian Jews in particular. If the term "Israel of God" is simply another way of referring to those who "walk by this rule," it would presumably refer to Christians (Jew and gentile; Martyn 1997a, 576, where he sees identity as being so radically redefined as to call the Christians "former Jews and former Gentiles"). If "the Israel of God" refers to a subset of those who "walk by the rule," it could refer to Christian Jews with Pauline views (e.g., Betz 1979, 323).

The double-blessing interpretation sits rather awkwardly with the layout of 6:16, since the verse names one group, then the pair of blessings, then the other group, rather than more straightforwardly keeping the blessings together and putting the recipients together. Eastman (2010, 373) and de Boer (2011, 404) avoid this by allocating each blessing to the adjacent group. Eastman (2010, 368, 373, 385–90) sees "the Israel of God" as ethnic Israel, arguing that this gives "mercy" a specific sense (linking this with Rom. 9–11), as Paul prays especially for Jews who have not accepted the Christian message (which Peter is taking to them). De Boer (2011, 407–8) thinks that this too quickly draws the meaning of "Israel" from Romans and does not fit the context of Galatians as well as does an alternative idea, that "the Israel of God" refers to the Jerusalem church and other Christian Jews who do not follow the Pauline pattern.

It is very difficult to reach a clear conclusion on this issue. None of the proposed solutions make the syntactical structure entirely straightforward and the phrase, "the Israel of God," is without precedent. The two extreme readings probably have the strongest arguments behind them. The reading that fits most easily into the rhetoric of Galatians is that "the Israel of God" "consists of all those, Jew and gentile alike, who believe in Jesus the Messiah" (Wright 2000, 226; cf. R. Longenecker 1990, 299; Dunn 1993, 345, with his composite group of all Jews plus Christian gentiles). On the other hand, the most straightforward way to take "Israel of God" is as referring to ethnic Jews (cf. Bachmann 2008, 101–23). As Eastman argues (see above), this does also give a reasonable rationale for Paul's wish for mercy. It may also not come as much "out of the blue" as people tend to think. Gal. 6:15 pointedly repeats both sides of the pair from 5:6: "neither circumcision . . . nor uncircumcision." Paul's gospel does not require uncircumcision. He remembers that point. It is not a surprise that he also remembers Israel in his prayer.

6:17. Finally, let no one cause me trouble, for I bear the marks of Jesus on my body. In considering the rhetorical care or artistry with which Paul structures his letters, the theories must always be limited by the extent to which he sometimes makes moves that appear rhetorically or artistically inept. After "finally" we expect a brilliant finishing touch, cementing Paul's argument and exhortation to the Galatians. Instead, we get what sounds like a self-concerned and petulant outburst. Paul does not even follow through on the angle expected in personal pleas, namely, an appeal based on the relationship between himself and the Galatians (contrast 4:12–20). Instead, he draws attention to himself as a living icon of the crucified Christ. This is made the basis for a plea that no one cause Paul trouble.

Let us look at this verse backward. The ending in Greek is *en tō sōmati mou bastazō* ("I bear on my body"). The reference is presumably to scars and other forms of bodily damage acquired through persecution or the hazards of itinerant ministry. Paul gives a long list in 2 Cor. 11:23–27, ranging from stoning to shipwrecks. Given the limited capabilities and availability of first-century medicine, the permanent harm done by these experiences must have been extensive. Paul's litany includes sufferings that no doubt produced a body damaged in multiple ways. He must have looked different from most other people, including his opponents at Galatia. As John H. Elliott argues, they may have cast aspersions on him about his deformity (2011). Paul turns his injuries around. What the Galatians can see in his body are "the marks of Jesus." Paul's injuries put him visually closer to Jesus than are other people, such as his opponents. Which teachers will the Galatians follow?

Stigmata probably carries a connotation of being shameful marks, rather than just marks. Pseudo-Phocylides 225 uses it of marks branded onto a slave. Given what Paul writes about Jesus elsewhere, the reference must be to the crucifixion. This verse is one of only eight or nine in which Paul uses "Jesus" without one of the qualifiers "Christ" or "Lord." In three of these, Jesus is linked to death, but this is not sufficient to demonstrate that the name was chosen in Gal. 6:17 for that reason. What is more interesting is the similarity to 2 Cor. 4:7–12. That text uses the name "Jesus" in a similar way and with other similarities to Galatians. Notice that Paul describes the apostles as persecuted (2 Cor. 4:9; cf. Gal. 4:29; 5:11) and links sharing in Jesus's death with sharing in his life (2 Cor. 4:10–11; cf. Gal. 2:19–20). The context of 2 Cor. 4, like Galatians, is one of difficult relations between Paul and the recipients, in which there appear to be question marks over Paul's ministry.

This suggests that Paul had a pattern of relating his bodily experience to Jesus's death, with the idea of the apostle's sufferings revealing Jesus's life, for the benefit of the churches. This suggests that in Gal. 6:17 Paul has in mind Christ's death and that he links that to his bodily life on quite a broad front, probably going beyond simply physical damage to a characterization

---

2 Corinthians 4:7–12

"But we have this treasure in clay jars, so that it may be made clear that this extraordinary power belongs to God and does not come from us. We are afflicted in every way, but not crushed; perplexed, but not driven to despair; persecuted, but not forsaken; struck down, but not destroyed; always carrying in the body the death of Jesus, so that the life of Jesus may also be made visible in our bodies. For while we live, we are always being given up to death for Jesus' sake, so that the life of Jesus may be made visible in our mortal flesh. So death is at work in us, but life in you." (NRSV)

of his life as one of danger and suffering. It also suggests that in 6:17 Paul probably has in mind some of the ideas in 2:19–20 (and conversely, in writing 2:19–20, he likely has thoughts of bodily suffering as well as other concepts of identification with Christ's cross). The Galatians too would probably hear something of 2:19–20 in 6:17. However, Paul does not want to use the reference to the *stigmata* to repeat the point of 2:19–20. He goes in a different direction.

Paul takes us back to the tone of the letter's opening. His first point was to assert his divine authorization (1:1). He expressed angry astonishment (1:6–9). Paul gave an exasperated denial of being a people pleaser. Instead, he is Christ's slave (1:10). Now in 6:17 he affirms that he bears the marks of his master's slave-like death. How could they seek to trouble him? Moreover, in troubling Paul, they are troubling the representation of Jesus's sufferings. It is as though they are troubling Jesus on the cross.

We react impatiently to what looks like self-focused defensiveness. However, there is here a depth of experience and suffering that should make us cautious. There is a mystery in the life of any servant of God who has suffered deeply in that service. Neither disciples nor commentators should rush to judgment.

6:18. The grace of our Lord Jesus Christ be with your spirit, brothers and sisters. Amen. There is no obvious rhetorical point being made in this particular grace wish. Apart from adding *adelphoi* ("brothers and sisters"), it is identical to Phil. 4:23 and very similar to 1 Thess. 5:28. After all the heat of the letter, Paul comes back to extending Christ's grace to these Galatians who—whatever they have done, plan to do, or plan not to do—are his brothers and sisters.

Theological Issues

Theology by Letter

And he puts down the pen. The words are now set on the papyrus. Maybe he hmm's and ha's a bit. Does this or that section want amending? Maybe? But no. Leave it there. Commit it to the messenger.

Words are a strange vehicle for God to use. So limited. So full of echoes of texts, good and bad. So risky. "In the beginning was the Word." The incarnation too was a sending, in a form that echoed other bodies. Even more risk—risk that led to death.

Yet God "raised him from among the dead." The sent one lives and brings life. In God's provision, the sent letter too has often brought life and will surely do so many times again.

Bibliography

Alexander, Loveday. 1993. "Chronology of Paul." Pages 115–23 in *Dictionary of Paul and His Letters*. Edited by G. F. Hawthorne and R. P. Martin. Leicester: Inter-Varsity.

Annas, Julia. 1996. "Plato." Pages 1190–93 in *Oxford Classical Dictionary*. 3rd ed. Edited by S. Hornblower and A. Spawforth. Oxford: Oxford University Press.

Arnaoutoglou, Ilias. 1998. *Ancient Greek Laws: A Sourcebook*. London: Routledge.

Arnold, Clinton. 2005. "'I Am Astonished That You Are So Quickly Turning Away' (Gal 1.6): Paul and Anatolian Folk Belief." *New Testament Studies* 51:429–49.

Baasland, Ernst. 1984. "Persecution: A Neglected Feature in the Letter to the Galatians." *Studia theologica: Nordic Journal of Theology* 38:135–50.

Bachmann, Michael. 2008. *Anti-Judaism in Galatians? Exegetical Studies on a Polemical Letter and on Paul's Theology*. Translated by Robert L. Brawley. Grand Rapids: Eerdmans.

———. 2010. "Bemerkungen zur Auslegung zweier Genitivverbindungen des Galaterbriefs: 'Werke des Gesetzes' (Gal 2,16 u.ö.) und 'Israel Gottes' (Gal 6,16)." Pages 95–118 in *Umstrittener Galaterbrief: Studien zur Situierung der Theologie des Paulus-Schreibens*. Edited by Michael Bachmann and Bernd Kollmann. Biblisch-theologische Studien 106. Neukirchen-Vluyn: Neukirchener Verlag.

Bagnall, Roger S., and Raffaella Cribiore. 2006. *Women's Letters from Ancient Egypt, 300 BC–AD 800*. Ann Arbor: University of Michigan Press.

Barclay, John M. G. 1987. "Mirror-Reading a Polemical Letter: Galatians as a Test Case." *Journal for the Study of the New Testament* 31:73–93.

———. 1988. *Obeying the Truth: A Study of Paul's Ethics in Galatians*. Studies of the New Testament and Its World. Edinburgh: T&T Clark.

———. Forthcoming. *Paul and the Gift*. Grand Rapids: Eerdmans.

Barth, Gerhard. 1993. "Πίστις." Pages 91–97 in vol. 3 of *Exegetical Dictionary of the New Testament*. Edited by H. Balz and G. Schneider. Grand Rapids: Eerdmans.

Basore, John W., trans. 1928. *Seneca: Moral Essays I; De clementia*. Loeb Classical Library. London: Heinemann.

Beard, Mary, John North, and Simon Price. 1998. *A History*. Vol. 1 of *Religions of Rome*. Cambridge: Cambridge University Press.

Becker, Jürgen, and Ulrich Luz. 1998. *Die Briefe an die Galater, Epheser und Kolosser*. 18th ed. Das Neue Testament Deutsch 8.1. Göttingen: Vandenhoeck & Ruprecht.

Betz, Hans Dieter. 1979. *Galatians: A Commentary on Paul's Letter to the Churches in Galatia*. Hermeneia. Philadelphia: Fortress.

Bird, Michael F., and Preston M. Sprinkle, eds. 2009. *The Faith of Jesus Christ: Exegetical, Biblical, and Theological Studies*. Milton Keynes: Paternoster; Peabody, MA: Hendrickson.

Blass, F., A. Debrunner, and R. W. Funk. 1961. *A Greek Grammar of the New Testament and Other Early Christian Literature*. Chicago: University of Chicago Press.

Boakye, Andrew. 2014. "Death and Life: Jesus' Resurrection, Israel's Restoration and Humanity's Rectification in Paul's Letter to the Galatians." PhD diss., University of Manchester.

Boer, Martinus C. de. 2011. *Galatians: A Commentary*. New Testament Library. Louisville: Westminster John Knox.

Bonhoeffer, Dietrich. 1948. *The Cost of Discipleship*. Translated by R. H. Fuller. London: SCM. German original published in 1937.

Bourdieu, Pierre. 1965. "The Sentiment of Honour in Kabyle Society." Pages 191–241 in *Honour and Shame: The Values of Mediterranean Society*. Edited by J. G. Peristiany. London: Weidenfeld & Nicolson.

Braxton, Brad R. 2002. *No Longer Slaves: Galatians and African American Experience*. Collegeville, MN: Liturgical Press.

Breytenbach, Cilliers. 1996. *Paulus und Barnabas in der Provinz Galatien: Studien zu Apostelgeschichte 13f.; 16,6; 18,23 und den Adressaten des Galaterbriefes*. Arbeiten zur Geschichte des antiken Judentums und des Urchristentums 38. Leiden: Brill.

Bruce, F. F. 1982. *The Epistle to the Galatians: A Commentary on the Greek Text*. New International Greek Testament Commentary. Grand Rapids: Eerdmans.

———. 1983. *New Testament History*. Garden City, NY: Doubleday.

Burkitt, F. Crawford. 1924. *Christian Beginnings: Three Lectures*. London: University of London Press.

Burton, Ernest deWitt. 1921. *A Critical and Exegetical Commentary on the Epistle to the Galatians*. International Critical Commentary. Edinburgh: T&T Clark.

Campbell, Douglas. 2005. *The Quest for Paul's Gospel: A Suggested Strategy*. Edinburgh: T&T Clark.

———. 2009. *The Deliverance of God: An Apocalyptic Rereading of Justification in Paul*. Grand Rapids: Eerdmans.

———. 2011. "An Attempt to Be Understood: A Response to the Concerns of Matlock and Macaskill with *The Deliverance of God*." *Journal for the Study of the New Testament* 34:162–208.

Castelli, Elizabeth A. 1991. *Imitating Paul: A Discourse of Power*. Louisville: Westminster John Knox.

Crook, Zeba A. 2004. *Reconceptualising Conversion: Patronage, Loyalty, and Conversion in the Religions of the Ancient Mediterranean*. Beihefte zur Zeitschrift für die neutestamentliche Wissenschaft 130. Berlin: de Gruyter.

Das, A. Andrew. 2000. "Another Look at ἐὰν μή in Galatians 2:16." *Journal of Biblical Literature* 119:529–39.

DeMaris, Richard E. 2008. *The New Testament in Its Ritual World*. London: Routledge.

deSilva, David A. 2011. *Global Readings: A Sri Lankan Commentary on Paul's Letter to the Galatians*. Eugene, OR: Cascade.

Downing, F. Gerald. 1998. *Cynics, Paul and the Pauline Churches*. Cynics and Christian Origins 2. London: Routledge.

Dunn, James D. G. 1993. *The Epistle to the Galatians*. London: A&C Black.

———. 2002. "Appendix 1: Once More, ΠΙΣΤΙΣ ΧΡΙΣΤΟΥ." Pages 249–71 in *The Faith of Jesus Christ: The Narrative Substructure of Galatians 3:1–4:11*. 2nd ed. Edited by Richard B. Hays. Grand Rapids: Eerdmans.

———. 2008. "ΕΚ ΠΙΣΤΕΩΣ: A Key to the Meaning of ΠΙΣΤΙΣ ΧΡΙΣΤΟΥ." Pages 351–66 in *The Word Leaps the Gap: Essays on Scripture and Theology in Honor of Richard B. Hays*. Edited by J. Ross Wagner, C. Kavin Rowe, and A. Katherine Grieb. Grand Rapids: Eerdmans.

Eastman, Susan. 2007. *Recovering Paul's Mother Tongue: Language and Theology in Galatians*. Grand Rapids: Eerdmans.

———. 2010. "Israel and the Mercy of God: A Re-reading of Galatians 6.16 and Romans 9–11." *New Testament Studies* 56:367–95.

Effenterre, H. van, and F. Ruzé, eds. 1994. *Nomima: Recueil d'inscriptions politiques et juridiques de l'archaïsme grec*. Vol. 1. Collection de l'École Française de Rome 188. Rome: École Française de Rome.

Eisenbaum, Pamela. 2012. "Jewish Perspectives: A *Jewish* Apostle to the Gentiles." Pages 135–53 in *Studying Paul's Letters: Contemporary Perspectives and Methods*. Edited by Joseph A. Marchal. Minneapolis: Fortress.

Elliott, John H. 2011. "Social-Scientific Criticism: Perspective, Process and Payoff; Evil Eye Accusation at Galatia as Illustration of the Method." *HTS Theological Studies* 67. www.hts.org.za/index.php/HTS/article/view/858/1454.

Elliott, Susan. 2003. *Cutting Too Close for Comfort: Paul's Letter to the Galatians in Its Anatolian Cultic Context*. Journal for the Study of the New Testament: Supplement Series 248. London: T&T Clark.

Elmer, Ian J. 2009. *Paul, Jerusalem and the Judaisers: The Galatian Crisis in Its Broadest Historical Context*. Wissenschaftliche Untersuchungen zum Neuen Testament 2/258. Tübingen: Mohr Siebeck.

Esler, Philip F. 1998. *Galatians*. New Testament Readings. London: Routledge.

———. 2003. *Conflict and Identity in Romans: The Social Setting of Paul's Letter*. Minneapolis: Fortress; London: SPCK.

———. 2012. "Identity Matters: Judean Ethnic Identity in the First Century CE." *The Bible and Interpretation*. www.bibleinterp.com/opeds/esl368002.shtml.

Evans, Craig. Undated. *Pseudepigrapha (New English)*. Translation module for Accordance Bible Software. www.accordancebible.com/store/details/?pid=PSEUD-E.

Fee, Gordon D. 2007. *Galatians*. Pentecostal Commentary Series. Blandford Forum, Dorset, UK: Deo.

Foerster, Werner. 1964. "Abfassungszeit und Ziel des Galaterbriefes." Pages 135–41 in *Apophoreta: Festschrift für Ernst Haenchen zu seinem siebzigsten Geburtstag am 10. Dezember 1964*. Beihefte zur Zeitschrift für die neutestamentliche Wissenschaft 30. Berlin: Töpelmann.

Gaston, Lloyd. 1987. *Paul and the Torah*. Vancouver: University of British Columbia Press.

Gaventa, Beverly Roberts. 1986. "Galatians 1–2: Autobiography as Paradigm." *Novum Testamentum* 28:309–26.

———. 2007. *Our Mother Saint Paul*. Louisville: Westminster John Knox.

Gempf, Conrad. 1994. "The Imagery of Birth Pangs in the New Testament." *Tyndale Bulletin* 52:303–6.

Girard, René. 1986. *The Scapegoat*. Translated by Y. Freccero. Baltimore: Johns Hopkins University Press.

Glad, Clarence E. 1996. "Frank Speech, Flattery, and Friendship in Philodemus." Pages 21–59 in *Friendship, Flattery and Frankness of Speech: Studies on Friendship in the New Testament World*. Edited by John T. Fitzgerald. Supplements to Novum Testamentum 82. Leiden: Brill.

Goddard, A. J., and S. A. Cummins. 1993. "Ill or Ill-Treated? Conflict and Persecution as the Context of Paul's Original Ministry in Galatia (Galatians 4.12–20)." *Journal for the Study of the New Testament* 52:93–126.

Goodburn, R., M. W. C. Hassall, and R. S. O. Tomlin. 1979. "Roman Britain in 1978." *Britannia* 10:267–356.

Goodrich, John K. 2010. "Guardians, Not Taskmasters: The Cultural Resonances of Paul's Metaphor in Galatians 4.1–2." *Journal for the Study of the New Testament* 32:251–84.

Goodwin, D. R. 1886. "Ἐὰν μή, Gal. ii.16." *Journal of Biblical Literature* 6:122–27.

Gorman, Michael J. 2008. *Reading Paul*. Milton Keynes: Paternoster.

———. 2009. *Inhabiting the Cruciform God: Kenosis, Justification, and Theosis in Paul's Narrative Soteriology*. Grand Rapids: Eerdmans.

Hagedorn, Anselm C. 2005. "Wie flucht man im östlichen Mittelmeer? Kulturanthropologische Perspektiven in die *Dirae Teiae* und das Deuteronomium." Pages 117–50 in *Kodifizierung und Legitimierung des Rechts in der Antike und im alten Orient*. Edited by M. Witte and M. T. Fögen. Beihefte zur Zeitschrift für altorientalische und biblische Rechtsgeschichte 5. Wiesbaden: Harrassowitz.

Hall, Robert G. 2002. "The Rhetorical Outline for Galatians: A Reconsideration." Pages 29–38 in *The Galatians Debate: Contemporary Issues in Rhetorical and Historical Interpretation*. Edited by Mark D. Nanos. Peabody, MA: Hendrickson.

Hardin, Justin K. 2008. *Galatians and the Imperial Cult: A Critical Analysis of the First-Century Social Context of Paul's Letter*. Wissenschaftliche Untersuchungen zum Neuen Testament 2/237. Tübingen: Mohr Siebeck.

Harmon, Matthew S. 2010. *She Must and Shall Go Free: Paul's Isaianic Gospel in Galatians*. Berlin: de Gruyter.

Harrison, James R. 2002. "Paul and the Imperial Gospel at Thessaloniki." *Journal for the Study of the New Testament* 25:71–96.

Harvey, David S. 2012. "'Upside-Down Honour' and the Spirit of the Faithful Son in Galatians." *Journal of the European Pentecostal Theological Association* 32:61–74.

Hays, Richard B. 2000. "The Letter to the Galatians: Introduction, Commentary, and Reflections." Pages 181–348 in vol. 11 of *The New Interpreter's Bible*. Edited by Leander E. Keck. Nashville: Abingdon.

————. 2002. *The Faith of Jesus Christ: The Narrative Substructure of Galatians 3:1–4:11*. 2nd ed. Grand Rapids: Eerdmans. 1st ed., 1983.

Holmes, Michael W., ed. and trans. 2007. *The Apostolic Fathers: Greek Texts and English Translations*. 3rd ed. Grand Rapids: Baker Academic.

Hooker, Morna D. 1990. *From Adam to Christ*. Cambridge: Cambridge University Press.

Horsley, Richard A. 2005. "Unearthing a People's History." Pages 1–20 in *Christian Origins*. A People's History of Christianity 1. Edited by Richard A. Horsley. Minneapolis: Fortress.

Howard, George. 1990. *Paul—Crisis in Galatia: A Study in Early Christian Theology*. 2nd ed. Society for New Testament Studies Monograph Series 35. Cambridge: Cambridge University Press. 1st ed., 1979.

Hubbard, Moyer V. 2002. *New Creation in Paul's Letters and Thought*. Society for New Testament Studies Monograph Series 119. Cambridge: Cambridge University Press.

Hübner, Hans. 1984. *Law in Paul's Thought: A Contribution to the Development of Pauline Theology*. Translated by J. C. G. Greig. Studies of the New Testament and Its World. Edinburgh: T&T Clark.

Hunt, A. S., and C. C. Edgar. 1932. *Private Affairs*. Vol. 1 of *Select Papyri*. Loeb Classical Library. London: Heinemann.

Hurtado, Larry W. 1979. "The Jerusalem Collection and the Book of Galatians." *Journal for the Study of the New Testament* 5:46–62.

Hutchinson, John, and Anthony D. Smith, eds. 1996. *Ethnicity*. Oxford Readers. Oxford: Oxford University Press.

Jewett, Robert. 2002. "The Agitators and the Galatian Congregation." Pages 334–47 in *The Galatians Debate: Contemporary Issues in Rhetorical and Historical Interpretation*. Edited by Mark D. Nanos. Peabody, MA: Hendrickson.

————. 2007. *Romans: A Commentary*. Hermeneia. Minneapolis: Fortress.

Kahl, Brigitte. 2010. *Galatians Re-imagined: Reading with the Eyes of the Vanquished*. Minneapolis: Fortress.

Käsemann, Ernst. 1969. *New Testament Questions of Today*. Philadelphia: Fortress.

Kertelge, Karl. 1990. "Δικαιόω." Pages 330–34 in vol. 1 of *Exegetical Dictionary of the New Testament*. Edited by H. Balz and G. Schneider. Grand Rapids: Eerdmans.

Kim, Seyoon. 1981. *The Origin of Paul's Gospel*. Wissenschaftliche Untersuchungen zum Neuen Testament 2/4. Tübingen: Mohr Siebeck.

Klein, Günter. 1991. "Paul's Purpose in Writing the Epistle to the Romans." Pages 29–43 in *The Romans Debate*. Edited by K. P. Donfried. Rev. and expanded ed. Edinburgh: T&T Clark.

Klinghardt, Matthias, and Hal Taussig. 2012. *Mahl und religiöse Identität im frühen Christentum / Meals and Religious Identity in Early Christianity*. Texte und Arbeiten zum neutestamentlichen Zeitalter 56. Tübingen: Francke.

Konstan, David. 1996. "Friendship, Frankness and Flattery." Pages 7–19 in *Friendship, Flattery and Frankness of Speech: Studies on Friendship in the New Testament World*. Edited by John T. Fitzgerald. Supplements to Novum Testamentum 82. Leiden: Brill.

Kooten, George H. van. 2008. *Paul's Anthropology in Context: The Image of God, Assimilation to God and Tripartite Man in Ancient Judaism, Ancient Philosophy and Early Christianity*. Wissenschaftliche Untersuchungen zum Neuen Testament 232. Tübingen: Mohr Siebeck.

Levy, Ian Christopher, trans. and ed. 2011. *The Letter to the Galatians*. The Bible in Medieval Tradition. Grand Rapids: Eerdmans.

Liddell, H. G., R. Scott, and H. S. Jones. 1996. *A Greek-English Lexicon*. 9th ed. with revised supplement. Oxford: Clarendon.

Lieu, Judith M. 2002. *Neither Jew nor Greek? Constructing Early Christianity*. London: T&T Clark.

Lightfoot, J. B. 1890. *Saint Paul's Epistle to the Galatians*. 10th ed. London: Macmillan.

Longenecker, Bruce W. 1998. *The Triumph of Abraham's God: The Transformation of Identity in Galatians*. Edinburgh: T&T Clark.

———. 1999. "Until Christ Is Formed in You: Suprahuman Forces and Moral Character in Galatians." *Catholic Biblical Quarterly* 61:92–108.

———. 2010. *Remember the Poor: Paul, Poverty, and the Greco-Roman World*. Grand Rapids: Eerdmans.

Longenecker, Richard N. 1990. *Galatians*. Word Biblical Commentary 41. Dallas: Word.

Louw, J. P., and E. A. Nida. 1988. *Greek-English Lexicon of the New Testament Based on Semantic Domains*. 2 vols. New York: United Bible Societies.

Lull, David J. 1986. "'The Law Was Our Pedagogue': A Study in Galatians 3:19–25." *Journal of Biblical Literature* 105:481–98.

Luther, Martin. 1949. *Commentary on the Epistle to the Galatians*. Translated by T. Graebner. Grand Rapids: Zondervan. www.gutenberg.org/files/1549/1549-h/1549-h.htm#link2HCH0003. Originally written in 1535.

Malina, Bruce J., and John J. Pilch. 2006. *Social-Science Commentary on the Letters of Paul*. Minneapolis: Fortress.

Marchal, Joseph A. 2006. *Hierarchy, Unity, and Imitation: A Feminist Rhetorical Analysis of Power Dynamics in Paul's Letter to the Philippians*. Academia Biblica 24. Atlanta: Society of Biblical Literature.

———. 2012. "Queer Approaches: Improper Relations with Pauline Letters." Pages 209–27 in *Studying Paul's Letters: Contemporary Perspectives and Methods*. Edited by Joseph A. Marchal. Minneapolis: Fortress.

Martyn, J. Louis. 1985. "Apocalyptic Antinomies in Paul's Letter to the Galatians." *New Testament Studies* 31:410–24.

———. 1997a. *Galatians: A New Translation with Introduction and Commentary.* Anchor Bible 33A. New York: Doubleday.

———. 1997b. *Theological Issues in the Study of Paul.* Studies of the New Testament and Its World. Edinburgh: T&T Clark.

Mason, Steve. 2007. "Jews, Judaeans, Judaizing, Judaism: Problems of Categorization in Ancient History." *Journal for the Study of Judaism* 38:457–512.

Matera, Frank J. 2007. *Galatians.* Sacra Pagina 9. Collegeville, MN: Liturgical Press.

Matlock, R. Barry. 2000. "Detheologizing the ΠΙΣΤΙΣ ΧΡΙΣΤΟΥ Debate: Cautionary Remarks from a Lexical Semantic Perspective." *Novum Testamentum* 42:1–23.

———. 2009. "Helping Paul's Argument Work: The Curse of Galatians 3.10–14." Pages 154–79 in *Torah in the New Testament.* Edited by Michael Tait and Peter Oakes. Library of New Testament Studies 401. London: T&T Clark.

Mattingly, H. 1923. *Coins of the Roman Empire in the British Museum (Augustus to Vitellius).* London: British Museum.

McLean, B. H. 2002. *Greek and Latin Inscriptions in the Konya Archaeological Museum.* Regional Epigraphic Catalogues of Asia Minor 4. British Institute of Archaeology at Ankara Monograph 29. London: British Academy.

Meeks, Wayne A. 1983. *The First Urban Christians: The Social World of the Apostle Paul.* New Haven: Yale University Press.

Meiser, Martin. 2007. *Galater.* Novum Testamentum Patristicum 9. Göttingen: Vandenhoeck & Ruprecht.

Meyer, Marvin W., and Richard Smith. 1999. *Ancient Christian Magic: Coptic Texts of Ritual Power.* Princeton: Princeton University Press.

Migne, J. P. 1800–1875. Patrologiae cursus completus: Series latina. Various publishers.

Mitchell, Stephen. 1982. *The Ankara District: The Inscriptions of North Galatia.* Regional Epigraphic Catalogues of Asia Minor 2. BAR International Series 135. British Institute of Archaeology at Ankara Monograph 4. Oxford: BAR.

———. 1993a. *The Celts in Anatolia and the Impact of Roman Rule.* Vol. 1 of *Anatolia: Land, Men, and Gods in Asia Minor.* Oxford: Clarendon.

———. 1993b. *The Rise of the Church.* Vol. 2. of *Anatolia: Land, Men, and Gods in Asia Minor.* Oxford: Clarendon

Mullins, Terence Y. 1972. "Formulas in New Testament Epistles." *Journal of Biblical Literature* 91:380–90.

Nanos, Mark D. 2002. *The Irony of Galatians: Paul's Letter in First-Century Context.* Minneapolis: Fortress.

Novenson, Matthew V. 2012. *Christ among the Messiahs: Christ Language in Paul and Messiah Language in Ancient Judaism.* Oxford: Oxford University Press.

Oakes, Peter. 2001. *Philippians: From People to Letter.* Society for New Testament Studies Monograph Series 110. Cambridge: Cambridge University Press.

———. 2005. "Re-mapping the Universe: Paul and the Emperor in 1 Thessalonians and Philippians." *Journal for the Study of the New Testament* 27:301–22.

————. 2009. *Reading Romans in Pompeii: Paul's Letter at Ground Level*. London: SPCK; Minneapolis: Fortress.

Oldfather, W. A., trans. 1925. *Epictetus: Discourses*. Loeb Classical Library. London: Heinemann.

Perrin, Bernadotte, trans. 1916. *Plutarch: Lives*. Vol. 3. Loeb Classical Library. London: Heinemann.

Pilhofer, Peter. 2010. *Das Neue Testament und seine Welt: Eine Einführung*. Uni-Taschenbücher Basics 3363. Tübingen: Mohr Siebeck.

Puca, Bartolomeo. 2011. *Una periautologia paradossale: Analisi retorico-letteraria di Gal 1,13–2,21*. Tesi Gregoriana 186. Rome: Editrice Pontificia Università Gregoriana.

Räisänen, Heikki. 1983. *Paul and the Law*. Wissenschaftliche Untersuchungen zum Neuen Testament 29. Tübingen: Mohr Siebeck.

Ramsay, William M. 1920. *St Paul the Traveller and the Roman Citizen*. 14th ed. London: Hodder & Stoughton.

Redekop, Vern. 1993. *Scapegoats, the Bible, and Criminal Justice: Interacting with René Girard*. New Perspectives on Crime and Justice 13. Akron, PA: MCC US Office of Criminal Justice; Clearbrook, BC: Mennonite Central Committee Canada Victim Offender Ministries.

Riches, John K. 1993. *A Century of New Testament Study*. Valley Forge, PA: Trinity.

————. 2008. *Galatians through the Centuries*. Blackwell Bible Commentaries. Malden, MA: Blackwell.

Robbins, Vernon K. 2013. "Opening-Middle-Closing Texture." *Dictionary of Socio-Rhetorical Terms*. www.religion.emory.edu/faculty/robbins/SRI/defns/o_defns.cfm.

Ross, W. D., trans. 1954. *The Nicomachean Ethics of Aristotle*. London: Oxford University Press.

Rowland, Christopher. 1982. *The Open Heaven: A Study of Apocalyptic in Judaism and Early Christianity*. London: SPCK.

Sanders, E. P. 1977. *Paul and Palestinian Judaism: A Comparison of Patterns of Religion*. Philadelphia: Fortress; London: SCM.

————. 1983. *Paul, the Law, and the Jewish People*. London: SCM.

Sänger, Dieter. 2010. "Die Adresse des Galaterbriefs: Neue (?) Überlegungen zu einem alten Problem." Pages 1–56 in *Umstrittener Galaterbrief: Studien zur Situierung der Theologie des Paulus-Schreibens*. Edited by Michael Bachmann and Bernd Kollmann. Biblisch-theologische Studien 106. Neukirchen-Vluyn: Neukirchener Verlag.

Schlier, Heinrich. 1989. *Der Brief an die Galater*. Kritisch-exegetischer Kommentar über das Neue Testament 15. Göttingen: Vandenhoeck & Ruprecht.

Schmidt, Karl H. 1994. "Galatische Sprachreste." Pages 15–28 in *Forschungen in Galatien*. Edited by E. Schwertheim. Asia Minor Studien 12. Bonn: Habelt.

Schnelle, Udo. 2005. *Apostle Paul: His Life and Theology*. Translated by M. Eugene Boring. Grand Rapids: Baker Academic.

Schreiner, Thomas R. 2010. *Galatians*. Exegetical Commentary on the New Testament. Grand Rapids: Zondervan.

Schüssler Fiorenza, Elizabeth. 1983. *In Memory of Her: A Feminist Theological Reconstruction of Christian Origins*. London: SCM.

———. 1984. *Bread Not Stone: The Challenge of Feminist Biblical Interpretation*. Boston: Beacon.

Schweitzer, Albert. 1931. *The Mysticism of Paul the Apostle*. Translated by C. T. Campion. London: A&C Black.

Sim, Margaret G. 2010. *Marking Thought and Talk in New Testament Greek. New Light from Linguistics on the Particles* ἵνα *and* ὅτι. Cambridge: James Clarke.

Smit, Joop. 2002. "The Letter of Paul to the Galatians: A Deliberative Speech." Pages 39–59 in *The Galatians Debate: Contemporary Issues in Rhetorical and Historical Interpretation*. Edited by Mark D. Nanos. Peabody, MA: Hendrickson.

Spawforth, Antony J. S. 1996. "Founders, City." Page 608 in *Oxford Classical Dictionary*. 3rd ed. Edited by S. Hornblower and A. Spawforth. Oxford: Oxford University Press.

Stendahl, Krister. 1976. *Paul among Jews and Gentiles*. Philadelphia: Fortress.

Stevenson, G. H., and A. W. Lintott. 1996. "Clubs, Roman." Pages 352–53 in *Oxford Classical Dictionary*. 3rd ed. Edited by S. Hornblower and A. Spawforth. Oxford: Oxford University Press.

Stirewalt, M. Luther. 1993. *Studies in Ancient Greek Epistolography*. Atlanta: Scholars Press.

Stowers, Stanley K. 1986. *Letter Writing in Greco-Roman Antiquity*. Philadelphia: Westminster.

———. 2003. "Paul and Self-Mastery." Pages 524–50 in *Paul in the Greco-Roman World: A Handbook*. Edited by J. Paul Sampley. London: Continuum.

Strobel, K. 2013. "Galatia." *Brill's New Pauly: Antiquity Volumes*. Edited by H. Cancik and H. Schneider. Brill Online. www.encquran.brill.nl/entries/brill-s-new-pauly/galatia-e417820. Accessed October 23, 2014.

Swanson, Reuben, ed. 1999. *New Testament Greek Manuscripts: Variant Readings Arranged in Horizontal Lines against Codex Vaticanus; Galatians*. Wheaton, IL: Tyndale; Pasadena, CA: William Carey.

Tait, Michael. 2009. "The End of the Law: The Messianic Torah in the Pseudepigrapha." Pages 196–207 in *Torah in the New Testament*. Edited by Michael Tait and Peter Oakes. Library of New Testament Studies 401. London: T&T Clark.

Vouga, François. 1998. *An die Galater*. Handbuch zum Neuen Testament 10. Tübingen: Mohr Siebeck.

Wakefield, Andrew H. 2003. *Where to Live: The Hermeneutical Significance of Paul's Citations from Scripture in Galatians 3:1–14*. Academia Biblica. Leiden: Brill.

Watson, Francis. 2004. *Paul and the Hermeneutics of Faith*. London: T&T Clark.

Wedderburn, A. J. M. 1985. "Some Observations on Paul's Use of the Phrases 'in Christ' and 'with Christ.'" *Journal for the Study of the New Testament* 25:83–97.

Westerholm, Stephen. 2004. *Perspectives Old and New on Paul: The "Lutheran" Paul and His Critics*. Grand Rapids: Eerdmans.

White, John L. 1986. *Light from Ancient Letters*. Philadelphia: Fortress.

Wiley, Tatha. 2005. *Paul and the Gentile Women: Reframing Galatians*. London: Continuum.

Williams, Sam K. 1997. *Galatians*. Abingdon New Testament Commentaries. Nashville: Abingdon.

Winter, Bruce W. 1994. *Seek the Welfare of the City: Christians as Benefactors and Citizens*. First-Century Christians in the Graeco-Roman World. Grand Rapids: Eerdmans; Carlisle: Paternoster.

Wischmeyer, Oda. 2010. "Wie kommt Abraham in den Galaterbrief? Überlegungen zu Gal 3,6–29." Pages 119–63 in *Umstrittener Galaterbrief: Studien zur Situierung der Theologie des Paulus-Schreibens*. Edited by Michael Bachmann and Bernd Kollmann. Biblisch-theologische Studien 106. Neukirchen-Vluyn: Neukirchener Verlag.

Witherington, Ben, III. 1998. *Grace in Galatia: A Commentary on Paul's Letter to the Galatians*. London: T&T Clark.

Witulski, Thomas. 2000. *Die Adressaten des Galaterbriefes: Untersuchungen zur Gemeinde von Antiochia ad Pisidiam*. Forschungen zur Religion und Literatur des Alten und Neuen Testaments 193. Göttingen: Vandenhoeck & Ruprecht.

Wright, N. T. 1991. *The Climax of the Covenant: Christ and the Law in Pauline Theology*. Edinburgh: T&T Clark.

———. 1997. *What Saint Paul Really Said: Was Paul of Tarsus the Real Founder of Christianity?* Grand Rapids: Eerdmans.

———. 2000. "The Letter to the Galatians: Exegesis and Theology." Pages 205–36 in *Between Two Horizons: Spanning New Testament Studies and Systematic Theology*. Edited by Joel B. Green and Max Turner. Grand Rapids: Eerdmans.

———. 2012. "Paul in Current Anglophone Scholarship." *Expository Times* 123: 367–81.

Zimmermann, Martin. 2013. "Lycia et Pamphylia." *Brill's New Pauly: Antiquity Volumes*. Edited by H. Cancik and H. Schneider. Brill Online. www.encquran.brill.nl /entries/brill-s-new-pauly/lycia-et-pamphylia-e712810. Accessed October 23, 2014.

Index of Subjects

Index of Modern Authors

Index of Scripture and Ancient Sources